BECOMING GOD-REALIZED
Stories From My Journey

— Bruce A. Smith —

BECOMING GOD-REALIZED
Stories From My Journey

ISBN 978-0-9973120-1-0 Perfect Bound

[ISBN 978-0-9973120-2-7 Hardcover]

© Bruce A. Smith, 2024
brucesmithstoryteller.com
The New Christs Publishing Co.
in association with the TARP Collective

All rights reserved. No part of this book may be reproduced or used in any manner without the prior written permission of the copyright owner. Plesase feel free to contact Bruce for permission at brucesmith@rainierconnect.com

Book Design, Cover Design, Self-Publishing Services:
Heidi Connolly, Harvard Girl Word Services, harvardgirledits.com
Author photos by Ashley Marie Studios of Olympia, WA

Testimonials

Becoming God-Realized is a passionate and sincere testament of the journey to a Master Teacher, and the life that unfolded in "making known the unknown." Bruce's storytelling had me enthralled to see where he was headed and what he learned. BRAVO!

— *Steve Klein, Ramtha School of Enlightenment Event Services Manager (retired)*

Bruce Smith's *Becoming God-Realized: Stories From My Journey* is a truly transformative piece of literature that transcends the ordinary. A testament to Smith's tenacity as an investigative reporter, this book cleverly weaves together profound narratives of spiritual awakening with the same rigor and meticulous detail that defines his journalistic work. *Becoming God-Realized* is more than a book; it is an invitation to embark on a spiritual adventure that promises to both challenge and enrich. Bruce Smith has gifted us a work that is as informative as it is inspiring, a true beacon for those seeking to ignite their own spiritual awakening.

— *Nicholas Broughton, DB Cooper researcher and investigator, who says that the "Home Run" story touched him deeply and ushered forth these kind words.*

[Author's Note: When I asked Nicky about his eloquent description of this book, he told me, "The words just came out...that happens sometimes." In communications during a channeled session and subsequent meditations with entities known as TARP, channeled via Gayle Thomas, TARP revealed to me that they delivered the above words to Nicky.]

Reading *Becoming God-Realized*, one gets the sense of a person on a search. Like most good inquiries, the questions posed here are often more important than the answers. This book is a candid, heartfelt, sometimes unusual recounting of that venture. One only has to read "Santa, Rudolph the Red-Nosed Reindeer and ZZ" to know Bruce Smith's intent is true and his book a clear extension of that. It is a crazy quilted ride with a most interesting author.

– *Philip J. Calabria, Camp Wauwepex Staff alum*

I know Bruce from having interviewed him twice for my podcast. When he asked me to comment on his latest book, *Becoming God-Realized: Stories From My Journey*, the first thing that came to mind is his gift of storytelling. Good storytelling draws you into the story, and Bruce did that with me. The other mark of this kind of skill is to leave the reader wanting to hear more. In several chapters I found myself with just that thought. I recommend *Becoming God-Realized*.

– *Dan Hall, founder and co-host of the "Anomalies" podcast and retired college professor*

THIS BOOK IS DEDICATED TO

My friend, Philip J. Calabria (1948-2024), as well as all those on a spiritual path, seeking to become greater than what they have been. May these stories lighten your load and quicken your step – and maybe even put a smile on your face. Regardless, please know you are not alone.

Table of Contents

1. What does "God-Realization" mean? — 11
2. Barbsie Comes Home for Christmas — 17
3. Santa; Rudolph, The Red-Nosed Reindeer; and ZZ — 21
4. Death of a Hero — 33
5. Wauwepex — 39
6. Gottman and Beck Find a Bear in their Bed — 49
7. Army Intelligence — 57
8. North to Chibougamou — 63
9. Not Going to Vietnam — 73
10. The Two Ghosts of Burston Street — 71
11. What to Say When Your Therapist Calls You Her Craziest Patient — 85
12. There is Justice in this World — 89
13. Untidy Beaches — 95
14. Take a Chance: No guts. No glory, etc. — 107
15. A Stepfather's Love — 111
16. The Man Who Divorced His Wife Over a Hat — 117
17. Mail Call — 121
18. Sex with Aliens — 125
19. Nice Guys — 141
20. A Full Moon and Fig Newtons — 143
21. Philmont Belts — 147
22. Any Place Can Be a Home — 153
23. On Becoming a Hunter — 155
24. Of Mice, and Men's Groups — 159

25.	On Being a Santa Claus	165
26.	Hey, Granddad, Thanks for the Banjo	169
27.	Don't Give Up Your Song	173
28.	Shoelaces	181
29.	A Good Samaritan in Tucson	185
30.	Miracle at the Crossroads	189
31.	Flight 800 and the Blue Angel	193
32.	Neil Diamond	207
33.	The Dixie Chicks	209
34.	Cheap Mickey	213
35.	On Being a Stagehand	215
36.	Arlo Guthrie	219
37.	The Bus Driver	223
38.	The Flute Player	229
39.	Pink Sky and Red Wine	233
40.	A Love Letter to You All	237
41.	Yuchi and Me, and Donald Trump	249
42.	TJ Doyle, Bill O'Reilly, and My 50th Reunion	253
43.	Tenney House	257
44.	A Last, Great Lesson from My Father	265
45.	Remembering Marty	269
46.	On Becoming a Presidential Candidate	279
47.	The Home Run	287
48.	Peering into the "In-Between"	293
49.	Endings and Beginnings	301
50.	Riding with the Orange Man	307
51.	On Betrayal	311
52.	On Age	319

53. Twists and Turns	327
54. On Gratitude	333
55. Trista	339
56. On My Way	341
57. Realizations	345
58. Revisiting the Aliens	349
59. Resistance and Resolution	359
60. A Song for the Journey	366

1

What does "God-Realization" mean?

God-Realization, to me, means knowing I am a divine being and it's my fundamental state of existence. I believe I am more than just my body, and I accept my potential for being unlimited, eternal, and immortal.

This understanding fosters the notion that everyone else is a God, too, whether they accept it or not. Bottom Line: we're all spiritual beings currently residing in a physical body. The goal is to have the experience of physicality—enjoying it, hating it, or just enduring it—but ultimately moving into a more evolved state of awareness. We learn as we live. As I understand the Big Picture of Life, having a body is not a diminished state because experiencing all the sights and sounds of this earthly reality is critical to our evolution. Where else can we sing a song, make love and war, ponder our mistakes, and celebrate our achievements? Ideally, in that process we evolve into wiser and more authentic beings, ultimately becoming so aware of ourselves and each other that we become like a Buddha or a Christ.

I am not fully God-Realized, yet, as I can't walk on water or heal myself. But I sense I'm getting closer, and in this book I detail some of the successes I have achieved and the steps I am taking to manifest this remarkable state.

My family describes me as a "spiritual seeker," and I agree with that assessment. However, the concept of God-Realization is hard for them to swallow, and I think it's comforting for them to know it is not an idea I developed on my own. Rather, I heard it from an entity named "Ramtha, the Enlightened One," who channels through the personage of JZ Knight.

Ramtha's teachings about being a God have inspired me profoundly. In 1990, I left my home in New York to study with him full time in Yelm, Washington, and for nearly 20 years I was an active student in Ramtha's School of Enlightenment, commonly called "RSE." During that time, I attended nearly every workshop and retreat offered. Since leaving active participation in 2009, I have continued my quest on my own.

However, my journey to God-Realization begs the question: Who or what is God? I don't believe "God" is a Supreme Being in the traditional sense of the Judeo-Christian religions. Rather, I feel God is something bigger, more along the lines of the "All-in-All," or the "Is-ness" that some Eastern religions profess. But more purposeful for me is what I gather from Ramtha—that God is an utterly unlimited creative force that Ramtha calls Primary Consciousness. Further, Primary Consciousness has brought you and me into life, and together we can be thought of what Ramtha calls Secondary Consciousness. Along with Primary Consciousness, we have co-created our world, and that's what I am embracing on this journey.

The stories on these pages are from that adventure. Each one is a stepping stone, revealing how I learned something important about myself, or helped in my realization of the grandeur of life. Some are simple, yet potent, such as learning that I actually loved someone—my little sister—a story told in "Barbsie Comes Home for Christmas" (Chapter 2). Others delve into the experiences that helped me cope with growing up in the suburbs of New York, like my time in the woods at Boy Scout camp, as described in the story titled "Wauwepex" (Chapter 5). Most, though, are birthed in the present day as I integrate a growing number of paranormal and inter-dimensional encounters into a comprehensive understanding of life. These experiences include abductions by Extra-Terrestrials, glimpses of orbs and energy forms, and even a few modest achievements in self-healing and physical manifestation.

As for my "regular" life, I grew up in a traditional upper-middle-class family on Long Island, New York, and attended Catholic schools until college. As a kid, my family and I lived in the tiny neighborhood of Floral Park Crest, just outside New York City, and I played Little League baseball next door for the Village of Stewart Manor. However, when I was 14, we moved six blocks east to the snooty town of Garden City.

My dad, Alan, was a business executive who commuted daily to New York City, and my mom, Frances, was a stay-at-home housewife. They ran a strict Catholic home for me and my sister, but I often felt like an outsider, as my thoughts and feelings were too outrageous to be warmly received. In short, I was the black sheep of the family. And rebellious. Tellingly, my first act of revolt was in fifth grade when I spent an evening in front of the convent of St. Anne's Elementary School shouting that my teacher, Mother Michaeline, was giving us too much homework. "Down with Mother Michaeline," I roared. "She gives us homework on the WEEKENDS!" That got me expelled until my mother repented on my behalf.

After that my family kept me at arm's length. I think I was just too outspoken to be held close to anyone's heart, and in response I became a raconteur—a "re-teller" of tales—to work my way back into the bosom of the family. At the dinner table, I told stories about the daily occurrences of my life, which seemed to earn me some respect. At least I captured everyone's attention for a few minutes while we ate.

As I got older, I expanded my repertoire. At holiday gatherings I'd describe epic family events, like getting stuck in a blizzard on the way to spend Christmas with relatives in Massachusetts (Chapter 3). By the time I was fifteen or so, I had become the master of ceremony for our family's color slide show on our summer porch, regaling our neighbors with accounts of recent vacation trips, such as getting soaked to the skin on a camping trip, touring EXPO '67 in Montreal, or visiting the iconic cathedral for miraculous healings in Quebec known as the Cathedral of St. Anne du Beaupré. I still remember seeing worn wheelchairs and dirty crutches hanging from the ceiling—a fierce testament to the power of belief or, similarly, the power of prayer.

Traversing through my teenage years, I discovered a deeper voice—one that was richly connected to my soul. This accelerated the friction between authority and me, and I dropped out of college, got fired from my Boy Scout camp, and went ski-bumming in Colorado for a winter, while I shunned my draft board (Chapter 9, "Not Going to Vietnam").

Eventually, I worked as an ambulance orderly for a year, and that led to an interest in medicine. I returned to college as a premed student, graduating from Hofstra University in 1974. Afterward, I coupled my youth work for the Scouts and the YMCA to build the foundational skills to be a recreation therapist in psychiatry, first at the Nassau County Medical Center (NCMC) in New York, and then later at the nearby Northport VA. Eventually, I got my masters in recreation from Lehman College in the Bronx.

At NCMC I started a passionate romance with a fellow therapist named Barbara Jean, whom I call "BJ," and lived with her for 14 years. After 10 years of doing psych work in New York, I left to start a business, a beachcleaning operation called Sandsifter. For eight seasons I sifted the beaches of Long Island and New Jersey, removing trash and debris through the screening plates of modified potato harvesters. By the late 1980s, I was knee-deep in environmental concerns, particularly the issue of medical wastes washing up in the greater New York area. It was through this environmental work that I first heard about Ramtha. (See Chapter 18, "Mail Call.")

Once I arrived at RSE, I developed another long-term relationship. This time with a schoolmate named Francesca, and we lived together for seven years. When I turned 50, I married a woman named Jen, but within a year we divorced. A year later, I married a second time to another RSE student. Even though it's been an unconventional marital road, I cherish all the women who have shared my life.

In the course of my studies with Ramtha, I began to nurture my creative talents, and started performing as a storyteller and singer-songwriter. Later, I added my grandfather's banjo and began strumming "story-songs" at folk festivals and on public-access radio. I never made much money, but the rich connections I've formed with my audiences have kept me going.

Along the way, I spent 15 months in Nashville crafting my musical chops, and that stint led to a five-year career as a stagehand. In turn, I wrote a freelance news column titled, "Stories from Backstage," which later earned me a reporting job at a weekly newspaper in Eatonville, Washington. That gig evolved into investigative journalism and, eventually, with writing a book on the infamous skyjacker, DB Cooper.

I even became an active candidate for the presidency of the United States in 2003.

The stories on these pages are all borne from these experiences. Some are tales I've told around the kitchen table with my family or campfires with friends—and even a few on loading docks with fellow grips. Many I've performed on stage as a professional storyteller, and the majority are simple accounts of love expressed or fears overcome.

Even though all these stories are true, several individuals have asked me to change their name to protect their privacy and I have endeavored to do so. Also, a few locales and some circumstances have been changed to protect the privacy of certain individuals. Nevertheless, all dialogue and interactions are truthful.

One more thing. If you'd like to get in touch with me, the best way is via email at brucesmith@rainierconnect.com.

2

Barbsie Comes Home for Christmas
Learning that I can love

In October 1959, my sister Barbara had open-heart surgery for a congenital birth defect. She was six years old at the time and I was 10. She called it "fixing the hole in my heart."

Open-heart procedures were dicey in those days, and Barbsie, short for Barbara, was one of the first kids to undergo the surgery. Only a handful of hospitals performed the procedure due to the complicated nature of maintaining blood and oxygen flows during the operation, which was achieved by utilizing a newly developed heart-and-lung bypass machine. As a result, my sister's operation took place in the special cardiac facility of St. Francis Hospital in Port Washington, New York.

The cardiac repair was successful but very stressful, and Barbsie got some nasty infections. She had to be hospitalized for months, far past the normal recovery time of two weeks, and was not well enough to come home permanently during that period. So, she was still confined to a hospital bed as Christmastime approached.

"We're asking Dr. Mannix if Barbsie can come home for Christmas," my mother informed me one night while I slurped a vanilla ice cream soda in the hospital's tiny sandwich shop. Being a kid, I was deemed a health risk to my sister, so I hadn't been able to see her since she had entered the hospital. As a result, I spent my "visiting" time alone with my soda, awaiting my parents' return.

My mother's news did not thwart my interest in getting every last drop of vanilla soda out of the tall glass container. Since I accompanied my parents on their daily visit to Barbsie only on an every-other-trip basis, the next time I went to the hospital was two days later. On the drive home that night I was sitting in the back seat of our family's Ford Fairlane when my mother addressed me, and it seemed especially important. She had turned in her seat to face me directly, and I leaned closely, resting my arms across on the tops of the front seats to support myself since my butt was hardly touching the back seat.

"Bruce, I have some very good news," my mom said. "Dr. Mannix told us Barbsie can come home on Christmas Eve, but she can only stay for three days. She'll have to go back the day after Christmas."

"Wow, Barbsie's gonna be home for Christmas," I said. "That'll be the greatest Christmas present I could ever get."

The words just tumbled out. I hadn't rehearsed them. I hadn't even known I felt that way. I didn't feel embarrassed either. Instead, I felt a tingly sensation inside. I wasn't sure why, but I let it flow, savoring it like a vanilla ice cream soda. But, even at 10 years old, somehow I knew this was deeper and sweeter.

"Barbsie has to be very quiet because she's still very weak," my mom continued, "so no rough-house stuff, understand? I mean it."

"Uh-huh," I answered, and then turned away. I saw snowflakes falling as we drove up Port Washington Boulevard past the Miracle Mile Shopping Mall, and I was struck by another magical thought. "Maybe we'll have a White Christmas, too," I said. "Wouldn't that be great?"

My mom smiled and nodded. "Barbsie's coming home would be your greatest Christmas present?" she asked. "She's really special to you, isn't she?"

"Yup." I was still leaning forward and she could see the big smile on my face.

"I don't think I've ever heard you talk like this before, Bruce."

I shrugged. I had never heard myself talk like that either, and I was confused, not knowing where the words had come from.

Now it was my mom's turn to smile. She, too, had just received a family gift — one of knowing that her son could love someone else. We drove home in a quiet bliss, and even when the snow turned to rain, we didn't lose a drop of that special glow.

Of Christmases past I remember Lionel trains, a big red Schwinn bike, and Tonka toy trucks. But most of all I remember a dark, chilly night on the north shore of Long Island and hearing the news that Barbsie was coming home for Christmas.

3

Santa; Rudolph, the Red-Nosed Reindeer; and ZZ

My first effort at creating a miracle, followed by real ones

If you expect Santa Claus to be a jolly, fat guy wearing a red suit and laughing behind his white, fluffy whiskers you might miss the real Santas in your life. The same, too, for Rudolph and his glowing red nose. I know, because on Christmas 1963, when I was 14, my family drove through a blizzard and met a real Santa Claus and a real-live Rudolph. However, our Santa was a short, skinny guy in a green jumpsuit and Rudolph drove a DPW truck with flashing orange lights.

1963 was the year my Aunt Teddy proclaimed, "Uncle Bunny and I aren't coming to New York this year for Christmas. We've driven to Long Island every year since Barbsie and Bruce were born, and now that they're old enough to travel it's only fair that you come to Massachusetts."

Aunt Teddy was called "The Boss" by more than just family. Therefore, her request ensured that my family would head north to their home in Shrewsbury, Massachusetts. We were scheduled to leave on Friday, December 23rd, the eve of Christmas Eve, but early that morning I was shocked to see my dad getting dressed for work.

"Hey, Dad, we're supposed to go to Shrewsbury today," I said.

"I know, son. I'll be back in a jiffy. I just have to drop off some papers at the office. Help your mom get things ready. When I return, we'll load the car and go." Then he left.

After breakfast my mom commenced a pre-vacation house cleaning that approached total home renovation. By 1 p.m. my father had not returned, and my mother focused her intensity toward him via the phone. Her shrieks got him on the next train out of Penn Station and back in our house by 3 p.m.

By the time we got our 1961 Rambler station wagon loaded with ski gear, Christmas gifts, suitcases, and bedding, and then stopped at the bank for cash for the trip, it was almost 5 p.m., perfect timing for the New York City pre-holiday rush-hour crush. To top things off, the day-long drizzle had turned into a downpour.

At the Cross Island Parkway, we joined the bumper-to-bumper traffic heading out of town. My mom didn't say anything about the sorry state our voyage was taking, but instead served tuna sandwiches and grapefruit juice. We finished our supper before we reached the Whitestone Bridge, only 16 miles from home.

Four hours later we had only traveled the 100 miles to New Haven, Connecticut, but there the traffic thinned. Despite the steady rain, we thought we'd be in Shrewsbury within two hours. But as we turned north on the Wilbur Cross Parkway, the outside temperature dropped quickly.

"I wonder if there is snow in Hartford," my mother pondered. "You know it always changes to snow in Hartford when it's raining here along the coast."

I knew that to be true, too. Prior, when we had left New York in a cold rain, it had changed to snow in Hartford, while Shrewsbury itself greeted us with a full-blown winter wonderland.

"They didn't forecast snow," my father replied. "They said it would be rain the whole way with a chance of snow at higher elevations. The roads will stay clear."

I don't think so, Dad, I thought, but kept it to myself.

As my mom and I had presaged, the rain turned to snow at Hartford. In fact, it had been snowing there all day.

The main roads were plowed, but it was snowing hard. A foot of snow was already on the ground. As we left Hartford and entered the hill country of central New England, all the lanes of the parkway emptied. By 10 p.m. we passed only an occasional snowplow, yet we kept on through a deepening snow and a darkening cold.

Twenty miles north of Hartford we climbed our first big hill. Halfway up, the car began to make noises: spritz, britz… sputz.

"What is it, Dad?" I cried out. "What's wrong?"

"I don't know. It sounds like the engine."

The car lurched and shuddered. I leaned over the front seat between my parents and watched the speedometer drop from 50 mph to 25.

We made it to the top of the hill, though, and after a quarter mile of level ground the engine cleared itself and we returned to highway speed.

"Maybe it was just a fluke," my father said. "It sounds like whatever was wrong is okay now."

"We should get it checked, Alan," my mother said.

"Well, if they checked it now, they wouldn't find anything wrong. Besides, where would we find a gas station around here?"

He was right. Northern Connecticut was a beautiful, snowy woodland — devoid of all service stations, especially at 10 p.m. on the eve of Christmas Eve.

My father relaxed and I did, too. I felt cold, though. The heat never reached the back seat of the Rambler, so I ordinarily wore my parka. My sister, too, felt a deeper cold, and we both put on another sweater and took blankets from the pile between us, wrapping them around our legs. I took a second blanket and put it up against the side door to block the chilliness creeping through.

On the next hill the engine began to sputter again, worse than before. "Alan, it's doing it again," my mother exploded. "What's wrong?"

"I don't know," my father spit back, "but getting all excited isn't going to help the situation."

"We have to find someone to fix it, Alan," she pleaded.

"Yeah, Dad," I added, "we'll never make it to Shrewsbury like this." We finally reached the top of the hill, sputtering at less than 20 mph.

"Okay, okay, you guys, we'll get off the road, but I hope we don't get stuck trying to get off the exit ramp. The last couple of exits haven't looked too plowed."

When we crested the hill top and reached level ground, the engine ran normally, again. "I don't know if we should risk it, Frances," my father announced. "Everything's okay now, and I don't know where a gas station's gonna be until we reach Worcester—and that's miles away."

My mother was quiet and I remained silent, too. But I knew we needed help. Fortunately, two sputtering hills later we saw a beacon of hope—a tall Mobil gas station sign advertising 24-hour service.

"Rescue, dead ahead," I shouted.

I guess my dad agreed because he drove off the exit, gingerly following the half-filled tracks of those who had ventured before us. At the bottom of the ramp, we could see the fully lit gas station advertising its 24-hour service. However, as we drove across the tarmac and headed toward the repair bay, a mechanic appeared in the window and waved his arms crosswise, like a football referee signaling an incomplete forward pass. He mouthed words we couldn't hear but could read his lips, which said, "We're closed. We're closed."

My mother rolled down her window. "What do you mean you're closed?" she shouted. "We need help. Our engine isn't running right."

"We're closed," he mouthed again, then turned and shut off the lights, including the sign that proclaimed 24-hour service.

"The-Sign-Says-Twenty-Four-Hour-Service-MISTER!" my mother roared, louder than our troubled six under the hood.

"Frances, calm down," my dad said. "He's closed. It's late. He wants to go home."

"How can you say that?" she screamed. "We need help!"

"We'll find it somewhere else. Roll up your window."

My mother complied with my father's instructions, muttering, "Now I know how Mary and Joseph felt being turned away from the inn. Twenty-four-hour service. Gawd!" she exclaimed, staring out the windshield as the blizzard's flakes streamed straight at us in a magical and cosmic kaleidoscope.

"Twenty-four-hour service...twenty-four-hour service...." she continued to mumble as we drove away. Then she took a deep breath, sighed, and we all settled in, wondering what would happen next.

I silently prayed for a miracle, envisioning that on the next hill our engine would run perfectly and we could continue without concern, gaily speculating on the engine gremlins that had given us a scare. I saw them as little buggers evaporating, going out the tailpipe and back into the darkness. (Forty years later I learned that this kind of mental envisioning is a technique in consciousness called the Observer Effect, and is used to shift realities.)

In the meantime, we came to a small hill. The engine sputtered a few times; not as badly as before, but the hill wasn't too steep. *Maybe my thoughts fixed the engine....* Then we came to a bigger hill and the engine began to self-destruct again. *How come my thoughts didn't fix the car?* "Maybe we should get off and find a motel," I finally said. "Fix the car tomorrow."

"I don't know where we'll find a motel, son. We might as well keep going as long as the car continues running."

"But Dad, the car could stop anywhere on the road and we'd be stuck out here. Maybe we should turn around and ask the guy before he goes if there are any motels around."

"Let's keep going, son, and see what we find."

The hills came regularly like slow rolling ocean waves. On each downhill my dad floored the gas pedal, almost skidding us out of the tracks in the snow. On each uphill the car faltered, the sputtering becoming a cruel, engine-slaughtering, ka-ka-knocking by the time we crested.

Then we saw it—a giant hill—but with a lit gas station sign on the summit. Again, my father put the pedal to the metal. We slipped out of the tracks in the valley, but my dad steered us back just before we started our climb. *Spritz, sputz, ka-bang-ga-kadanga, sputz.* Twenty-five mph, 20, 15, 10, 5. I saw the gas station ahead on the right.

"We can push it from here if we have to," I shouted.

Goodall's Garage proclaimed a red neon sign atop the bay doors. All the lights were on inside. It had to be open.

We pulled onto the exit ramp. Blessedly we found tracks cutting through the 12 inches of snow leading past the pumps and directly to a bay door. As we approached it magically opened, but I didn't see anyone in the shop. My dad drove straight in.

"Dahn't turn it aff," said a voice with a strong Bostonian accent. A small, slender man dressed in a green one-piece uniform walked toward us from his office. He wore a red five-pointed star on his chest, signifying a Texaco mechanic.

"What's the mahta?" he asked as we stepped out of the car.

"The engine's misfiring," my father said. The man in green stuck an exhaust hose on the tailpipe and closed the bay door. My sister and I breathed in the warm, dry heat blasting from the propane floor heaters.

My father popped the hood, and the mechanic leaned in. We all got close. Seeing my father's hesitation, I spoke. "It misfires bad," I said, "especially on the hills going up. But it's okay on the downhills. I didn't think we'd make that last one."

"Do you think it's serious?" my mother asked.

He shrugged and gave us a whimsical-but-reassuring, "Hmmm."

In the shop, the engine ran smoothly. The mechanic pulled the accelerator cable a few times. "Rhum...Rhumm... Rhum-mmMMMMM." The engine sounded great.

I wondered why it hadn't done that in the snow.

The mechanic checked the wires to the spark plugs and pulled one off. The engine lagged. He put the wire back near the head of the spark plug so that it almost touched, causing an intermittent firing.

"Did it sound like that?" he asked us.

"Yeah," I said. My dad got alongside the mechanic.

"We just had a tune-up," my father said. "It can't be the spark plugs."

"Yeah, they look fy-ene," said the mechanic, voicing the same idiosyncratic New England slang that my aunt and uncle used for words ending in "-ine."

"Then, what is it?" asked my father.

"Dahn't know for sure, but Ah have a good idea."

The mechanic walked over to his trash barrel, pulled out an empty Valvoline oil cardboard box, and tore off a section about 1 foot x 2 feet. He slid this sheet of cardboard behind the front grill, but in front of the radiator.

"These new Ramblahs have a lot of space between the cooling fins," he said. "On a night like tanight, a lot of the frozahn ice and snow can fly past the fins and land on the spark plug wires. They melt and short out the wire, giving ya the intamittent misfire. On the uphill ya'll notice it, baht on the downhill, where ya don't need the same power, ya won't. This cahrdboard shield will block out the snow."

"But won't it cause the radiator to heat up?" my father asked.

"It might, so keep ya eye on the gauge. If it runs too warm, tear aff a corner. Let a little more air flow past the fins. Baht it's cold out and getting colder. Where ya' going?"

"Worcester," my father said.

"Shrewsbury," my sister and I corrected.

"Shawn't be a problem. That's only 40 miles, I'm sure ya'll be fy-ene."

I breathed a sigh of relief. Everyone felt the same. My mom asked the little man in green if she could use his phone to make a collect call. She wanted to let Teddy and Bunny know our situation.

"Sure, lady, raht on the desk."

My mom was back in two minutes saying, "Teddy picked up on the first ring. She's been sitting by the phone for the past two hours wondering where we were. She's had Bunny camped out next door at the Liuvetski's, calling the State Police of New York, Connecticut, and Massachusetts every 15 minutes to see if we'd run off the road. Plus, she's got the Michalski boys shoveling the driveway to keep it clear for us. They've got 18 inches on the ground and expect more."

Wow, I thought, the skiing at Ward's Hill would be great.

We climbed back into the car and thanked our benefactor. My mother told him we had tried to get help at the Mobil station down the road, but that they had closed in our desperate faces.

"How come you were still open for us?" she asked.

"Ah guess Ah knew ya were coming," he said, chuckling. "Baht now Ah guess Ah can go home, too. Merry Christmas, folks."

"Merry Christmas to you too, mister," I called out. "You really saved the day for us."

"Thank you, Mr.-Man-Who-Wears-The-Star," said my sister quietly through her open window.

"You're very welcome, sweetie," he replied. "Ah hope Santa will be very good to ya this year," he added, winking at her.

"He already has," my mother replied.

We backed out of the repair bay and headed for the highway. He returned our waves, then turned out his lights. We were on our way and he was gone. But he has never been forgotten.

We rejoined the empty lanes of the parkway and the car ran fine. An hour later we arrived in Worcester. My mother's side of the family lived in the Worcester, Massachusetts area, so we had visited there many times and knew the roads. In fact, it felt like home. In my mom's family everyone is of Lithuanian decent, with the older generation having "come over on the boat."

In Lithuania, the family name was pronounced *Zhiez-Zhish-Cuss*, but stateside my uncles shortened it to two syllables, each using a variety of "z's" and vowels. My cousins in Brockton were *Zizes* and my mother's immediate family in Worcester picked *Zizis*. But Uncle Henry in Canada stood out with *Zizys*. Since no one in the family could agree on how to spell the family name, my mom's friends always called her, "ZZ."

So, when I was a kid and answered the phone, if the caller asked for "ZZ," I knew it was somebody from the old neighborhood. It gave me a warm feeling, too, since the Worcester crew was the fun side of the family. They joked and drank beer, went swimming and fishing every weekend in the summer, and always had time to play with kids. Going to Massachusetts for Christmas seemed like a good idea to me. Plus, the nearby Wards Hill offered great skiing for newbies like me.

As we passed through Worcester and headed to my aunt and uncle's home in the neighboring town of Shrewsbury, we descended cautiously down the hilly Route 9, which was totally devoid of traffic. Finally, we crossed the Quinsigamond Lake Bridge and entered into Shrewsbury — almost there! Besides the feeling of relief that we were near the end of our ordeal, we were also greeted by a unique Yuletide display.

Ahead of us all the traffic lights blinked rhythmically every few seconds — red and green, red and green — like a greeting from Santa's realm. Plus, all of the stores alongside the roadway in the White City Shopping Mall still had their windows lit, so it felt like we had discovered an abandoned Santa's Village. But the greatest gift lay ahead: a set of orange lights strobing across the wintry sky.

Stopping a few feet shy of the lights, we discovered they belonged to a Shrewsbury Department of Public Works snowplow parked sideways in the middle of the roadway. As we rolled to a halt, the driver hopped out of the cab and approached. My father rolled down his window, but instead of speaking to my dad, the DPW guy leaned in and looked across the front seat at my mom.

"ZZ, is that you?" he called out.

My mom reached far to her left to get a good look, then shouted, "Eddie!...Eddie Tomalevich! Is that really you?"

"Yeah, Z, it's me."

"My Gawd, Eddie, what are *you* doing here? I haven't seen you since high school!"

"Me?" he roared. "I'm driving a snowplow. There's a blizzard out here in case you haven't noticed, so let me ask you, ZZ, what the hell are you doing out here?"

Our laughter warmed us like thick grog from Tiny Tim's table.

"Bunny called me an hour ago," Eddie continued, "saying his crazy New York relatives were driving up and were sure to need a plow to get through. Since I'm the Superintendent of Public Works, I figured I'd better make sure you'd be okay. I wouldn't want Teddy Zizis' kid sister to end up in a ditch. I'd never hear the end of it."

ZZ and Eddie shared a more private laugh together, knowing fully what Teddy's wrath could be like.

In a minute we were following behind Eddie's International Loadstar 6000 as it threw a giant wave of snow 40 feet to the side, while his orange halogens blasted through a darkened New England night. Seeing the strobe lights flash across the snowdrifts, I knew the joy and wonder Santa must have felt on that night long ago when he, too, needed a Rudolph to guide himself home.

4

Death of a Hero
The first passing of a friend

Some say heroes are made, not born. Perhaps. I've only known one hero, and I say they're simply ordinary guys who know how to do the right thing when trouble happens.

My hero was named Jimmy Gunderson, who was 16 when he risked his life off the coast of Long Island to save a man who was having a heart attack. The story didn't make the evening news, but in my hometown of Garden City everyone proclaimed Jimmy a hero.

Jimmy was a buddy from a YMCA summer camp, one that our moms had arranged for us to attend together. For three summers we were cabin mates at Camp Hi-Rock in the Berkshire Mountains of Massachusetts. Back home on Long Island, however, we would only see each other occasionally—family affairs mostly, as our mothers were old college friends. But the first fish I ever caught was off the stern of Jimmy's family cabin cruiser as we trolled the waters of Hempstead Harbor.

Jimmy was a nice guy. You probably would have liked him; most people did. He was good-looking too, but not an Adonis-type. He was more of an All-American guy, tall and lanky, with freckles and a great smile. Like most heroes, I think, he was self-assured. Certainly, Jimmy always seemed to know what he was doing, and always helped others in whatever they were trying to do. In short, he was a really good buddy to go camping with.

I heard about Jimmy's life-saving heroics a couple of days after it happened. Jimmy had been invited by his girlfriend's family to accompany them on a weekend of sailing around Long Island. On their first night, they were under full sail at 9 p.m. on a mostly moonlit summer's night, a few miles from Jones Beach on Long Island's southern coastline. With the gentle swells on the ocean and a steady breeze from the southwest, everything was just right.

Then the girl's father, who was at the helm, keeled over with an apparent heart attack. Fortunately, Jimmy and his girlfriend were on deck. Jimmy grabbed the tiller and brought the boat into the wind, bringing it to a stop. Then Jimmy grabbed the father and, with the girl helping, rolled him into a prone position so he could administer CPR. That wasn't the easiest thing to do, as the deck space was small and the boom and sheet ropes were sloshing back and forth. Plus, the boat was heaving in the swells.

Within moments the mother joined them on deck, and they started taking turns with mouth-to-mouth resuscitation and external heart massage. This was back in the '60s when not many people knew CPR, so Jimmy had to show the women how to do it.

The father was in bad shape. No heartbeat, no breath, pale skin. With the mother and daughter working on the father, Jimmy went back to the helm. The boat didn't have a radio, though, and this was before the age of cell phones, so there was no chance of getting help — no Medivac chopper or Coast Guard cutter coming to their rescue even though assistance was only 15 miles away at Fire Island Inlet.

But Jones Beach is one of the most popular beaches in the world, so even at 9 p.m. there would be people around — walking the boardwalk at least, if not the actual surf line.

Jimmy put the boat on a beeline for the shore. Once they passed the breakers and sandbars, maybe about a half-mile off shore, Jimmy began to tack back and forth parallel to the beach, shooting off flares to get everyone's attention. People started running down to the water, but all the shouting from Jimmy and the women was simply lost in the roar of the waves. So, Jimmy gave the helm over to the mother, and dove in.

Jimmy swam to shore through a half mile of dark Atlantic. If you've ever gone swimming at night, alone in the ocean, I don't have to tell you how scary it is. But if you never have, it's hard to accurately describe how waves can suddenly break onto you, and you need to be ready to take a last-second breath before the inundation. Plus, you never really know where you are until you ride the crest of a wave and see the lights along the shoreline.

Somehow Jimmy got to shore. After a phone call, the Coast Guard dispatched a chopper, and a para-rescue guy lowered himself down to the deck of the boat and strapped up the father, who was, unfortunately, DOA at the hospital.

Jimmy was given a special award for bravery by the Boy Scouts, and I attended the ceremony wearing my own Boy Scout uniform. Somehow, though, Jimmy looked different from me. Maybe I just recognized the special way he wore his. It had a faded look to it, and he seemed comfortable in it, as if it breathed along with him.

That was the last time I saw Jimmy. Six years later I got word about Jimmy's death from my mom, who had heard about it in a grocery store check-out line.

Jimmy had just graduated from college and was married. One night, he and his wife attended a party at her old sorority house. During the festivities, when the house was getting hot and stuffy, Jimmy and his wife, and another couple, went out on a balcony to get some fresh air.

Suddenly the balcony collapsed, killing Jimmy. No one else was critically hurt, and on the way down I'm sure Jimmy did what was necessary to push the others out of the way to make sure they'd be okay. He really was that kind of guy.

However, when I sent a copy of this manuscript to Jimmy's parents and asked for permission to publish it, his mother replied: "It's a wonderful story, Bruce, and of course you have our permission to use it as long as you change our family's name, but that's not what happened to Jimmy. Would you like to hear what really happened?"

"Of course!" I replied. "But I don't need to know if some little details are off, like the rescue taking place at midnight instead of 9 p.m."

"Oh, no, it's nothing like that," she answered. "The father didn't have a heart attack. He was drunk and fell overboard."

I listened with amazement as she continued.

"Jimmy was invited on the sailing trip because the guy's wife refused to go with him. She knew he was a serious alcoholic, and worse, was a terrible sailor. But worst of all, he thought he was a terrific sailor."

Jimmy's mother and I agreed that was a deadly combination of personality traits.

"When the father went overboard, Jimmy and the girl threw him a life-buoy, but by the time Jimmy maneuvered the boat back to where the father had been floating, they couldn't find him. The wind and waves had blown him in an unknown direction. Unfortunately, they didn't have a search light to scan the area effectively, so Jimmy put the boat into shore."

"Well, how did I hear the heart attack version?" I asked. "Everyone in my family knows that Jimmy saved a guy who had a heart attack at sea. My sister even wrote a story for her creative writing class in high school using the same story line I have."

"I have no idea how the heart attack version popped up," she replied. "But I want to tell you that Jimmy was very much a hero that night, regardless of the circumstances of the father. The Coast Guard told me that night, when we went down to Jones Beach to pick up Jimmy, that if he had dove in a half hour later when the tide turned, the outgoing tide would have been too strong for Jimmy to overcome, and there would have been two victims that night instead of one rescued alcoholic."

I was shocked. "What a strange twist," I finally uttered. I pondered what psychological forces must have been at work to elevate a sad but common story of an out-of-control alcoholic to a version that had more appeal.

Regardless, Jimmy's mother was correct. Jimmy put his life on the line for a guy who needed his help. When trouble happened, he knew what to do. That, I know, is the truth.

5

Wauwepex
Wisdom and solace in the woods

Wauwepex was the Boy Scout camp that saved my life, or at least my soul. It was a place I loved, and still do, for it was a place where I felt absolutely alive and true to myself. As a kid born in the suburbs of New York and dealing with uptight parents, I reveled in the peaceful wilderness of Wauwepex.

Wauwepex was 600 acres of scrub pines and sandy soil, part of what is now known as the Pine Barrens of Long Island. The camp was centered around a pristine lake named Deep Pond, with no buildings along the lake shore. Further, the soils of Wauwepex have never been farmed, so it looks just like the Indians saw it when they called these lands Paumonok.

In general, I loved all the typical things that come with summer camp: swimming, canoeing, camp fires, and sing-alongs. Most of all, I just relished being in nature. From 1961 until 1965 I was a camper. Starting in 1967, I was a camp staffer. So, by the time I turned 21 I had spent half my life at Wauwepex.

I've come to realize that Wauwepex has had a value for me far beyond the fun and freedom of youth, for, oddly, many of my memories of camp now trigger regret or shame. As I dig into those experiences during my meditations, I can now see that Wauwepex was a place I could safely make mistakes, especially big ones.

I first got drunk at Wauwepex, and I got fired for the first time there. The second as well. I first expressed my anger at adults there, too, and on a hilltop overlooking the lake I discovered how complicated having sex with a virgin can be.

But Wauwepex was sacred and gentle. I relaxed in some deep subconscious ways, and felt profoundly safe. In fact, I felt so secure that I would swim at night in Deep Pond, even swimming upside-down with my snorkel mask in place and looking at the stars through the surface of the water.

I first went to Wauwepex when I was 11. My Boy Scout Troop, 166 of Garden City, would go for overnight camping trips there once a month, sleeping in four-man lean-tos or two-man tents. In the winter we stayed at one of several little cabins situated around the camp. I loved the camaraderie—20 Scouts gathered around a campfire or nestled in bunk beds near a big stone fireplace. Our Scoutmaster, Mr. John Peters, was a great guy. He made hot cocoa for us every evening over a Coleman stove in the kitchen area when we were in cabins or lean-tos, and one time when I forgot my sleeping bag, he scrounged up enough blankets to keep me cozy.

Our two-week summer camp outing was sheer bliss. Every day I would keep count of how much time I had remaining in my stay. *Three days down, eleven more to go!* I silently told myself.

I loved the freedom to do what I wanted, even when it meant being part of some organized activity. In my first couple of years, Mr. Peters or our senior Scouts led instructional sessions to teach us camp skills, like recognizing poison ivy or how to pitch a tent. Usually, these lessons were geared toward earning our next "rank." We started as "Tenderfoot" Scouts, and then became 2nd Class as we mastered basic outdoor skills.

Next came the tasks for 1st Class. These included cooking dinner over a fire, knowing Morse Code, and demonstrating rudimentary aspects of first aid, such as putting a splint on a broken arm or securing a twisted ankle. We also had to learn how to sharpen axes and knives, make emergency shelters, and follow the tracks of animals. I loved every minute of it.

At summer camp, most of these skills were taught in the morning immediately after breakfast. Following these sessions we typically went to another organized activity, like target shooting at the rifle range, listening to an Indian Lore presentation, or attending a wood-working program at the craft lodge. As Mr. Peters said, "The purpose of Boy Scouting is to have fun while learning how to do things."

Not only was John Peters the best Scoutmaster I ever had, he was also the best leader of young men I have ever seen. He was firm but kind. He was also soft-spoken and differential—he gave his Scouts a lot of lee-way to do things. But he always kept an eye on our whereabouts so nothing got out of hand. He particularly trusted his older Scouts, who generally ran the day-to-day operations, like supervising the cleaning of the latrines, sending mess-hands down to the dining hall 15 minutes before a meal to set the tables, and organizing the evening camp fire.

The hierarchy of my troop was simple: Mr. Peters was the sole adult leader. He was assisted by a Senior Patrol Leader, who was usually our oldest Scout, often 16 years old. Next was an assistant Senior Patrol Leader, who was usually 14 or 15 years old. The regular Scouts were an assortment of 11-, 12-, and 13-year-olds, and during most summers we had about 25 kids at camp.

Since my troop was sponsored by St. Anne's Church, we were all Catholic and went to mass every day at the outdoor chapel. Although I liked the chaplain, a Franciscan friar named Dave Reedy, daily mass got to be a hassle for me. I was chronically guilt-stricken and I never received communion, the host-taking that Catholics do at mass. That worried

Mr. Peters. When he asked me why I didn't take communion, my squirming, shrugging, and grumbled professings that nothing was wrong seemed to keep him at bay. For the rest of the summer he left me alone with my weighty conscience. Looking back at this dimension of my spiritual life, I can't remember what the issues were—there was nothing major—but I sure felt unholy. Maybe it was an endemic unworthiness that unsettled me. I just didn't feel clean enough to receive communion.

Regardless, the major fun events at Wauwepex focused on all the traditional summer camp activities. In the mornings, those Scouts not receiving some lesson in the campsite went off to merit badge instruction, such as lifesaving, rowing, or nature life. In the afternoon, all the Scouts had two sessions available—one could be swimming and the other could be canoeing. Or neither. Nobody forced us to do anything. It was the first time in my life that adults weren't keeping tabs on me.

There was also some free time in the afternoons before dinner when I could shoot archery or do leather work at the craft lodge, an old log structure that was built when the camp first opened in 1922. Its wooden-slatted floor was sloped and misshapen, and reeked of "oldness." But the biggest time for personal activities was after dinner, and I was often back at the craft lodge and painting neckerchief slides or tooling a leather belt.

My first phase at Wauwepex ended after five summers, when I was 15. Even though most guys leave Scouting when they reach their mid-teens and Scouting becomes "not cool," my relationship intensified. In the summer of 1966 when I was 16, instead of Wauwepex I went to Philmont Scout Ranch in Cimarron, New Mexico. There I joined with 40 other Scouts from my home council of Nassau County for a 30-day adventure backpacking through the Sangre de Cristo Mountains.

The following summer, at 17 years old, I returned to Wauwepex and joined the camp staff. I was assigned to the camp ranger, Johnnie Jones, and his maintenance crew. My father had suggested I learn how to do something with my hands, so I volunteered to be a "fix-it" guy. Besides Johnnie, I worked with another Boy Scout, Charlie P., a swarthy Italian guy from Franklin Square who was a few years older than I was, and who distinguished himself by owning a car. Charlie also had a girlfriend, so he was my window into the world of being a "young adult."

Johnnie was like a second father to me, and I worked for him for three summers. His first words to me have stayed with me all my life: "I have two rules. First, if you don't know how to do something, tell me and I'll show you. Second, if you break something—a tool or some fixture or something—tell me right away so I can fix it and not be surprised later when I need it. Shit happens. It's a fact of life. Don't worry, I promise not to yell or get mad." He never did.

Later on, he told me some other rules of life, such as: "Never ask a man to do something you're not willing to do yourself." Simply, Johnnie and Charlie taught me the honor of hard work, even when it's messy. The three of us went on garbage runs every morning—it was how we started our day—picking up the slimy burlap bags from each campsite that Scouts had filled with the detritus of outdoor living. To their credit, Johnnie and Charlie were usually as knee-deep in the muck as I was.

They also taught me how to drive stick shift—in the camp's old pick-up truck, a '52 Chevy. I also learned how to use a power saw, pour concrete, and bang a nail without splitting the wood. In addition, I mastered how to splice telephone lines, connect electrical systems, or unplug sewer pipes. I even fought a small forest fire.

Plus, I helped maintain the truck engines and learned a few tricks on how to change a flat when the lug nuts won't come loose. I witnessed a sign painter at work and learned how to use a stick as a steadying guide by placing it under the hand holding the brush.

Eventually, Johnnie warmed to me enough to take me to town to get supplies and hardware. If the day was hot and sunny, we stopped at the Wading River Beach on Long Island Sound for a "bikini check." It was the first time I had ever gone girl-watching. Johnnie and Charlie even taught me how to cuss—not too profanely—but it was a start.

Once or twice after work, Charlie took me to the Greenbrier, the local tavern in Wading River. I had my first beer there. Charlie also rescued me from my first serious drinking binge—at a bachelor's party for another camp stalwart, Bob LeSal. At Bob's open bar I had 13 delicious drinks that I think were Seagram's and Sevens. When my inebriation prevented my hand from holding the glass tightly and it slipped out and crashed to the floor, the bar closed, ending the festivities. Charlie took me back to our tent, and I experienced my first Spinning World Sensation. I vomited for an hour and then dealt with the resulting hangover. Johnnie laughed the next day when he saw me, never showing me any pity.

By my third season on camp staff, Charlie was gone to a "real job," fixing cars in Stewart Manor, and I was Johnnie's main guy. Marty, who later became my best friend for a few years, had also arrived, and one night near the end of the summer he asked me to go to the Greenbrier. I jumped in his car and off we went. But I hadn't asked permission to leave camp as was required, and when my transgression was discovered, I was fired. It wasn't unexpected. Johnnie had told me earlier that I was on "thin ice" for my increasingly outspoken attitude and non-compliant behavior toward those in authority, particularly the bossy members of an honor society called the Order of the Arrow, generally referred to as "the OA."

One night, I was about to close down the maintenance shop when a call came in asking if I could transport a recent food delivery to one of the dining halls that was catering an OA ceremony. I agreed, jumped in a camp truck, and delivered the foodstuffs. Somewhere someone handed me a can of beer, which was a very strange occurrence and one that had never happened to me before. I drank most of it while hanging out with the kitchen staff and, feeling buzzed and happy, decided to drive around the lake, a beautiful cruise at 10 p.m. On the lake road I came upon the OA guys leaving a ceremonial encampment. I stopped, rolled down my window and shouted, "The OA sucks," then tore off.

The next day, Johnnie told me how precarious my employment status was. He also informed me that he wasn't too happy with me *personally*. I was making Wauwepex look bad, and putting a sour taste in the mouths of senior staff. One more misstep, Johnnie said, and I would be gone. That occurred two days later with Marty at the Greenbrier.

But I was also tired of being a maintenance guy. I was much better suited for working directly with kids and teaching camping skills. Marty knew that, and he got me re-hired the next summer as a provisional Scoutmaster. These staffers were assigned to troops of Scouts who didn't have an adult leader from their home district. Wauwepex specialized in those kinds of campers, and we had at least five provisional troops at any given period of time. Beginning in mid-summer 1970, I was leading one of those units.

1970 was also a time of turmoil in the country. The massacre at Kent State had just happened, and Wauwepex was not immune. Besides the churn of politics in the air, former camp staff who had just returned from a tour of duty in Vietnam were looking to be rehired at their old camp jobs. As a result, we possessed a weird mix of former Marines and hippie war protesters. For me, marijuana got added to the swirl. Topping it off was a growing sense that I didn't want anyone telling me what to do.

Worse, though, the fun and freedom that I felt as a camper was missing as a staffer. I began to chafe at my camp responsibilities in quiet, mysterious ways. Additionally, by mid-summer I had decided to drop out of college, Lehigh University. I was bursting at the seams.

I wasn't alone. I was part of a rebellious, liberal crew of provisional Scoutmasters, and I loved those guys immensely.

One night, two of them, Geoff and Bill, came by my troop's campsite on an overnight hike away from Wauwepex, and invited me to the Greenbrier. Again, I was discovered and fired — my second dismissal.

As I moved into adulthood all my camp experiences rolled into a huge, complex ball of sweet memories and a bubbling, seething cauldron of guilt and shame for all the irresponsible things I had done as a Wauwepex staffer. Nightmares followed me into wakefulness. The panic was severe, and it built to an unbearable crescendo. Sleepless and in agony I meditated, then decided to confront these terrors and see why they were coming into my consciousness. I asked my soul to reveal to me what Wauwepex meant to me in deeper ways. I had to find out what was haunting me.

In consciousness, I realized that Wauwepex was, and is, holy ground to me. I breathed in the bliss of sweet memories, and pushed onward. I focused on the dreams and the anguish. Then, gently and simply, the realization arose that Wauwepex was truly a unique place for me — it was absolutely safe, especially emotionally. I realized I was psychologically secure enough to make Really Big Mistakes at Wauwepex, maybe the only place for me to do that since I grew up in such a strict, Catholic, upper-middle class environment. I saw that Wauwepex had been a place for me to experiment with life — to express my desires and to feel my power — no matter how clumsily or at what expense.

Ten years after my last year at Wauwepex, I wrote my old camp ranger, Johnnie Jones, on Father's Day. I sent him a card and told him how much he meant to me. I also found the courage to tell him that I considered him a second father.

A decade after that, I visited Wauwepex for the first time since my youth. Johnnie was gone, but his son, Wally, was the new Ranger. Wally and I talked about the old days, especially how much the camp meant to me. I told Wally that his father was very important to me, and he responded, "Yeah, he got that Father's Day card, and it meant a lot to him, so thanks. By the way, you're not the only one to tell my dad he was kind of a father figure *or* send him a card!" I smiled.

A couple of years afterward I received a phone call from a Boy Scout official at the Nassau County Council headquarters. The fellow said he wanted to talk about Wauwepex and the strange "magic" it had.

"I've heard from so many Scouts," he said, "especially camp staffers, that Wauwepex was a special place—personally and in other ways. What made it so special? I don't hear Scouts or staff at our other camps, Onteora or Alpine in upstate New York, talk about their camps in the same way. Not even close."

"Wauwepex is special," I replied. "I'm not sure what it is, but part of it might be the land itself—Wauwepex is still virgin ground since it was never farmed. It's pure, unlike most of metropolitan New York. Wauwepex has always been a pine barren, and the soil is so thin you can even see the underlying white sands in a lot of places. Yet, the aroma of pine is rich and sharp, especially in August when all the needles on the ground turn bone-dry and get crackly when you walk on them. The lake is gorgeous, too. It's deep and blue. The forests are open, and the woodlands feel free. The trees are so scrubby and spaced so far apart that you never feel closed-in, or suffocated, like you do in an upstate forest."

The official asked me to reach out to other Wauwepex staffers and encourage them to call in with their thoughts. The guy said he wanted to see if he could find a way to instill the Wauwepex magic into the Council's other camps since Wauwepex was being "retired" as an active camp.

"Wauwepex has been receiving campers every summer since the 1920s," the official said. "The forests are depleted of firewood around every campsite, and the ground is compacted, especially on the trails. Wauwepex needs a rest. We're not abandoning the place, and we'll continue to use it during the fall and spring for troops on the weekends."

I endeavored to contact Geoff, Bill, and the rest of the crew, but to no avail. I never heard back from the BSA official, either.

Now, in my 70s, I went back to Wauwepex a few summers ago. It's still resting, but I walked around the lake and smelled the pine needles. All the pit latrines are gone now due to county health regulations and have been replaced with large, heated bath houses. But in every other regard, Wauwepex is just the same.

Note: In 2022, the Theodore Roosevelt Council of the Boy Scouts of America (TRC-BSA) — the local chapter that took over from the Nassau County Council — announced it was subject to a $1 million contribution to the overall $850 million national settlement with the 80,000 men who have been sexually assaulted during their time in Scouting. Approximately 1,000 young men of Nassau County were molested while in Scouting, many of them reportedly while camping at Wauwepex. Unlike many other local BSA chapters, the TRC did not have to sell Wauwepex or any other camp lands, and found the $1 million needed with contributions from private sources and the sales of TRC-related assets.

6

Gottman and Beck Find a Bear in their Bed
I see myself growing into manhood

Gottman and Beck were two Boy Scouts I traveled with on the previously mentioned cross-country trip to Philmont Scout Ranch. We were part of a busload of Scouts from Long Island, en route to spend 10 days trekking through the Sangre de Cristo Mountains, a landscape the Philmont staff called "God's Country."

Perhaps you can guess the story. We're camping and a bear went into Gottman and Beck's tent, scaring the daylights out of them. Of course, it's fun to know how it happened, but in this case, it's more important to know what didn't.

Our troop was an eclectic group of Scouts from all over our Nassau County Council, and everyone had to be at least 14 years old to qualify. Gottman and Beck barely satisfied that requirement, and most of the Scouts were older. I was 16, as were most of the guys, with a few at 17.

I knew a handful of the Scouts from Wauwepex or Jamborees, but we were mostly strangers to each other. Even though they were only two years younger than I was, Gottman and Beck were clearly different. Not only were they the youngest, they were also the smallest. Plus, they were the least sophisticated kids on the bus. Worse, Beck's father was one of our four Scoutmasters. As a result, the two kids were viewed as pariahs. Hence, they clung to each other. They were a complete pair, so much so that they seemed to morph into one person. We even called them by their two names together—it was always "Gottman-and-Beck." They would even be assigned to duty rosters together as if they were one person, doing clean-ups, collecting firewood, or cooking meals. Naturally, they were tent mates, too.

Once we arrived at Philmont, the 40-man troop was subdivided into four patrols of 10 Scouts each. Gottman and Beck were assigned to my patrol, which was headed by one of our Scoutmasters, a wise and kindly man named Mr. Henderson, who was an English teacher during the school year.

Another important element of our patrol was the presence of Colton Baskett. Colton was a weird Boy Scout. To begin, he was 17 but an "old" 17, appearing to be caught between "too cool" and "total nerd." As a result, he was a loner. Colton was one of those lost Boy Scouts who were too hip to still be passionate about being a Scout, but unable to figure out what else he wanted to do with his life. Some parental figure probably stuck him on our Philmont bus because they didn't know where else to put him that summer.

I was a fringe guy, too, and Colton and I were the "leftovers" when camping partners were selected. By default, we became tent mates. Even though we never became friends, Colton pulled his own weight and was a decent camping buddy.

Gottman and Beck did okay, too. They never lagged behind on our daily treks, which sometimes were tough 20-mile hikes with heavy packs filled with several days' worth of provisions. They never told funny jokes or a cool story, but they never whined either, which put them in good standing with me. After humping across 100 miles of the Rockies, our patrol had become a tight group, which made the events at a campsite called Cimmaroncito all the more surprising.

Cimmaroncito was a crossroads type of campsite in the sprawling Philmont ranch, which is over 120,000 acres. Philmont has over 20,000 Scouts traipsing across its landscape every summer, and Cimmaroncito was one of those places where a number of trails intersected. The night we were there we joined a dozen other Scout groups. With all this traffic Cimmaroncito maintained a ranger station, food depot, and even had a little country store where we could buy candy bars, soda, and potato chips.

Cimmaroncito was high in the southeastern flank of the Rockies, known as the Sangre de Cristo Mountains, and nestled in a lush, alpine-like valley. It was the epitome of "God's Country" — a green, unspoiled wilderness, and refuge for my troop who had just come from a night of "dry" camping — a form of backpacking away from any rangers or re-supply. We didn't even have access to fresh water.

As a result, we were excited to arrive at Cimmaroncito to get new food — mostly dehydrated stews, veggies, and pastas — take hot showers, and drink lots of cold water.

Cimmaroncito was manned by several rangers who greeted us as we arrived in late afternoon. They told us about the services, and they invited us to take hot showers in exchange for bringing firewood to stoke the fires for the next day's group.

They also warned us about the fire risks and asked us not to build our campfires too high, as they didn't want the woods and its dry tinder exposed to any errant sparks. Further, to protect the pristine landscape we were instructed to pitch our tents on the wooden platforms the staff had established, and to build our cooking fires in the stone circles which were designed to minimize fire risks.

But chief among their concerns were the bears, as Cimmaroncito was a mecca for them. As a result, we had to hang our food caches from tree branches. We were instructed not to bring any candy or food stuffs into our tents.

After supper, Colton and I decided to go for our showers along with our patrol leader, Danny, and his brother, Jimmy.

Gottman and Beck stayed at the campsite to clean-up, along with the rest of our crew and Mr. Henderson.

After a wonderful 45-minute shower I felt transcendent. I could feel my body getting toughened by all the miles. It wasn't a boy's body anymore, and it felt good. Our foursome was in a similar state of mind, and we radiated a sweet camaraderie, a brotherhood.

In the midst of this reverie, Colton blurted out: "You guys will never guess what I did to Gottman and Beck!"

"I have no idea, Colton," I said. "Whaddaya do?"

"I put some Insty-Grape jam under the floor boards of Gottman and Beck's tent platform."

"Oh, no Colton, you didn't," I said.

Danny called him an asshole for pulling a stunt like that. Danny was not only our patrol leader; he was also the only one who could use cuss words without recrimination.

By now we were walking back to our campsite and saw a campfire blazing sky-high with about 30 Scouts and several adult leaders standing around it.

"Must be those Scouts from Los Angeles," I joked.

"Yeah, they don't think they have to obey the rules!" Danny added.

Then I returned to the matter of the grape jam under Gottman and Beck's tent. "Colton, that sweet stuff is gonna attract bears like you wouldn't believe," I said.

"That's the point!" he rebutted. "The bear will scare the crap out of Gottman and Beck."

"Geez, Colton," Danny chimed in, "that's all we need is to have Gottman and Beck scared out of their gourds by some stupid bear smelling the grape jam and snooping around. They were doing okay, too, but now they're probably gonna want to run off and see their mommies...."

"Or get switched to the patrol that Mr. Beck is leading," offered Jimmy.

"And that'll screw up our schedule and everything," Danny retorted.

Colton was saddened that no one was enjoying his practical joke. He continued trying to convince us that his jam move might be funny. No one believed him.

By then we were passing another campsite. We were startled to see another roaring campfire, with a ton of Scouts standing around it.

"Must be more Scouts from California," I laughed.

"Or Jersey," Danny said. "Our cousins live in Trenton and they love burning things down. Right, Jimmy?" The brothers laughed, but I wasn't sure what the family secret was exactly.

After passing the second fire, Danny got Colton to agree to remove the grape jam from Gottman and Beck's platform.

"It's better to be safe than sorry," Danny counseled. Colton demurred.

But when we entered our campsite, we found it dark and empty.

"Where the hell is everyone," queried Danny. "Hey, anyone here?" he called out, but there was no answer.

In response, I decided to build a campfire, and Jimmy helped. Danny went off with Colton to fix the grape situation, and when the flames of our fire reached a few feet I added some larger logs. With the extra light we could see our guys running back, followed by a dozen strange Scouts and a few adults.

"GOTTMAN AND BECK WERE ATTACKED BY BEARS!!!" they shouted over and over. They were hysterical, and circled Jimmy and me, shouting and flailing the air with their arms.

Danny and Colton joined the circle, and their faces dropped when they grasped the seriousness of the situation.

"Are Gottman and Beck okay?" Danny asked. "Where are they?" A cascade of questions and shouts surged.

Russ, a solid 15-year-old from our patrol, pushed forward and answered our questions.

"Yeah, Gottman and Beck are okay, kinda. They were crying their eyes out the last I saw them, but now they're down at the ranger station in the infirmary. A bear came in their tent when they were lying down, and they started screaming. They tore through the back of their tent, which collapsed on the bear. The bear went crazy and ran off into the woods."

"All the bears in the valley are here, too!" another member of our patrol offered. "We could see them in the trees at the edge of our campsite!"

"Oh, my Gawd," I muttered.

Then the crowd parted and Mr. Henderson entered the circle. "Boys, do you know anything about this?" he asked.

I looked at Danny, then Colton, who was looking at the ground. Danny turned toward Mr. Henderson and caught his eye. He flipped his head, indicating to Mr. Henderson that he should join him away from the group for a little private conversation. Danny wasn't a super Scout—he only had the rank of first-class—but Danny knew a lot about tough fathers and what to do when trouble hits the fan. It was clearly time for Danny to step up to the plate and tell Mr. Henderson what had happened.

At the fire, Russ gave us more details.

"I was in my tent when I heard Gottman and Beck screaming and the bear roaring, so I got my knife and flashlight and went outside. Gottman and Beck were running through the woods like crazy people—screaming all the time. I tried to chase after them, but I didn't want to get too close to the bears, so I came back to the campsite and shouted for everyone to follow me and we went down to the next campsite—some San Diego guys—and told them what was happening and that we needed protection, and that they had to build up the campfire and all that. Soon a bunch of those guys were going to all the other campsites and telling them what was going on—and everyone could see the bears in the woods. I started throwing rocks at the bears, but some Scoutmaster told me to stop because he said it would provoke them—but I was just trying to scare them away and keep us safe. I was frightened, I guess. Everyone was. The guys who left to warn the others had flashlights and long sticks, and they went as a group—everyone was staying together. Soon the rangers got here, and one even had a rifle!"

Danny and Mr. Henderson silently returned and tapped Colton on the shoulder. Together the three pivoted, slipping away into the shadows.

An hour later, Mr. Henderson returned. He told everyone that the rangers were armed and were patrolling the campsites. He said we could safely return to our tents. "Try to get some sleep, boys," he said.

As I crawled into my sleeping bag, I saw him and Danny stoking the fire. I was nearly asleep when Colton came in and removed his sleeping bag.

"Where ya going, Colt?" I asked.

"I gotta sleep in Gottman and Beck's tent. The jam is gone, but I gotta put the tent back up. There's a broken pole. I think I can fix it with a stick."

"Whew, Colton. I hope you'll be safe."

"Yeah, me, too."

Colton made it through the night, and the next day was given a reprieve. I think Danny must have prevailed on Mr. Henderson to show mercy, and Colton stayed with the patrol. Not surprisingly, he was a model Scout for the remainder of his time at Philmont.

The next day Gottman and Beck rejoined the group as we pulled out of Cimmaroncito, and they, too, showed restraint. They never said a word about the incident, and they never plotted revenge against Colton.

As we hiked past the ranger station, I could see vestiges of the bear rampage from the night before. Overturned garbage cans and flipped metal food caches were strewn all over the place. Bags of flour and dehydrated meals were torn open, making the whole scene look like a snowstorm had hit during the night.

One stupid practical joke had caused all of this, and there didn't seem to be any way to patch it back together. Cimmaroncito would need time to return to its idyllic calm. I certainly hoped no other Scouts would be attacked or traumatized in the days to come. The ripple effects of Colton's jam joke were enormous. So was the potential for more unrest.

I suppose having Colton sleep in Gottman and Beck's tent was a sublime act of frontier justice, but what if the bears had come back and attacked Colton, or even killed him?

What then?

Would Cimmaroncito have been closed to all hikers for the rest of the season? Would the rangers be compelled to shoot or relocate all these bears? If anyone was injured, how devastating would the legal difficulties be for Philmont? What about law suits? What would become of the Boy Scouts of America?

It's easy to imagine how one little packet of jam could have brought Philmont and the BSA to its knees.

Note: Gottman and Beck's names have been changed to protect the innocent. But Charlie and Elliott, if you get wind of this story, please give me a call. I'd love to hear how you are doing.

Note II: I was so transformed by Philmont, and by extension New Mexico, I adopted the Zia symbol — the sun sign ubiquitous throughout the state. The symbol is a circle with four lines radiating out from its four quadrants. Some say it represents the cycle of life — birth, childhood, adulthood, and death. Others describe it as the flow of time — morning, afternoon, evening, and night. But for me it speaks to all of it and illumines the grandeur of life.

7

Army Intelligence
My first encounter with governmental surveillance

The closing of America's borders to many Muslims by the Trump Administration in 2017 brings to mind the political struggles of the 1960s and 1970s, especially the shooting of four students at Kent State University by Ohio National Guardsmen on May 4, 1970 during an anti-war protest.

This story is about a buddy of mine from my old neighborhood of Floral Park, named Kenny, who joined with me in a protest against the Kent State Massacre. He later paid a huge price, courtesy of the US Army, and his experience reveals the enormous capacity of the government to conduct surveillance of the public, particularly college demonstrations.

The day after the Kent State shootings, colleges across America erupted with outrage against the government and the Vietnam War. Many universities went on strike, with faculty canceling classes and students occupying administration buildings. Since I had dropped out of Lehigh the prior September, I gravitated to kindred spirits protesting at the campus of Hofstra University, where Kenny and many of our hometown friends had enrolled.

Although Kenny had dropped out of Hofstra prior to the Kent State incident, he was still hanging around, especially with his fraternity buddies. By mid-afternoon of the protest, Kenny and I — independently of each other — and thousands of other young people coalesced in the main quad of South Campus, adjacent to the principal administration building that had just been commandeered by students of the SDS — Students for a Democratic Society. A small stage had been built on the steps of the building, and speakers were beginning to foment a rally.

They touted the idea that we should march down Hempstead Turnpike — the main drag from Hofstra to the nearby town of Hempstead — and hold a second, more visible rally to voice our rage. Organically and peacefully, we began moving from the quad to a local street, and then headed to Hempstead Turnpike a couple blocks away.

I joined the throng, and as we funneled past the side streets onto the main thoroughfare, a dozen police cars appeared. A phalanx of officers directed us onto the three westbound lanes of the roadway, holding back traffic so we could cross safely.

As we marched, word passed quickly that we would re-group at A&S, the giant department store in town that was the commercial hub of central Nassau County. A&S stood for "Abraham and Strauss," and was so popular that everyone called it by its initials. In the flowering of the '60s, it had also become a symbol of American consumerism and decadence, and thus was a suitable destination for a day of protest.

Marching along the pavement, I marveled at walking on a spread of concrete where thousands of cars would normally be speeding along. It was intoxicating. Glancing around, I noticed some students walking on the double-yellow line that separated us from the eastbound lanes, the ones that still contained vehicular traffic. Peering more closely, I realized those special students wore red armbands. I didn't know any of them, and I later learned they were all members of various fraternities. As such, Kenny was among them. He later told me the fraternities had been asked by the cops to act as guardians since they could mobilize their members quickly. There was a real risk in marching to A&S even though the traffic behind us was detained by the cops. Eastbound traffic still flowed, albeit at only 20 mph. Given the political and cultural tensions in the country, it was not unthinkable that a crazy right-winger might want to plow into us.

But nothing happened. The rally at A&S was anti-climactic. The demonstration soon dissipated, and we dispersed as darkness approached.

Six months later, Kenny told me he was going to volunteer for the Army. I was aghast. Kenny listened to the same music I did, and he had already sampled a bit of LSD as I had, so I figured he was anti-war. Certainly, he had never presented himself as a gung-ho guy for global American hegemony. Besides, he seemed smart enough to know his presence in the Army could mess up his mind, let alone risk getting himself killed.

Kenny assured me he had a plan, though. As a volunteer, he was given a guarantee by the Army he wouldn't go to Vietnam as long as he passed all the requirements to remain in his chosen field of radio electronics. Kenny saw it as a realistic career move at a time when little else was going on in his life that either made sense or felt satisfying. A lot of men felt that way, but it was tough to accept Kenny's decision, and he went off into the Army without my blessing. It signaled the end of our friendship.

Nevertheless, I would hear from him periodically throughout his early Army experience. First, from boot camp at Fort Dix, New Jersey, and then from Monterrey, California, where he went for advanced electronic training. After about a year or so, the Army taught him Russian in preparation to station him in Alaska and monitor Soviet military radio transmissions. Kenny was enthusiastic at the prospect of living and working in Alaska—the wilderness appealed to him as much as having something worthwhile to do with his time.

However, his assignment was canceled the day before he was scheduled to depart. Kenny was summoned by his commanding officer to the HQ. As Kenny entered, his CO opened a file and took out some photographs. He flipped a few of them in Kenny's direction.

"What the hell are these?" the CO asked.

They were pictures of Kenny walking down Hempstead Turnpike in 1970 with a red arm band on.

The CO then told Kenny that his security clearance had been revoked. Therefore, he was no longer eligible to monitor Soviet military communications. As a result, his electronics outfit no longer had any use for him, and he was being reassigned to advanced infantry training in Fort Polk, Louisiana, which was often called the "Gateway to Vietnam."

Kenny was stunned. So was I when he told me the story. How did the Army get the pictures of the march from two years before? Sure, we all knew that the FBI was taking pictures of all the anti-war rallies, but Kenny was so insignificant. He wasn't SDS or a protest organizer. He was just a young kid trying to keep his fellow students safe during a protest.

Plus, how did anyone know his name? He was a dropout, and only an "associate" member of his fraternity. He probably wasn't even on any roster of "the brothers."

So, how did he get identified at the only protest rally he ever attended? More importantly, how did those photographs find their way to an Army officer's desk two years later and 3,000 miles away?

The fact that the Army was able to identify Kenny and track him shows that the Army has incredible access to information—thousands of photographs and plenty of informants who can identify every individual of note. Plus, a huge staff to catalog that name and still be able to retrieve it years in the future.

Was my friend really that much of a security risk? Was it really unsafe for our country to have Kenny listen to Russian radio chit-chat? The reality is that the Army was clearly concerned, and they had the means to do something about their fears.

Which begs the question: If the military can track someone as far from public recognition as my old friend Kenny, then what can they do with someone who writes a story like this?

8

North to Chibougamou
My first independent foray

Driving north from New York City, the road eventually ends 750 miles later in a Canadian mining town called Chibougamou. When I hitchhiked there in 1969, the last 150-mile stretch of highway was unpaved gravel, and that helps make Chibougamou unique in my travels. Yet, in other ways it is even more distant from where I grew up on Long Island.

In 1969, I was full of adventure and only slightly curious to see if Canada might be a place to live since I had just dropped out of Lehigh and had lost my draft deferment. Hence, the notion that I might have to join the throng of draft protestors relocating to Canada was real, but tucked deeply in the back of my mind. More importantly, hard-hat bozos in New York were beating up on hippies like me. Bumper stickers in my neighborhood loudly proclaimed: *America – Love It or Leave It!* So, I was eager to find people who would be more accepting and more life-affirming. My journey to Chibougamou was certainly a lengthy trip, but it started long before I stuck my thumb into the northbound traffic of the New York State Thruway.

Instead of returning to Lehigh for my third year, I left all that I had known and started hitchhiking northward, first to Montreal. It was the first time in my adult life that I wasn't doing what others told me, or what I thought they wanted me to do. In my pocket I had my life's savings: $70.

Montreal is the biggest city in Québec—*La Belle Province*, the Beautiful Province. Even though I had gotten only a D+ in French at Lehigh, I was eager to try out my chops and *parlez Français*. Besides, Montreal is bilingual, so I knew I could fall back on my native tongue if the French got too tough.

As a kid my family had vacationed in Quebec, and I had seen the old fortress of the Chateau Frontenac and the ramparts along the Plains of Abraham where the French colonialists lost to the British in the decisive battle for Canada. All that enchanted me. Since I had never been to Europe, Quebec offered the next best thing, and my thumb got me there for free.

For the first leg of my trip, I called my friend Manny to see if he would like to join me for the run to Montreal. He had been a buddy in the freshman dorms at Lehigh, someone who had always been ready for adventure on a moment's notice. He agreed, and I met him at his new college, NYU. We then headed to the Bronx via the subway and, after a short walk from the station, we got on an entrance ramp to the Major Deegan Expressway. There we put out our thumbs.

As I was to learn repeatedly, if you have enough patience and balls you can get a ride anywhere. So, after withstanding the violent gloom of the south Bronx and a couple of NYC cops who didn't want a bunch of long-haired hippies on their highway, we got our first ride.

Just north of the NYC line, the Deegan becomes the New York Thruway, which splits at Albany into I-90 westward to Buffalo and the I-87 "Northway" to Montreal. We took the Northway, a beautifully scenic highway, and by 9 p.m. were approaching the Canadian border. Still on the American side, our ride got off at an exit called "Chazy-Sciota," which made me think of "Crazy Sciots," as if the area were named after a band of pioneers from Scotland who went psychotic in the northern wilderness.

Whatever the origins of Chazy-Sciota, we did meet unusual people there, or at least one. As we descended the exit ramp, Manny asked the driver if he knew of any place where we could roll out our sleeping bags and "crash for the night," the slang term for having an impromptu roof over our heads.

The driver said he did, and he drove a few miles east of the highway, where he dropped us off at what he termed a "commune." Manny and I walked into the main structure among a cluster of farm buildings. The people we met were friendly; however, no one could tell us if we could spend the night, which made us nervous. We kept making small talk while waiting, but for 20 minutes no one would confirm that we could stay.

Eventually, we were ushered into a small room, and a burly guy with a huge beard motioned for us to sit down. He asked if we had ID.

ID? This is a commune! Who has ID on a commune? Isn't a commune where hippies go to tune out, turn on, and drop out?

Fortunately, Manny and I both had our New York State drivers' licenses, which back in those days didn't have a photo on them. As we handed them to the hairy guy, I thought: What's he gonna learn from an ID that doesn't have a photo? But I knew instinctively that the guy asking the questions needed something in his hands to look at to assuage his anxiety.

After a few minutes of staring at the licenses and turning them over in his hands, he gave them back to us. Then he faced his commune friends and said that it would be okay for us to spend one night, which we spent nestled atop a huge pile of old clothing stacked in an outbuilding.

As we left the next day, Manny asked me if I thought the bearded guy was Abbie Hoffman.

"Nah," I said. It seemed too preposterous that we would cross paths with him, even though the *Village Voice* was claiming that Abbie was hiding out on a commune in the northern reaches of New York State. But now I know the usually insurmountable divide between celebrities and common folk is often penetrated by the vagaries of life.

So, yes, now I do believe our host was the Cultural Revolutionary, Abbie Hoffman.

The next day Manny and I arrived in Montreal. Chickening out on the French, we headed to the English-speaking bastion of McGill University, where we found an all-night rock concert in progress. Around 2 a.m. we spread out our sleeping bags in a little alcove off the multipurpose room that was filled with hundreds of rockin' kids.

At dawn we had to leave after only three hours of sleep. On the steps of the building we met a guy who spotted our packs and sleeping bags, and offered to let us stay with him for a couple of days.

My strongest memory of that time is the anger our host felt toward Manny and me for messing up his bathtub. One morning, Manny took a shower before I did and left an incredible amount of body hair strewn on the porcelain surface of the tub. I followed in the shower and, feeling detached, or at least not responsible, I didn't do anything to clean up my buddy's mess. Now, however, I rarely bathe in anyone's home without thinking of that shower stall in Montreal, and it still bothers me that I didn't cover for my friend.

After Montreal, Manny returned to New York, and eventually his law degree. I continued on to Quebec City, hitching down Sherbrooke Boulevard, the longest urban street in the world.

La Cité de Québec is 150 miles northeast of Montreal, and it is the only city that has thoroughly enthralled me. The walled Inner City, the cobbled streets, the tiny alleyways—it all thrilled my soul. I suppose Venice or Paris can do that to other people, but Quebec City is my medieval paradise.

One special memory of Quebec City is how I felt its enchantment so strongly that I was emboldened to walk up to a beautiful woman and tell her my thoughts. I even asked to take her picture, and with a smile she complied. All this was done in French, too.

On the other side of the same magical coin, I also felt desperately lonely. One night, eating by myself in a Chinese restaurant, I propped up my pack on the seat across from me for company.

A third memory is my discovery of a distinct culture very different from my own. For me, the clearest dramatization of this was the graffiti from the *Parti Québecois*, the French separatist movement advocating secession from Canada and known to Anglophiles as the Quebeckers' Party. Their graffiti impressed me. Somehow it looked very real, as if the passions behind it were still vibrating in the paint. This was surprising to me since I had just come from a country being ripped apart over the issues of racism and the war in Southeast Asia. But no one in New York was suggesting that we anti-war folks all move to California or some other hippie place and then secede from the United States. In contrast, many *Québecois* felt they needed to leave the Canadian Confederation. That personal sense of identity — and feeling assaulted by the dominating English culture — was wholly new to me.

After a few days in Quebec City, I decided to hitchhike north to James Bay and visit the Inuit people. The idea just popped into my head, and it seemed like a cool thing to do, even though the map showed a road only going halfway.

I'll figure out the second part when I get up there.

Heading northward from Quebec City is a nondescript highway that winds through the *Parque du Laurentides* and then to the farm country surrounding *Lac Saint Jean*.

As I passed through the Laurentian Mountains the weather began to get chilly. It was early October, and I remember seeing vibrant blue skies dotted with puffy white clouds, delivering an exquisite clarity and vitality that was unlike anything I knew back home in New York.

Strangely, I started smoking cigarettes for the first time in my life—Lucky Strikes. I thought they tasted pretty good, too, especially the first puff. They also seemed to warm my fingers as I stuck out my thumb.

Another weird experience befell me as I passed through the Laurentians—I left all connection to the English-speaking world. Virtually no one spoke English. I was surprised. It felt like something had flipped in the Natural World. *What is this? No one speaks the language I do?* I realized I had a deep-seated belief that since I spoke English, everyone else should, too.

Nevertheless, I learned that I was *fait du pouce*, literally, "making of the thumb," or hitchhiking *en Français*. Another phrase that still stays with me is: *epouché les potates,* or "peel the potatoes." By this time, I had run out of money so I was working odd jobs. In the northern reaches of Quebec City I worked in a bar and grill, peeling the potatoes for the *pomme frites* fry man. In exchange, I stayed in a nearby apartment building, whose facilities I was told were usually filled with the ice hockey team the bar owner sponsored. The players received free room and board and a couple of bucks to play a good brand of "Junior" level hockey.

The *potates* I peeled were turned into homemade French fries and served in the bar. At the time, I had never heard of a restaurant doing that, but now I know it is common practice in rural, mom-and-pop types of establishments. The *frites* were fresh and tasty, and whenever I have a French fry these days, I often think of all the potatoes I peeled in Quebec. But if I were to return to La Belle Province, I probably couldn't get my old job back because most people these days eat their *frites* with the skin still on their *potates*.

Another surprise to me about *les frites du Québec* is that the *Québecois* eat them with malt vinegar, not catsup. It's an excellent tradition and I think Americans should switch over.

After four days of *epouché*-ing, I made my way to the town of Mistassini, on the north shore of Lac Saint Jean. I was now about 200 miles north of Quebec City.

Around sunset I asked the young guy who was giving me a ride if he knew of a place where I could spend the night. He suggested I try the Trappist monastery. In English he told me, "The monks have a long tradition of taking in travelers who have no money and need a place to stay."

The monastery had a large wooden door that was mounted into a stone wall that looked as if it was part of a castle. I knocked. With the darkness of early evening, the scene took on the overtones of a Frankenstein movie, but I didn't feel afraid. I felt reassured knowing I wasn't the first guy to ask these monks for a free room.

A monk of about 60 opened the door. He was no taller than 5 feet and wore the brown-hooded robe customary for Trappists. In an English-French mix I explained who I was, and he welcomed me in. Even though it was close to 8 p.m. he asked me if I had eaten dinner and offered to feed me. I wasn't hungry, but I was impressed by his hospitality. He showed me to my room. It was a typical monk's cell—small, sparse, and meditative. I thought it was great. I felt very warm and secure, and slept well on my little cot. But the 6 a.m. call to breakfast was too tough to answer. Usually, I don't wake until 8 or 9 a.m., and I don't eat breakfast until 10 a.m. at the earliest.

However, the monastic schedule did give me an early start on the road to Chibougamou. Since there is very little between Mistassini and Chibougamou, I got a through-ride and was in Chibougamou by mid-afternoon. As usual, the big question was: *Where am I going to stay?*

I wandered into a small music store and soon a saleswoman asked me if I needed any help. I blurted out most of the French phrases I had been practicing during the long hours of standing on the road with my *pouce* out.

I explained I was traveling, out of money, and looking for a place to stay in exchange for working any odd job. She looked confused. I didn't know if it was my French or my request. Probably both. Fortunately, her English was better than my French, and between the two languages we understood each other.

I learned she lived with her sister and brother-in-law, and I might be able to stay with them. She said she would have to ask them first, which she did over the phone. They agreed to take me in.

Their house was a small, working-class home. I slept in the living room on the couch, which was about 5 feet long. It had no arm rests, so my feet dangled over the edge. The living room was pretty small—just big enough for the couch and a TV stand. I remember the house because it had no siding, only lots of exposed tar paper. Many houses in the neighborhood were like that. Even though the brother-in-law worked full time in the local copper mine, they didn't have enough money to install siding or insulate the house properly, so it must have gotten very cold in the winter.

Speaking of winter, in Chibougamou I was surprised to see all the cars dangling the male end of an electrical cord out their front grill. The brother-in-law explained that it was for the engine block heater. The winters were so cold that in the mornings the engines had to be heated before they would turn over.

In addition, he told me the tires would flatten in the cold, and would require a few miles of slow driving before they would expand back to their original, round shape. As a result, the brother-in-law went to work with the *thwrop, thwrop, thwrop* of misshapen tires sounding in his ears.

I was beginning to see people who lived a much different life than I did.

The *jeune fille* who befriended me was a couple of years older than I, and very good looking. She was ambitious and worked two jobs. Besides the music store, she worked several nights as a barmaid in one of the local taverns. She told me that she wanted to make a lot of money so she could leave Chibougamou and support herself for a few months in a city like Montreal. There, she wanted to become an airline stewardess for Air Canada.

That evening we talked for a few hours, past the time her sister and brother-in-law went to bed. I began to feel romantic toward my friend and I reached out and grabbed her wrist, saying, "I'd like to touch you."

"You already are," she said icily. I quickly let go, and we went to our separate rooms.

The next day I visited her in the music store. The incident the night before, although leaving a bad taste in my mouth, did not make her any less friendly in the light of day. But I suspected that she felt a bit of contempt toward me. Nevertheless, she suggested that I visit her that night at her second job tending bar. Since the Montreal *Canadiennes* were playing that night and the hockey game would be on the tavern's TV, it would be the place to be in Chibougamou.

Hockey is one of my favorite sports, and I played it briefly at Lehigh. As for viewing *Les Canadiennes* in Chibougamou, it felt wonderful watching one of the best hockey teams in the world while sitting among dozens of their hometown fans.

As the *Canadiennes* kicked the butts of some NHL team from America, I nursed a *Labatt Cinquante* — a Labatt 50 — while my friend served beers and drinks to the hordes of men screaming at the TV screen.

But every now and then the bar owner would call her over to him, and she would leave the room for about 15 minutes. I didn't think much of it until I moved my seat in the course of the game, and with a new angle I could see her ascend a staircase on the far side of the tavern. She entered a second story that had a few rooms.

On two occasions I saw her climb these stairs, and on the second I realized a guy was following behind her. It didn't dawn on me until much later that she might have been turning tricks up there.

The next day, I decided to explore Chibougamou and see exactly where the road north led. I walked down Main Street. The city's pavement turned to gravel about a mile out of town, and then it became a rutted jeep trail. Eventually, it turned into someone's driveway. Getting to the Inuit people was clearly a little trickier than I had first envisioned. When I told the locals of my intentions they said, "You're either gonna have to fly, or wait a few weeks and take a Ski-Doo or dog sled."

But, as I stood on that jeep trail at the end of the road and looked at the cool, wet fir trees, I knew I had reached some kind of special destination. I didn't have to see any Inuit for I had gone as far as I could go, and for me it was a very special place. Since then, I have traveled to many wonderful locales. Some of them are on maps, others are in poems and songs, and a few precious ones are in my dreams. Many of them are unique, but they all trace their roots back to Chibougamou.

And to this day, I have never met anyone who has ever been to the end of the northern road in Chibougamou.

9

Not Going to Vietnam
My first big manifestation

One of the impacts of dropping out of Lehigh was losing my draft deferment. Since the Vietnam War was still going on, I risked heading there. But deep in my bones I knew I wouldn't go.

I hadn't been ignoring the draft, though. I had applied for Conscientious Objector status, which was denied. Further, traveling to Chibougamou gave me a view of the world far beyond America and Vietnam, so I had a detached feeling about the war. Besides, the Viet Cong were not bothering me, and the conflict seemed as if it was somebody else's problem.

Nor did patriotic calls to duty touch me, especially after I went to D.C. for a "March on Washington." There, I saw tanks ready to roll against the protesters, and it confirmed to me that America was not a country I was willing to die for, let alone kill others.

Vietnam just wasn't my fight. I didn't drop one bead of sweat worrying about it. Instead, I continued to live my life and follow my dreams.

Eventually that wanderlust led me to Steamboat Springs, Colorado to go skiing for the winter of 1969-1970. While I was there, the round-about process of my *not* going to Vietnam revealed to me how the miraculous can manifest in surprising ways.

One night I awoke with a sharp cramp in my lower right abdomen, accompanied by a raging fever. Heading to the bathroom to take some aspirin, my hands shook so badly I needed two hands to turn the door knob. Instinctively, I knew I was having an appendicitis attack and resolved to head to the hospital the next day.

Steamboat Springs had one doctor, who operated out of a tiny 22-bed hospital. There was no Emergency Room as such; I just walked into the lobby. Positioned there was a desk and nurse's station, where I described my condition to the nurse-receptionist. She motioned to a gentleman sitting next to her.

"Dr. Price will see you shortly," she said, a tad formal for the obviously informal surroundings.

Dr. Vincent Price, who bore a striking resemblance to his namesake actor, stood and waved me into an examination room. Within moments he confirmed my diagnosis of appendicitis.

"I suggest I operate on you right away," Dr. Price said. "Do you have a problem with that?"

"Nope," I said. "Go ahead."

I returned to the nurse-receptionist, who took all my pertinent information and oddly asked me to take a shower. Maybe she assumed that as a ski bum I was grungy and stinky, or she just felt that everyone should be as clean-as-a-whistle for surgery.

After bathing, she guided me into the surgical room where Dr. Price was ready to go. Later that day, I awoke from the anesthesia and Dr. Price was standing next to my bed.

"How do you feel?" he asked.

"Okay, I guess," I replied. "Pretty weak, though."

"Well, I've got some good news and some bad news," Dr. Price said. "What would you like first?"

"The good news, I guess."

"Well, the operation was a success, and you'll be skiing in a week."

"Great. So, what's the bad news?"

"Well, when I read the notes from the nurse, I saw that you're only 20. So, I had to call your parents in New York and get permission to operate. I spoke with your father. Of course, he gave me the okay, but he also told me to tell you that your local draft board has sent you a draft notice. Your induction medical is scheduled for next week. Um...I hope it's okay with you, but I took the liberty of calling your draft board and informing them that you were under the direct care of a surgeon in Colorado and would not be able to make that appointment."

I never heard from the draft board ever again.

Note: The draft lottery had kicked in while I was hitch-hiking through Canada, and I received #232. My draft board reportedly drafted to #235 that year, so, mathematically, I should have been drafted. But I wasn't. Did my draft board lose my paper work after Dr. Price called? Or did my Conscientious Objector request shove me into the "troublemaker" pile? Or did my consciousness nestle me in a place that was safe? I believe the latter.

10

The Two Ghosts of Burston Street
The mystical makes itself known

In 1971, I went back to college, this time at Hofstra University. After a short stint in the dorms, I moved into a duplex house with six other students on a nearby road named Burston Street. Three fellows lived upstairs, four of us downstairs. We downstairs guys lived as a mini-commune, and we called ourselves the Burston Boys. Every night we four ate dinner together, and we divvied up the chores. One week I'd cook; the next, wash dishes; the third, shop; and the fourth, clean the bathroom.

One day during my cooking week, I told my housemates I'd be making spaghetti for dinner and it would be ready at seven o'clock. Everyone concurred, and we went off to our classes.

On my return, I rode my bike through the side yard. Through the kitchen window I saw somebody standing at the stove stirring our spaghetti pot. *Why is someone else cooking the spaghetti? It's my week. And, why are they starting the meal now? No one else will be home for another hour.*

In the time it took for me to lock my bike, walk up the stoop and open the door, whoever had been at the stove was gone.

But when I entered the kitchen, I could see the shadow of somebody walking down the corridor toward the bedrooms.

Three quick strides got me across the kitchen, but just as I turned into the hallway, I saw the shadow enter Conrad's room, the first bedroom on the left.

What timing. When I see Conrad in the kitchen he walks into the hallway. When I go into the hallway he walks into his room. I wanted to congratulate Conrad on his great sense of synchronicity, so I walked boldly into his bedroom.

But no one was there.

WAH? That's weird, I know I saw somebody. Maybe it was a trick of light. Maybe a trucker flashed his headlights on the main street next to us, and Conrad, or whoever it is, went into another room.

I walked to the end of the hallway, to Matty's room. The door was closed and I tried to open it, but it was locked. "Knock, knock," I tapped and called out. "Hello, Matty, are you in there?" No answer.

Hmmmm. Maybe they went into my room. It's right across from Conrad's.

I looked in, not questioning why someone would go into my room, but no one was there, either.

I quickly went to the last bedroom, Alan's. It was next to the kitchen. "Alan," I called out, knocking loudly on his door. "Are you in there?" No answer.

Oh, my Gawd! I know I saw somebody. But not knowing the phone number for Ghostbusters, and not wanting to tell 911 that I had been invaded by an apparition, I figured the next best thing was to go see my buddies in the upstairs apartment and calm myself.

Leaping up the steps two at a time, I arrived in a flash. I banged on the door and in two seconds one of the upstairs guys opened it.

"What's up, Bruce? C'mon in."

"Thank Gawd you're home, Kevin."

"Want a beer or something?"

"Yeah, thanks, but not a beer. I need a cup of coffee, or better, something mellow, like chamomile tea…Kev, I think I saw a ghost. Downstairs…."

"Really? Hmmmm…. It's funny that you should be telling me this," Kevin said, heading to the kitchen while I plopped on a nearby sofa.

"Why?"

"Because the last three nights, me and the other guys up here have been hearing something strange on the roof. It's woken us up and we've gone out with flashlights to see what it was."

"Whadidya see?"

"Nothing."

"Whaddaya meaning nothing? How could that be?"

Kevin shrugged.

"Then, whadidya hear?" I continued.

"Well, each night it was the same thing," Kevin explained. "We'd hear a heavy thud on the roof, and then a scrape across the shingles."

"Maybe it was a tree limb banging on the roof," I offered.

"Yeah, that was what we thought at first. But we didn't see any limbs doing that."

"Maybe it was a limb that came down in the wind?"

"Yeah, we thought of that too, but this happened three nights in a row. And, we didn't see any limbs on the roof, and there were none on the ground. We've got trees near the house, but none are close enough to make that sound."

"Well, maybe it was an animal?"

"Nah. It was too heavy a thud. It sounded like somebody jumping on the roof, or walking hard across it. It wasn't a chipmunk or squirrel."

"Maybe it was a dog?"

"A dog? Have you ever seen a dog on a roof? No, Bruce, it wasn't an animal; the sounds were too heavy."

"Maybe it was kids throwing trash up there, ya' know, playing a prank."

"We thought of that, too, but we didn't see any trash. No bricks, garbage cans, or car tires. Nothing. That's the thing Bruce, we didn't see diddily-squat, three nights in a row."

"Whaddaya think is going on?"

"I don't know."

Just then we heard a noise downstairs. We froze and listened. Footsteps made their way through the kitchen and into the hallway. Then a toilet flushed.

"Ahh..." we exhaled and smiled, knowing instinctively that ghosts don't pee. Kevin and I went downstairs to inform whichever housemate had come home that we lived in a haunted house.

"Hey, Bruce, where's the spaghetti?" Matty called out as Kevin and I walked into the downstairs kitchen.

"Matt, have we got a story to tell you," I said. "Sit down; the spaghetti's gonna be late tonight." Kevin and I told him what we had told each other.

While we recounted the recent events, the rest of our housemates came home and joined the discussion. To my amazement everyone had something to add to the story. Each of my housemates had seen or heard something weird during the past three months. Conrad had the most chilling sighting.

"I thought the ghost was you, Bruce," he said. "I was lying in bed one day and I needed to make a phone call."

Downstairs we had one phone, mounted on the wall in the hallway with a 20-foot extension cord so anyone could sling it into their bedroom.

"But someone was on the phone," Conrad continued, "and I thought it was you. My door was open and on the hallway wall I could see a silhouette of a big guy, about 6 feet and 200 pounds. I thought it was you leaning with the phone tucked between your shoulder and neck."

Conrad continued with a rapt audience.

"I heard you, or whoever it was, talking, although I couldn't make out exactly what you were saying because your voice was too low. After waiting 10 minutes I said, 'Hey, Bruce. C'mon, I gotta make a phone call', but you didn't answer. A couple minutes later I shouted, 'C'MON Bruce, get off the phone.' But still no answer, and you, or the ghost, stayed on the phone. I got angry and shouted, 'HEY, GET OFF THE PHONE!' I got up, and walked into the hallway. But when I got to the hallway, no one was there. You had been there just the second before, and the phone cord was still swishing back and forth like you had just hung it up.

"Since you didn't walk past me or go into your room, which I would have seen since it's right across from my doorway, I figured you were in the kitchen. But when I went into the kitchen you weren't there, and the door was locked. No one had left because I would have heard the door closing and locking. I freaked out at that point, and went to stay with my cousin in Jersey."

"So, that's why you left," Matty said. "I remember you were gone because it was your week to wash dishes, and I ended up doing them. I was wondering why you left and didn't tell anybody." Conrad squirmed at Matty's comments, but it brought some human-sized levity back to the moment.

"How come," I asked everyone, "none of you guys told me you'd been seeing stuff and hearing weird things, huh? What kind of friends are you? Letting me live in a haunted house and not telling me? Then, one day I come home and get the willies scared out of me…" We laughed, but a part of me was hurt.

"Maybe somebody in the astral plane needs our help and they're trying to get our attention," Alan suggested.

We all agreed, and began a discussion on the various causes of inter-dimensional stress that might cause a ghost to stick around our house on Burston Street, and what we could do to assist their moving on to higher realms of consciousness.

For the next month we chanted and meditated, and asked the spirit how we could help, but got no response. No one saw or heard anything weird ever again. Until 16 years later.

Then, I was sitting in a small auditorium at the University of Washington in Seattle for a men's gathering with Michael Meade. Seated two rows in front of me was a long-haired blonde fellow that I knew from somewhere. But where? It distracted me to the point of social boldness, and on the next break I approached him.

"Excuse me," I said. "I know you from somewhere but I don't know your name...." He interrupted me with a big embrace.

"Bruce, it's *so* good to see you!" he roared. "How ya' been?"

"Er...um... good to see you. But who are you?"

"Alan, from Burston Street."

"Oh, yeah. Right!" It all came back to me. *Alan and me and all the guys in the duplex back in Hempstead when we were going to Hofstra.* "Oh, Alan, it's good to see you, too. It's been a long time."

Since we were in Seattle, we New York transplants went to a Starbucks for lattes and reminiscing. Along with the vapors of steaming hot coffee, the questions floated in the air: *What brings you to Seattle? When did you leave New York? Do you remember...?*

"Did you ever go to medical school?" Alan asked.

"Nah. Thank Gawd I didn't. It would have driven me crazy. How about you? What are you doing?"

"Selling commercial real estate. Not too exciting, but it pays the bills," Alan replied. He sipped once, and in a growing lull he sipped again. Then his eyes twinkled, and he took a new tack. "Do you remember the ghost at Burston Street?" he asked.

"Of course I do, Alan. I've told that story 100 times."

"And do you remember the Pentecostals, from next door? They were something, eh?"

"Thanks for reminding me of the Pentecostals," I said. "I had forgotten about them for the past 16 years, Alan, thank you very much." I relished my mock indignation.

Our nextdoor neighbors, a small independent Pentecostal Church, had been a sore point with the Burston Boys. The Sunday parking nightmare the Pentecostals triggered on Burston Street and the neighboring roadways was not a problem for me, but it was for the Village of Hempstead, which sued them and demanded mitigation. In response, the Pentecostals bought our duplex and cut down all the trees and shrubs in our yard to make a parking lot for their church. The *coup de grace* was their 30-day eviction notice.

Worse than losing my home was seeing an end to the Burston Boys. I knew the Pentecostals needed a place to park their cars, but their evangelical popularity rendered me homeless and an emotional orphan. At the time I was pissed, but now that Alan had offered me one more opportunity to forgive and forget I decided to do so, and I congratulated myself on my maturity.

"Hey," Alan continued, "did you hear about Conrad?"

"No, what?"

"He died of AIDS three weeks ago in San Francisco."

"Oh, my Gawd." I was stunned. Conrad was the first individual I knew personally to die of AIDS.

"No, Alan, I didn't know. Heck, I didn't even know that Conrad was gay. I just thought he was weird."

"Well, he was weird *and* gay, and now he's gone."

Conrad lived in San Francisco? We all moved away from New York? I was unable to speak, I felt so detached. How can people I lived with for years get AIDS and die, and I not know of it? Why didn't I keep in touch with The Burston Boys? They were family when I didn't have any, at least emotionally. Three of us even moved out west, all within a day's drive of each other, and I didn't know it. Why?

I looked up at Alan, perhaps to ask him, but I was surprised to see him smiling.

Conrad's dead and you're smiling? How dare you! But I began to smile, too. I knew what he was thinking. Then, I knew that he knew that I knew what he was thinking. Alan raised his latte mug and I raised mine. Alan toasted, "Conrad, if you're listening…."

I finished, "We hope you go back to Burston Street and haunt those Pentecostals."

We clinked our mugs together, and returned to the auditorium.

A year later, on the morning of July 4th, I awoke at first light feeling exceptionally peaceful. Oddly, I was not perturbed in the least to see a radiant glow at the foot of my bed. I watched calmly as the soft, pulsing light became denser, and formed into the shape of a person. When it came into full clarity, I was surprised to see one of my old Burston buddies.

"Conrad, what are you doing here? You're supposed to be dead," I said.

"I am," he answered with only a hint of his trademark smirk. "I just wanted you and Alan to know I went back to Burston Street to haunt those Pentecostals. I got 'em good."

I laughed, and nodded an acknowledgment: *Way to go, Conrad.*

He smiled sweetly at me, winked, and then he was gone.

11

What to Say When Your Therapist Tells You You're Her Craziest Patient

I have always believed in UFOs, even as a little kid. In fact, I thought it odd others didn't.

My fellow true believers and I have a few theories we place a lot of stock in, and the main one is that aliens are already here. Secondly, we believe there are plenty of alien races, including at least one species that looks exactly like us—so much that the only way to tell them apart from regular human beings is to touch them and see if they are clammy-cold. If they are, they're aliens.

They're clammy-cold because of a third theory: They have evolved to such a degree that they no longer have the DNA to carry emotional expression. Thus, their bodies have no "emotional warmth" and are cold to the touch. That's why they're here on earth—to study our emotions and develop a plan to get themselves back to "normal" body temps. One might wonder why Extra-Terrestrials who are advanced enough to get here would have a genetics problem back home, but those kinds of questions are rarely asked in the UFO World.

Regardless, a few years ago during a sleepless night a thought struck me. *If I'm an Extra-Terrestrial and want to study emotions — but don't want anyone to touch me so that they can find out I am a clammy-cold alien, the best job to have would be that of psychotherapist.*

I knew that because my therapist, Sally, had never touched me during my seven years of treatment. The prevailing rationale was that avoiding physical touching would block any emotional entanglements between us.

Then the realization hit. *Oh, my Gawd. What if my therapist is an alien?* I mentally wrestled with this dilemma for hours, but there was simply no way out — either my therapist was an Extra-Terrestrial or she wasn't. There was no in-between.

Worse, if she wasn't an alien, was everything I believed just total crapola? No UFOs, no aliens, no governmental cover-ups? *Gawd Help Me, is the X-Files just a TV show?*

On the other hand, if my therapist was an alien and found out that I knew what she truly was, what would she do? Beam herself up to her mothership and force me to face my life all alone? Or beam us both up and conduct advanced emotional studies?

The next day I had an appointment with Sally. As I entered her office, I didn't know what to say. Once seated, I couldn't speak.

"Having trouble getting going today, Bruce?" she asked in a soothing voice.

"Yeah."

"So, what's up?"

"Well, um...." I decided to leap into the abyss. "I think you might be an alien."

"Oh, I thought you knew I was Jewish."

"Jewish?" I laughed. "Yeah, I know you're Jewish. I mean an Extra-Terrestrial-type-of-alien. Not a Mexican-fruit-picker-kind-of-alien."

My therapist looked very confused and concerned.

"Let me get this straight, Bruce. You think I'm from outer space, that I'm not really from Earth?"

When she said it like that it did sound a bit crazy, but this was not a moment to debate the semantics. "Yeah, I guess that's what I'm saying."

"Oh, no…oh, no…." my therapist said between gasps. She slowly slumped into her chair.

I began to explain my theories of the alien invasion of Planet Earth as a way to make her feel better, but it didn't work. She wrapped her arms around her chest and began to rock back and forth.

"Ohhhh, Bruce… this is the craziest thing I have ever heard in my life."

I became euphoric. The Craziest Thing? *Whoopee – that makes me the Craziest Patient!* I felt like I was having an adrenal Fourth of July because I knew some of her patients were combat vets from the war in Vietnam…and I *was crazier than them*! I felt like I had just been elected to the Psychiatric Hall of Fame. It felt special, and I felt good.

My therapist on the other hand, looked like hell. She was falling apart right in front of me.

Oh, my Gawd. I've got to rescue her. I guess she's seeing all her hard work going down the drain.

I switched from UFOs to talking about my mother, Catholic school, and my latest bout of sexual impotency. By the end of my session my therapist was back to her old self. As I left her office, I tapped my chest, thinking, *I did a good job in there today.*

So, I'd like to share a piece of advice: If you're in psychotherapy and you Gotta Go Big, then, *Just Do It*. But know that when you do, your therapist might have an anxiety attack and you might have to help them out.

Lastly, if your therapist can't handle your Super-Sized Crazy, then give me a call. We'll find someone who can.

12

There is Justice in this World
Learning that synchronicities abound

Back when I owned my beachcleaning business, there came a time when I needed to sell one of my pickup trucks, a beat-up ol' Ford with 154,000 miles on it. I put an ad in the paper asking $1,000, and was amazed at how many guys thought this $1,000 beater was going to be a dream machine. So, when I had a live customer, a guy much like myself who wanted to buy the truck as a run-around rig for his masonry business, I was glad to accept his $650 offer.

Down we went to the garage to take the plates off my truck and affix the ones he had brought. "Took 'em off one of my other trucks until I get this one registered," he said. Then we went back to my kitchen to sign-over the title and exchange the money. Surprisingly, he whipped out a check to write the $650.

"Wait a minute, buddy. This is a cash deal," I said.

"Oh, don't worry. It's a good check," he answered.

What could I do? No one else wanted the truck once they saw it. Do I take a chance on this guy? He seemed okay and I enjoyed his company, so.... *Heck, it's only $650, and I do want* *to get rid of the truck.* Finding parking for it was a hassle and I wanted to move on to more important things.

So, I accepted the check. We shook hands and away he went. A week later my bank informed me that not only was it a bad check, it had been written on a closed account. I had been totally set up and conned. I was angry and embarrassed. The warrior in me said that this sucker was gonna be sorry that he even thought about screwing with me.

I called the police. That was a joke. After my anger toward them settled down, I called my insurance company. Heck, it was like a stolen vehicle. The money from an insurance company is just as green as from a legitimate buyer. However, my insurer refused my claim and told me the matter was a civil dispute, a contractual disagreement that had to be resolved in the courts.

So, I filed a complaint at the local small claims court, a place many contractors like me knew well from collecting unpaid accounts. My court date was set for two months down the road, but I didn't really think I was going to get my money back. After all, why would the guy show up in court? But maybe I could get a lien on his business assets. I knew it was a long shot, but the $7.50 court fee made it worth a try.

Fortuitously, the phone number the guy had written down on his check happened to be a good number. In fact, it was his sister's. In addition, it had even been his until the sister threw him out of the house for pulling too many stunts like the one with me, or so she said.

With the phone number I knew the general area where he lived and that was good for my anger. I went cruising in his neighborhood in hopes of spotting my truck and snatching it back. No such luck, however, and after a few trips through his part of the county I gave up. Nothing happened for a few weeks, then Fate played her hand.

Passover that year fell on the same weekend as Easter. In my Judeo-Christian household that meant all my kinfolk were at my place for the weekend.

Fortunately, BJ's daughter, who was living with us for the spring and summer, was an insomniac. That meant she was still up when my business phone rang at 6 a.m. on Easter Sunday. The answering machine clicked on before she could pick up the receiver, so she just let the caller place his message. Then she came upstairs.

"Bruce, I think you'd better get up. One of your trucks is gonna get towed."

I bolted out of bed. All of my vehicles had been in the garage since the beginning of the weekend, so I knew it was the stolen truck that was about to be towed.

I ran downstairs and listened to the message. It was a guy with a heavy Greek accent who hadn't had his wake-up coffee, and it was tough to discern what his name was exactly or his phone number—but it was clear he was the owner of a diner and my truck was blocking something in his parking lot.

I checked the yellow pages for a restaurant in the town where the sister lived. BINGO! I found the diner and called the number. The Greek guy answered. He still hadn't had a cup of coffee, but his attitude and English both improved when I told him I'd be right down.

"You will?" he replied with perfect diction.

"Listen, mister, you're doing me a favor," I said.

I arrived at the diner in 40 minutes—not too much traffic on Easter Sunday in suburban Long Island. Driving to the diner, I felt like a warrior going to snatch a member of his tribe who had just been taken hostage. Pulling into the parking lot, I immediately saw my truck and what was so offensive. It had evergreen bushes sticking out wildly from the cargo area, and anybody walking by in their Easter outfits could get snagged by the branches.

I went inside to see the owner, who by now had had some coffee. He confirmed it was my guy who had left the truck the night before, saying he couldn't get it started and would be back in the morning.

Ah, I had beaten him to it!

The owner of the diner knew how to get in touch with me since my telephone number was painted on the side of the truck and the thief had apparently been too discombobulated to remove it.

I put my spare key in the door lock. It fit! Inside, though, the cab was a mess. Coffee cups, Micky D wrappers, and tons of mud covered the floor. I felt violated seeing my truck so badly trashed. Anyway, I put the key in the ignition. The engine turned, but didn't catch. Rhrummm, rhrummm, rhummm, a few more tries, and nothing. The fuel gauge read empty, so I switched tanks. Low, but still some fuel. Still the engine didn't fire. I popped the hood to see if all the electrical connections were good. Everything looked okay. Turned the key again, but now the battery sounded like it needed a rest. It had to be out of gas or not getting gas—even if the second tank read okay.

I poured in a gallon of fuel from a spare can I carried, and sure enough the truck started right up. I left my good truck in back of the diner and drove the stolen rig to a gas station to fill it up. Mission accomplished. Victory shouts and war hoops all the way down Route 109 through Farmingdale!

I parked it at a friend's house a few miles away and took a taxi to retrieve my second truck. Then I returned home to get a second driver to ferry the stolen rig back to home base.

Later, when I was cleaning the truck, I discovered what had happened. I found the gas cap key to the auxiliary and main tanks off the key ring and covered by mud and sand at the bottom of a footwell. Apparently, the guy had lost the key and couldn't put any fuel in the tanks. As a result, he'd drained the main tank completely and switched into the auxiliary, driving until it was almost bone dry. However, when he pulled up to the diner he'd parked on a slight incline, nosing the truck uphill. The auxiliary is a long, slim tank along the underbelly of the truck, so when he parked uphill the fuel that was left sloshed all the way toward the rear of the tank and away from the fuel lines in the front. All he would have had to do was put the truck into neutral, coast backwards a few feet to level ground and let the fuel flow forward. Then the engine would have fired.

Isn't it amazing how it all came together? Remove one little piece of the puzzle and I wouldn't have gotten back my truck. First, my stepdaughter was awake and heard the call. Then my phone number was still on the truck and the owner of the diner called it. And then, the thief had written a legitimate phone number on the check. He'd even ended up parking uphill.

As Dennis, the mechanic for my trucks said when I told him this story, "Bruce, there really is justice in this world."

13

Untidy Beaches
My first encounter with governmental and media cover-ups

In July of 1988, the beaches of New York and New Jersey were walloped by wash-ups of syringes and medical wastes, including bloody bandages. In disgust, people stopped coming to the beach for the remainder of the summer. More troubling, the syringes continue to wash ashore to this day, but no one knows about it because the media doesn't report it. That's because beach managers and politicians keep it a secret to maintain the billion-dollar beach industry. Nevertheless, I'll tell you what I know, how I think it got started, and my speculations on why this travesty continues.

As described in another story, I was the owner and founder of Sandsifter Beachcleaning Company, the biggest commercial operation of its kind in the metropolitan New York area. My clients were many of the small and mid-sized beaches of Long Island and the Jersey Shore. I was also the local sales representative for Cherrington Beachcleaner, the manufacturer of the machines I used. Through my efforts to sell these machines coupled with my sifting services, I became acquainted with most of the beach managers in the region.

The wash-ups in 1988 radicalized me and I became an environmental activist. As events unfolded, it also became my first experience with a governmental cover-up and media complicity.

The needles first appeared on the July 4th weekend, and wash-ups continued intermittently into the first two weeks of August. During that time, approximately 800 syringes were found scattered along the Long Island coast, and by mid-summer the needle deposits also included a nasty mix of bandages, ooze, and used medical packaging. Besides not swimming, people stopped fishing and boating, and I read in the newspapers that our local economy took a $7 billion hit. I believe that loss blunted the investigation into who was responsible.

Nevertheless, early in the official investigation, environmental agencies, such as the United States Environmental Protection Agency (US-EPA), offered plausible scenarios to explain these events. They suggested that a tragic confluence of weather, badly engineered sewers, and diabetics and drug addicts tossing their needles into the streets or toilets were the culprits.

However, that narrative doesn't jibe with information shared with me over a cup of coffee by a grunt-level Federal worker during a Congressional hearing on the medical waste in the winter of 1989. Specifically, this Park Ranger stated that the major concentrations of syringes her team discovered, were not on Long Island, as the media had reported, but on Staten Island, just south of the Verrazano Bridge. In addition, the majority of these Staten Island syringes were found at one location—an unused, derelict beach named North Beach. In fact, all these syringes—estimated to be nearly 2,000—seemed to have plumed out southward from that point since very few were found north of North Beach. These discoveries were never revealed to the public.

"Do you know what this means?" I asked her incredulously.

"Yes," she replied. "The syringes were dumped at North Beach."

"Have you told your bosses?" I continued.

"Yes," she answered. "I passed on the information weeks ago."

"Has anyone done anything about it?" I stammered. "I haven't heard anything like this on the news."

My confidante only smiled, and shook her head from side-to-side.

"They're covering it up?" I asked.

She smiled again, and shrugged.

"You're afraid to talk about this, aren't you?"

She nodded.

"Why cover this up? Who at EPA could gain from that?"

She shrugged and looked around. She appeared frightened.

"Thanks for telling me. This is really big information. I appreciate it."

She smiled and returned to the hearing.

But a one-time disposal of syringes does not comport with other environmental disasters occurring at the same time and in the same waters, such as the reported die-off of nearly 1,000 Atlantic Bottlenose dolphins off the coast of New Jersey, or the historic hypoxia event in the western third of Long Island Sound, where 100 square miles of water ran out of oxygen at all depths of the water column—from the surface to the bottom.

These events and other long-term problems, such as a 90% decrease in the production of seaweed in Long Island's waters during the eight years I cleaned its beaches, suggests a larger problem. As a result, I felt compelled to take an active role in finding a solution. I joined the Citizens Advisory Group of the Long Island Sound Study (LISS), a joint Federal, state, and local clean-up program. Also, I became a member of a professional association of solid-waste handlers and sewage treatment operators. In this process, I became acquainted with the New York State Department of Environmental Conservation (NYS-DEC) findings on marine-related matters, such as contamination of seafood from pollution, and beach closings due to sewage.

But to understand any of these larger issues, it's best to start at the beginning with the syringes, and follow that story as it unravels.

The official narrative for the source of the 1988 medical waste was based on how New York City handled rain on its streets. In those days, New York City, especially Manhattan, routed much of its street-storm water into its sewer system. It's called a Combined Sewer Overflow system (CSO), and is typical of the older cities along the East Coast. New York's system was built to handle the average flow of sewage, plus a rainfall of 1/4 inches per hour. Any more and the whole kit-and-kaboodle of excess rain, toilet waste, and street trash gets diverted past the sewage treatment plants and dumped directly into the waters of New York Harbor.

The EPA estimated in 1988 that NYC diverted 10% of its CSO flow directly into area waterways due to excessive rain from thunderstorms. Even though officials in the investigation claimed that the summer temperatures of 1988 were above average, which meant more frequent and more intense thunderstorms, their claims were later proven false by environmental activists.

Specifically, thunderstorms typically dump a 1/2 to 1 inch of rain per hour, thus exceeding the CSO's limit. Officials further stated that this above-normal flush pushed syringes from street drug use into the sewers, thus flooding the harbor with thousands of needles. In addition, health officials speculated that many diabetics were disposing their needles into their toilets, thus adding greatly to the mess. However, no conclusive data has ever been presented to prove these allegations.

With the 10% diversion, though, it's plausible to assume a few of the city's estimated 150 million syringes used each year end up in the harbor. But thousands depositing themselves on our beaches? And why only 1988? These were the first troubling questions to arise with the street-flush scenario.

Further, the fact that I never saw a syringe on a beach before or after 1988 defeats the official story. It tells me that something special happened in 1988 besides the weather or bad plumbing. Through the following years, I investigated more deeply. What I learned told me that the syringe problem was more complex and perverted than I had originally thought. My first discovery was that the syringes were not unique to 1988, nor a single dump at North Beach.

One ally in my research, Cindy Ziff of Clean Ocean Action in New Jersey, told me the syringe wash-ups continue to the present day. In addition, my cousin, a docent at the Fire Island Lighthouse, found a bag of 20 used needles at Robert Moses State Park in 2010.

Initially in 1988, especially when I heard about North Beach, I suspected the source of the syringes was a change in the disposal of medical wastes from hospitals and doctors' offices, rather than needles washing into the sewers during rain storms. Through the late 1970s and 1980s, the Joint Commission on the Accreditation of Health Organizations (JCAHO) became more aggressive on the disposal of hazardous medical waste because of the AIDS epidemic. Hospital administrators labeled virtually anything that had a little bit of human fluid, such as finger bandages, as hazardous medical waste. As a result, the medical waste disposal business skyrocketed.

At professional gatherings, I met individuals from the EPA and the DEC who told me the only place this medical waste could be disposed of legally on the East Coast was in a mass burn incinerator in South Carolina. They also told me the cost of the disposal charged by the carting firms was $2,000 per ton. Since the average carting truck carried 20 tons of waste, each truck was grossing $40,000 per trip to South Carolina.

In the early search for culprits to the beach wash-ups, it was often inferred, such as the TV news reporting "what the man in the street is saying," that the syringes were dumped by unscrupulous carting companies. One intrepid TV crew even got videos of a roll-off truck dumping its load into the East River at the old Brooklyn Navy Yard. However, no medical wastes were found—it was all construction rubble—and the guy got arrested. At the beginning, I didn't believe blatant dumping happened to the medical wastes. With the carting firm bosses making piles of money, why would they want to kill the goose that was laying the golden egg?

That fundamental view, coupled with the North Beach information I had received from my friendly Park Ranger, allowed me to form a speculative scenario of how the syringes washed up. I think the bosses of the carting companies were clean on medical waste, but somebody further down the food chain was not. I think a guy who drove a legitimate disposal truck to South Carolina, who knew the routine and watched his boss pocket $40,000 per truck, wanted to get a little action for himself.

I believe this individual, or a few, set up their own independent medical waste disposal business. They probably offered great deals to low-income clinics and small veterinarian offices—outfits that did not generate large amounts of syringes and operated on a shoestring budget. Nor did these customers have reason to suspect, nor the means to check, if their new disposal company was legit.

These drivers probably collected a bag of syringes here and there through the early months of 1988, perhaps even 1987 or earlier. I bet their original idea had been to toss a bag or two into the back of the trucks they were driving to South Carolina. Perhaps it worked for a while, but in the spring of 1988 they got caught in a squeeze due to increased JCAHO scrutiny. Waste transfers at hospital loading docks were carefully weighed, manifests signed, and the load secured with locks. Off-loading in South Carolina was also tightly regulated, so the drivers couldn't discard their syringes.

I speculate that they stored their waste in a self-lock storage unit for a period of time, but by the summer their problem reached critical mass.

"Why not throw it in the harbor?" one of guys probably said. "The tide will take it out. It'll sink, and no one will be the wiser. If it floats, no one can trace it to us."

"Yeah, good idea," his buddy probably replied. "And I know a great place, too. North Beach on Staten Island. We can go there late at night with a fishing pole and a couple six packs of beer, and if anybody asks, we're just a couple of guys fishin'. But if the coast is clear we can throw a couple bags into the water. In a couple of nights, we'll be rid of this stuff."

As a result, 2,000 syringes entered the water at North Beach. The 1,000 syringes identified by the EPA tracking team stayed close to North Beach. The remainder—another 800 or so—floated on the wind and tide. When they hit the beaches of Long Island, all hell broke loose.

With all the eyes of the world upon them, I suspect that the carting dons went to work quickly. They probably suspected that a few bozos in their operations were doing a little side business, and likely found them right away. I imagine the bosses dealt with them effectively, and any remaining syringes left in offending storage sheds were quickly emptied into a legitimate waste truck and hauled to South Carolina. This happened around the second or third week of August, 1988. By the end of the third week of August, the syringes stopped coming and I never saw another again—until my followup research revealed otherwise.

Nevertheless, in the run-up to the 1988 Labor Day weekend there were no syringes reported on any beach for a couple of weeks. The business and political sectors turned up the heat on the environmental and media collective to get people back to the beach and salvage some of that $7 billion in lost revenue.

During the last week of August, 1988, I attended a meeting at Nassau County's huge shoreline conference facility, Nassau

Beach, to discuss the syringe crisis. In attendance were nearly 1,000 beach managers, sewage treatment plant operators, and environmental officials.

The head honcho of EPA Region II launched the meeting in lighthearted fashion by saying that he needed help convincing his wife that it was safe to take the kids to Long Island's iconic Jones Beach, and wondered out loud "who wore the pants in his family." He received vociferous and good-natured applause from the mostly male audience.

He said it was important to get people back to the beach in order to resuscitate the local economy, and presented the current beach problem as wholly one of public relations. He asked the assembled if they would agree to a joint press release stating that the syringe issue had been resolved, and that the beaches were now safe.

I jumped to my feet and protested vigorously. I said we didn't know the source of the waste—at the time I didn't—nor were there any on-going water samplings for pathogens other than bacteria. "We don't know if there are viruses," I challenged, "or algae and their toxins, or inorganic hazards such as poisons. There might even be radiation out there. We just don't know. How can we, in good conscience, tell the public that the beaches are safe?"

The upbeat crowd went silent, and I sat down.

"You got 'em kid," the guy next to me said, patting me on the back. "Good job."

"Thanks," I replied. "Where ya from?"

"I work at a sewage plant in Great Neck," he said. "I'm glad you said what ya did. We've been seeing stuff float up on our beaches for weeks and we should be closing the beaches, but the bosses don't want us to. The people on the beach are screaming when they see the stuff wash in... They blame us, but it's not us. I don't know where the stuff is coming from, but it looks like shit, smells like shit, so I figure it's gotta be shit. But it's not from our plant."

"The City's?"

"Maybe. But the funny thing is I really don't know what it is. Some days it's really slimy stuff. But, most of the time it's cake—fluffy, solid stuff that is brown or yellow or black. The scientists tell us it's dried algae from hypoxia blooms in the Sound, but I don't know. All I know is that I've never seen it before, and personally, I doubt that it's algae. I've been in this business long enough to know what algae looks like. But what we're getting this summer isn't algae, or if it is, it's very different algae."

"Wow."

"Yeah, wow. That's why I'm glad you said what you said. I don't think anybody really knows what's going on."

Following that pivotal meeting at Nassau Beach, I never saw or heard a press release on behalf of any professional body claiming the waters were safe. Nor did the people return to the beaches of New York that year.

That winter I began speaking at libraries and community centers, sharing what I had heard from the EPA and DEC. I described what I had seen as a beachcleaner, telling my bits and pieces of the wash-up story, tales of environmental degradation, sewage runoffs, and unsafe beaches.

One piece of "insider" information that always made people groan was revealing that the state's criteria for safe swimming beaches is a fecal bacterial count low enough so that *only* 15 people out of 1,000 get sick from sewage contamination. Not "too safe" for those unlucky 15, but okay for the other 985 swimmers.

I continued to wonder about the wash-ups during the winter and the following summer. Why weren't the North Beach syringes discussed and factored into the clean-up strategies, which focused only upon developing a fleet of "skimmer boats" to scoop up floating syringes near CSO discharge points. Further, why was the EPA guy at the Nassau Beach meeting convinced the beaches were safe in August 1988, even though his wife was just as scared as the rest of us? Did he know something we didn't and he wasn't telling us?

In 2005, I determined to find out. Upon close examination of the reporting by the New York Times back in July 1988, I discovered that they pulled their initial team of veteran journalists, Ralph Blumenthal, Philip S. Gutis, and Sam Howe Verhovek, after their July 9 to July 25 postings, which had begun to reveal links between clinics undergoing Medicaid fraud investigations and the medical wash-ups. Were the syringes intentionally dumped by unscrupulous clinical staff pushing back against federal and state indictments? Was the syringe dump on a hot July 4th a ploy to gain leverage in a corruption scandal?

Or was the first syringe wash-up from a bunch of medical waste truckers on Staten Island, after which other criminals saw the potential of polluting beaches as a way to paralyze problematic investigations?

Regardless, by late July, Blumenthal, Gutis, and Verhovek were replaced with junior reporters who mostly filed bland pieces based upon press releases from governmental Public Information Officers (PIOs).

Why did the Times dumb down their reporting, and even possibly whiff on the Medicaid hustle?

I phoned Ralph Blumenthal at his new assignment as the Houston Bureau Chief for the NY Times. I asked him point-blank why he and his team were pulled off the story, but he said that he had no memory of the entire incident.

Philip Gutis, despite becoming the communications director for the prestigious Natural Resources Defense Council—the premier environmental organization run by Robert F. Kennedy, Jr.—never returned any of my phone calls or emails, even though his secretary told me she knew he had received them.

As for Sam Howe Verhovek, I have never been able to contact him. However, I determined that he left the New York

Times and took a new job at the *LA Times*, and was later reported to be their Tokyo Bureau Chief. Currently, Sam Verhovek is rumored to be working as an environmental consultant in Seattle.

But since reports of syringe wash-ups in the NY area persist to this day, I suspect criminals continue to thwart investigators with medical waste dumpings. In 2010, officials at Jacob Riis Park reported over 500 syringes washed up in one day, which they quickly attributed to an intentional dumping by criminal elements. So, the potential has been recognized.

More problematic though, beach officials have come to realize that if they don't publicize the wash-ups, the public is none the wiser. Plus, the power of the criminals is reduced. So, everyone wins.

Back in 1988, I think the major players knew the initial syringe problem ended by the third week of August. I think they knew because I think the carting bosses—or elements within organized crime who controlled the Medicaid fraudsters—told them. I suspect the price of getting the whole story was silence. I figure the power brokers at the EPA and the DEC, plus the politicians and the media—perhaps even the *New York Times*—agreed to keep quiet. That silence continues to this day.

As for the dying dolphins, the sewage cake on Great Neck's beaches, and the severe hypoxia event in Long Island Sound, I don't know why they occurred or if there is any connection to the medical waste wash-ups.

Regardless of how it all happened, the following season, 1989—my last summer cleaning beaches—I heard loud and clear their collective sigh of relief as I sat upon my beach-cleaner, sifting the glorious sands of my beloved New York beaches.

14

Take a Chance
No guts, no glory, etc. Romantic Division

She was 40. I was 25. I took a chance. Or rather, I let her take the chance and start a romantic relationship with me.

We were both new in our jobs and worked well together, so there was a freshness and excitement to our work lives. I had just graduated from college and in my first real job working as a Recreation Therapy Aide in the psychiatric division of the Nassau County Medical Center (NCMC).

Barbara Jean, "BJ," was just starting out as well. A few years earlier, BJ had decided she didn't want to be a full-time mother and housewife anymore and returned to school. She earned a master's in dance/movement therapy, ultimately finding a clinical position in the Recreation Department at the NCMC. As an aide, I often assisted in her sessions, first in an out-patient program called Day Hospital, and then later on the locked, short-term, in-patient psych unit.

We were a fantastic team. She was smart, graceful, and very intuitive — one of the finest therapists I have ever seen. I respected her greatly, and BJ in turn admired my work. It was the first substantive friendship I'd had with an adult.

Our professional relationship grew quickly. Our after-session debriefs were substantive and insightful, first focused on our patients' participation or lack thereof, and later evolving to include hospital politics and world events. Those conversations led to shared lunches, and soon we were recognized as a working pair—two therapists who led dynamic therapy groups together. During that first year we also began sharing an office.

Our colleagues were uncomfortable with our closeness, however. My boss told me that another therapist in our department had complained: "When I have a disagreement with either Bruce or BJ, it's like I'm arguing with both of them." Our "two-ness" was that powerful.

Another dimension arose as well when BJ decided she wanted a divorce. After 18 years of marriage and five kids, she felt the pull to spread her wings a little further, and that included a romantic relationship with me.

We never really talked about it. We discussed her divorce and her frustrations in her marriage, but not about us as a potential couple. However, one day during a professional conference in New York City we got a hotel room and became lovers.

Our affair moved awkwardly in those first months. We didn't flaunt our romance at work, but we didn't hide it, either. Shared lunches expanded to glasses of wine after work, and then dinners. But in the evenings, she went home to her new apartment, and I returned to my little 8x12 cubbyhole of a room in a house I shared with three other guys.

I was happy, but I struggled, too. First with the intimacy of a real, full-blown adult relationship and the new feelings and fears—such as being an instant father-figure to her five kids. Then, with the judgments of my co-workers. Socially, the 15-year difference between us was problematic for me as well. When we spent time with her friends, the gals were all her age, but their husbands were 10 to 15 years older, so I ended up hanging out with guys my father's age. They were okay fellows, but I was uncomfortable.

The other side of that coin was the fact that I was closer in age to BJ's kids than I was to her. BJ's oldest child was only nine years younger than I was. Oddly, all of this strangeness condensed into a realization that BJ had none of the musical records I had. Hers were all jazz classics from the '50s and '60s, and mine were a motley collection of contemporary folk and rock, such as Bruce Springsteen, Crosby, Stills, and Nash, and Celtic legends like the Chieftains. In some bizarre existential way, I longed for a girlfriend who had the same musical — and cultural — tastes as I did. For instance, BJ had spent the '60s raising her kids while I was hitchhiking to Chibougamou.

By summer I couldn't handle it anymore. I broke up with BJ, jumped on my Honda motorcycle, and zoomed off to the White Mountains of New Hampshire. I spent a week backpacking and tried to figure out why I'd gotten mixed up with an older woman.

When I returned, I was thankful for my work and the stabilizing routine it provided. Blessedly, BJ and I continued to run our sessions together as if nothing had happened between us.

I began dating women my own age, especially those with Grateful Dead or Rolling Stones albums. But the depth of those conversations paled in comparison with the ones I'd had with BJ. The lack of a deep soul-connection was apparent to me, but I didn't know what to do about it. I was stuck.

I went into therapy and tried to make sense of my life. By the autumn I was okay. My life wasn't exciting, but it was manageable.

Then I broke my leg. I was playing touch-football with some of my patients and slipped on wet grass. I hyper-extended my leg and cracked the head of my tibia. The Emergency Room put my leg in a full cast, so I couldn't ride my motorcycle. In response, BJ drove me home in her Ford station wagon. Hobbling on crutches, she helped me into my cramped living quarters, where I had to sleep on the floor since I couldn't climb into my loft bed. Once I was settled, BJ went grocery shopping for me, then came back and made dinner. After eating, she laid down beside me and we held each other close.

We stayed that way for the next 14 years.

Yes, I left her to head off to Yelm and Ramtha, but I greatly savor those years.

Glad I took the chance.

15

A Stepfather's Love
Marching on Gay Pride Day

I hesitated at the curb, then stepped off. For a moment I felt strange standing on a spot of pavement I had been watching others walk across for the previous few hours. Looking around I slowly breathed in my acceptance—I was really in the 1985 New York City Gay Pride Day March.

I was marching because BJ's daughter, Laura, is a lesbian and I wanted to show her my love in a public way. That's tough to do. Her brother and sisters received festive parties when they were married, or they themselves hosted big shindigs when their kids had a birthday. But what kind of celebration could I sponsor for my adult step-kid who was also a homosexual? Birthdays? There didn't seem to be a societal equivalent for public displays of parental pride.

The plan to march began over a beer at one of our family's frequent gatherings. I told Laura of my desire to do something for her, a "coming of age party, perhaps," and suggested a big square dance or a summer picnic.

"Yeah," she responded, "I can just picture your parents mingling with all my dyke friends who'll be wearing rows of studded jewelry in their ear lobes, and shirts that say, 'A

Woman Needs a Man like a Fish Needs a Bicycle.'" She and I listed other family members who would flinch in the company of her alternative-lifestyle friends. More than half our relatives made the list.

"So, what can I do?" I asked.

"Why don't you and Mom march with me on Gay Pride Day?"

"Whoa," I said. "I don't know if I'm ready to spend all day with a couple thousand gays."

"A hundred thousand," she corrected.

"Two, a hundred, whatever—it's more than I can handle. A room full of your friends is okay, but not every gay in New York City."

"My Gawd, I never knew you were so homophobic," she replied.

I didn't know I was that homophobic, either. I wondered how a liberal guy like me could be so uptight. After all, no one I voted for ever got elected. After a momentary pause, Laura interrupted my pondering.

"You don't have to march all alone," she said. "You and Mom can march with P-FLAG."

"Who's P-FLAG?"

"Parents and Friends of Lesbians And Gays. They'll have a group marching, and you can go with them."

"But who are they?"

"They're folks like you who have a kid like me." Then she leaned toward me with a twinkle in her eye and put her hand on my knee, saying conspiratorially, "You won't have to worry about all those gay guys coming on to ya—the P-FLAG'ers will protect ya. Ha, ha, ha...." To my credit, I laughed, too.

Although I was uncomfortable with the prospect of spending all day in a city full of gay men and women, I knew deep inside I wanted to march. Laura and I approached her mom and outlined the plan.

"Sure, let's do it," BJ said. I was surprised and impressed at the lack of hesitancy in her voice. She then gathered her daughter and me in a three-way hug.

The day of the march, BJ and I decided to join half way. The expectation of political confrontations at St. Patrick's Cathedral led us to forego the first half, so we planned to join the P-FLAG contingent at Washington Square Park for the last mile of the march. However, the disturbances uptown slowed the flow, making us hours early for our rendezvous. We waited, and watched a world that was having fun, even if it felt strange to me.

"Dykes on Bikes," a motorcycle gang of lesbians, performed precise figure-eights with their machines, none of which was a Harley. I was impressed.

"Lesbians for Patsy Cline" confounded me, though. Why were they attracted to Patsy? Was Patsy Cline a closet lesbian, or did lesbians just like country music?

The most striking groups were those clusters of men who had AIDS. One crew, called the "Gay Men's Health Crisis," had dozens of members who looked like holocaust victims—thin and gaunt. Although stooped, they walked so purposefully that they brought tears to my eyes. Each of their careful steps said to me, *I may be dead tomorrow, but today I am alive and proud to be here.*

After several hours, P-FLAG reached us. I saw a band of maybe three dozen people. "Here they are," BJ said, "let's go."

I stepped off the curb, but cringed. Familiar, but still troubling fears made me sweat. For support, I looked around at my marching buddies. Some looked like veterans of every progressive political movement since the labor union struggles of the 1930s. They wore vests filled with political buttons, and their eyes had a glazed, single-minded focus. A *yenta* came over to BJ and me and asked, "Are you new to P-FLAG?"

"Yes, we are," we replied.

"Would you like to join?" She handed me a pen and an application. I shrugged and gave her back the pen, but kept the paper.

Some P-FLAGers looked meek and withdrawn. Others appeared relaxed and open. A few families walked together — parents strolling with their gay son or daughter, their arms around each other. Seeing them, I said to myself, *that's what this is all about.* I missed my stepdaughter, who had opted to march with her group of "Lesbian Thespians" further ahead of us. But I understood her desire to be with her friends, and I felt proud that her family was strong enough to be in two places.

Soon the march entered the West Village, which appeared to be the bastion of gayness in New York City. Turning into West 4th Street, I heard the shouting of thousands of voices and the roar of their applause. It sounded like a tsunami of the heart.

I tried to remember what groups preceded us and why they might earn such a response. I didn't think "Dykes on Bikes" or "Lesbians for Patsy Cline" would generate that kind of cheering. Perhaps the groups of AIDS survivors touched the crowd the way they had moved me.

Moving deeper into the West Village, the crowd swelled enormously. Men and women leaned out of every window, all the fire escapes were jammed, and any perch on the street such as a mail box or street lamp had somebody on it. The sidewalks were packed like a human lava flow, surging down into the street, and up stoops and alleys. Everyone was shouting, cheering, clapping, or giving righteous power salutes. Again, I wondered, who's this for?

Suddenly, I realized that the crowd was looking right at me and my fellow P-FLAGers. I gripped BJ's hand hard. "Wow," I said, "they're cheering us."

"Yes, it's really something, isn't it?" she said.

I looked into the faces at the edge of the crowd. My eyes caught many, and with some I slowly nodded, and they nodded back. I realized the P-FLAGers were giving these tens of thousands of gay men and women a universal parental acknowledgment: *You're okay, and we're here to tell you that.*

I began to weep. I was moved being part of this parental love, even though I was family to only one. BJ clutched me, steadied me. I put my arm around her to hide from the tide of emotion that made it hard even to breathe. I could only glance at the crowd briefly before turning away to gather my composure.

By the end of the march I was spent, light-headed, and happy. Laura found us within a minute or two. I don't think BJ and I were too hard to locate.

That evening the three of us roamed the streets of the West Village enjoying the festival. And even though I was nervous using a local tavern to pee, the whole scene began to feel like family.

16

The Man Who Divorced His Wife Over a Hat
Don't mess with my hat, please

I like hats. I've had Panamas, Stetsons, baseball caps, Indiana-Jones-type hats, and balaclavas. BJ bought me many of those hats, but not recently. She doesn't like my wearing a hat, especially indoors.

In retrospect, I must have been unaware of how often I wore them. Perhaps it was a gradually acquired taste because I haven't always worn a hat, but now I do. I find I need a brim to shield my eyes from sun glare or bright lights because my eyes are getting more sensitive. As a result, I usually wear a hat indoors. Further, if I'm not wearing a hat when I leave the house, I don't feel fully dressed.

I remember the first moment BJ objected to my hat-wearing. We were at the movies. She leaned over and nudged me, saying, "Honey, no one else in the theater is wearing a hat." I looked around. Even though she said, "No one else is wearing a hat," I knew she meant no other *man* was wearing a hat.

"Son-of-a-gun, you're right," I said, craning my neck and looking around. "Lots of bald-headed men here tonight."

That was my way of flipping her off because I knew her real message was: *Stop being weird and embarrassing me.* I didn't feel like capitulating, so, the hat—a Sandsifter baseball cap—stayed put.

On the way home we had a "hat talk." Essentially, she was asking, "Why do you feel the need to wear hats indoors, especially at the dinner table?" But the deeper issues were: *"Why are you so weird? Can't you be normal?"* We didn't touch that one, though.

My defense consisted of complaining about her foibles, especially her cold hands and feet, and how she shocked me awake in bed every night by snuggling after I'd gotten cozy and warm.

That night when I dressed in my pajamas, I also put on my baseball cap. Unbeknownst to me, BJ dressed for bed with wool socks, mittens, and a scarf. When we spotted each other, we laughed so hard tears streamed down our faces and made sweet love that night. Still, a year later we separated when I left for Yelm and Ramtha.

Before I had ever heard of Ramtha, though, I had developed a very strong desire to relocate from suburban New York to the country, citing the Smokey Mountains of western North Carolina as my preferred go-to place. On our vacation in October 1988, BJ and I had driven to the Appalachians to start Scouting for a home, or at least getting warmed up to the idea of living in the country. Tellingly, we drove in my pickup truck, not her yuppie Nissan sports car.

In Galax, Virginia, I pulled into a truck stop to get gas and learn if their famous fiddle convention was happening any time soon. While I fueled the pickup, BJ went inside to get a diet cola. When I walked in to pay for the gas, I saw a half dozen truckers near the counter or in the aisles. They all wore Stetsons or baseball caps that read, "Detroit Diesel" or "Caterpillar." In addition, the two women working the registers each wore orange baseball caps that proclaimed: "Disney World." I sidled up to BJ. There was only one thing I could say:

"Honey, you're the *only* one not wearing a hat."

Note: The title of this story is a riff on the famous narrative written by the neurophysiologist, Dr. Oliver Sachs: "The Man Who Mistook His Wife for a Hat."

17

Mail Call
My journey into the mystical begins

Taking the unfamiliar and unsolicited tabloid-sized newspaper out of my mail box, I skimmed through the first few pages until I hit an article about back-to-the-earth folks in Yelm, Washington. However, after reading their strident fanaticism regarding a One World Order and global corporate conspiracies, I shoveled the paper into the waste-paper basket as if it were on fire.

"Christ," I shouted, "this newspaper's a cult."

Twenty minutes later, though, I felt pulled by an inner force to examine it again, and dug it out of the garbage. With a strange calmness I smoothed the crumpled paper and turned to the front page.

Windwords proclaimed the masthead, the lettering bordered by swirling clouds. Reading the main article, titled "The Nature of Reality," I discovered the newspaper reported the latest spiritual teachings of a channeled fellow named Ramtha.

Channeled...hmmm. *Cool.* Although I was no disciple of any guru, I had spent a lifetime floating comfortably in and out of the New Age. I had read extensively, including books on the "sleeping prophet" Edgar Cayce, and the channeled messages in *Seth Speaks*. In fact, I had two friends in Frenchtown, New Jersey who were top-notch palm readers and channelers.

As for *Windwords*, I liked what I read. Ramtha seemed to see the "big picture" in a way that made sense to me, on subjects like reincarnation and finding the "God Within." However, my fascination fully ignited when he talked about "earth changes." Besides being the owner of Sandsifter, I was also becoming an environmental activist—especially after the catastrophic medical waste wash-ups. In addition, I had a close affinity with Native American shamanic traditions, particularly those of the indigenous activist Sun Bear. I knew well of his earth-change prophecies.

So, I easily accepted Ramtha's predictions of how life would end as we know it. My professional labors had taught me sea levels were rising, the world's climate was changing, and my local environment collapsing. I had witnessed first-hand a 90% decline in seaweed production in Long Island's waters during the prior eight years. Nearly all marine life—especially the fish and clams—had declined decisively since I had been a kid swimming at the beaches I cleaned. Ramtha's teachings validated all that I knew, and he spoke with such a progressive insight that I knew he was legit.

I joyfully read the rest of the newspaper, then put it away on a shelf.

A month later, a second issue showed up in my mail box. Hungrily, I read it at one sitting. Several weeks later, I began looking in my mail to see if a third *Windwords* would show up. It did, and I devoured it. With this third issue, though, I realized how much I enjoyed learning the nitty-gritty of unlimited consciousness from Ramtha, encapsulated in his chief message, "Behold God." The flip side of that teaching as I received it, is: If you take full responsibility for everything that happens in your life, you then have the power to create anything in your life. In fact, Ramtha calls his students "masters" since his teachings extol them to be the master of their lives.

So, wanting to be the master of *my* life and not having to rely on Fate to continue delivering my mystical mail, I whipped out my credit card and called *Windwords*.

"Hello," I called out to the woman who answered, "I don't know how you got my name and address, but I want to thank you very much for sending me a trial subscription to your wonderful paper, and now I would like to buy a year's subscription." I gave her my name.

"Err…" she replied, "Are you the Bruce Smith that lives in Sea Cliff, New York?"

"Yup. That's me."

"Well, our computer shows that you already have a subscription."

"No, you don't understand," I replied, "I want to *get* a subscription. I've been getting a free copy for the past three months; I guess it must be a trial subscription, correct? But now I want to get my own."

"We don't offer trial subscriptions. You're getting a regular subscription right now."

"I couldn't have," I said. "I've never heard of you folks until your newspaper started showing up in my mail box three months ago. I've never called you and I have no record of paying you any money. How could I have gotten a subscription without paying for it?"

"Maybe someone gifted you with one?"

"No way! No one has told me that they've done such a thing, and nobody I know *would* do it. Everyone I know thinks this stuff is a cult, and they think I'm crazy just for reading your newspaper."

"Well, all I can tell you is that you are paid in full for another nine issues, so… enjoy them."

I was stunned and didn't know what to say. Social convention propelled me to say something, but all I could utter was a weak, "Thanks."

From that moment onward, I always felt that someone else had indeed sent me the subscription to *Windwords*. But he probably didn't use a credit card, cash, or pay for it by check. Probably just splashed a little bit of energy onto the magnetic computer tape that encoded my mailing address.

Thanks, Ramtha. Best mail call I've ever gotten.

18

Sex with Aliens
Engaging the nitty-gritty of the unknown

This story is my account of being abducted by aliens. Since it's based solely upon my memories, it may not be true—at least in the usual sense of that word. But I know it has *a* truth, one that lies beneath the remembered events of the case. It may reflect a truth so deep that it speaks to the part of us that does not need facts or evidence, or even logic. Or, it might be a truth that comes from another world or dimension, and thus has no words in this one. Regardless, it is not fiction.

My first conscious recall of having contact with Extra-Terrestrials (ETs) occurred in October, 1989 at my friend Jeff's house in McKenna, Washington. I had been staying with Jeff while I attended a retreat at RSE, and one night I awoke abruptly and sat upright. I was fully awake and sweating profusely. I was also aroused sexually. I knew somehow that aliens were right outside the house, and were waiting for me to accept their visit. In my mind I intuitively knew—perhaps by telepathy—that they wanted to have sex with me and were asking for my permission. Through my life-long studying of the ET phenomenon, I knew they needed my sperm to create a hybrid race, as their species needed human chromosomes to develop the physiologic and genetic structures necessary to hold emotions. Apparently, as their race had devolved over the millennia, emotionality had left their bodies. As a result, they wanted to reconfigure their species by incorporating the emotional dynamism of humans. This confirmation of my studies came to me that night as a complete chunk of information, spontaneously and instantly.

Being aroused, I wanted to say yes, but I was scared. I stalled for time.

"I would love to help you out," I said telepathically, "but I really can't handle something like this right now. Why don't you come back in six months or so and we'll talk?"

With that, the intensity of the moment was gone and I knew they had left. I got out of bed, made tea, and paced the house for an hour.

The next day I told Jeff about the wacky dream I had had in his home the previous night.

"They don't sound so wacky to me, Bruce. Stuff like this happens to others and it sounds like it's happening to you."

"C'mon, Jeff. Sex with aliens?"

"You never know," he replied.

The next night it happened again. But when I awoke, I was lying rigidly on my left side, paralyzed. The aliens asked to have sex again, and I begged off. "Like I told ya, come back in six months."

But they did not leave, nor did they release me. Angry at being dominated, I willed my mind to say words I had learned from Ramtha for critical moments like this: "From the Lord God of my Being, I command my arm to move."

Slowly, I was able to raise my right arm and swing it behind me, as if I was pointing to something at the far end of the room. My eyes followed my arm's movement, and I saw a UFO. Somehow, I could see it through the walls of Jeff's house.

The craft was saucer-shaped on the upper half, with a dome on the top. The lower half of the ship was tapered, much like an ice cream cone. Think of an empty ice cream cone with a plate on top, and a huge dollop of ice cream on the plate. In addition, the dome had red and green lights glowing on the lower rim area, and above them were rectangular windows that were back-lit. I could see figures within. They seemed smallish in stature, and they were looking at me, or at least out their windows in my direction.

The cone part had porthole windows, and light shone out from there as well. It was so colorful I exclaimed, "Wow! That is so beautiful." I was not afraid. Rather, I felt enchanted, almost awed.

The UFO was just outside the house, perhaps 100 feet away. Only later did I wonder how I could see the spaceship through the wall of the house. In addition, the craft was hovering a few feet off the ground, and somehow the 80-foot-high Douglas Firs that usually exist in that spot were missing. From the bottom of the cone to top of the dome the UFO appeared at least 100 feet tall.

Although I could move my arm, I was unable to free anything else. I couldn't move my legs, nor could I turn from my left side. Then the UFO blinked out. It was like someone turned off a switch and the UFO disappeared. Suddenly, a thought came into my mind: *If you want to play, you gotta pay.* I do not know if it was a telepathic communication from the aliens or my own intuition. I believe it was the latter, because a moment later the UFO blinked on again, as if in confirmation of what I was thinking. But this time the UFO was in drab grays, black, and white. The lack of color confirmed to me that if I wanted to continue seeing the UFO's full display, I would have to surrender fully to the aliens and their agenda. I refused. As if in confirmation of my telepathic message, the UFO blinked out again, and I have never seen it since.

Although I had felt myself to be totally awake when I saw the UFO, upon awakening in the morning my rational mind declared that all experiences that happen while asleep must be dreams no matter how real or fantastic they seem at the time.

"I don't know, Bruce. It sounds pretty real to me," Jeff replied when I updated him on my most recent encounter.

"Oh, c'mon, Jeff. UFOs only happen to other people, not me," I said without thinking. After a moment of pondering, I added, "Jeff, what should I do?"

"I don't know. Maybe you should talk to someone?"

"Gawd, Jeff, are you crazy? You want me to tell people that I've been invited to have sex with aliens? And what's worse, I really would like to but I'm too scared. On one hand I feel debauched, and on the other I feel spineless."

"What are you going to do?"

"I don't know. Nothing right now."

That's how we left it. The following day I returned home to Long Island, New York. Once in the security of my old routine, I told my therapist, Sally, about my "dreams."

"Bruce, it sounds to me your subconscious is crying out for attention. It is telling you your deepest longings, your deepest romantic desires are not being met, and they seem so unattainable, so out-of-this-world, that for you to feel truly satisfied you're going to have to find a girlfriend in outer space."

Sally spoke so authoritatively I believed her.

However, a few weeks later the aliens came back. While I was asleep, and in a presumably lucid dream state, I saw an oddly shaped woman enter the bedroom I shared with BJ. The being glided to my side of the bed, and appeared to be about 5 feet tall. She was slender and had an Asian-looking face. She looked cute and wore a black-haired wig, but it was askew.

Telepathically, I called out, "What's with the wig?" She quickly rearranged it on top of her head, and ever since then I've named her "Suzy Wong," after the NYC cabaret artist of the '60s and '70s.

After this telepathic exchange, Suzy mounted me. I turned my head toward BJ. "What about her?" I said mentally.

"She's not part of this. Don't worry," Suzy replied.

Suzy was on top of me for a few minutes and I suppose I ejaculated into her. I know I was fully aroused, but I have no memory of an orgasm.

During this coupling, two Grays came into the room. One was the traditional-looking type—a short figure with big head and black, almond-shaped eyes. The second was a short, dumpy guy with a round head and a silly-looking grin.

After a few moments of afterglow, Suzy and her Gray companions left, but I don't remember seeing where they went. Apparently, I had fallen asleep at that point.

When I awoke, I was greatly troubled. I had just "cheated" on BJ, and with her in the same bed. More troubling, I'd enjoyed the sex, too. As a result, I felt morally bankrupt. Empty. *And I'm trying to get enlightened at Ramtha's school?* My life felt upside-down.

Fortunately, I had a therapy session that day. When I told Sally, she assured me once again that I was having vivid dreams due to my deeper longings for a more satisfying relationship. That made a lot of sense to me because I had been in therapy with Sally for several years due to my ambivalence about BJ, recently amplified by her staunch objections to my studying with Ramtha. In fact, I had begun contemplating leaving Long Island and relocating to Yelm. The song by Clint Black, "I'm Leaving You a Better Man," ran through my head daily. Internally, I knew I was preparing to end my relationship, but externally I didn't say anything.

With those kinds of pressures, I was squirming with tons of anxiety. One day it spilled out, and I told BJ of my dreams and Sally's psychoanalytic interpretations. BJ demurred, and it seemed like she thought I was just going through an extended crazy spell. First, I was in therapy to talk about our relationship, then I took several trips to a school for enlightenment, and now I was having sex with Extra-Terrestrials to save their world? *Oy vey. Maybe I'll be back to normal by spring???*

Normal didn't return, though. In the second week of January, 1990, I left BJ and moved out of the house, and started living with my parents. However, BJ insisted that we try marital therapy and I agreed. We had about four or five sessions together, and even though she screamed and howled through most of them, I convinced her the relationship was over. We concluded the details quickly, with attorneys making simple arrangements for a buy-out of my share of the house and everything else was split equitably. From the vantage point of my parents' home, I planned for the future.

Along the way, I met a woman named Karen at a New Age book store. She was reading one of Ramtha's books and I introduced myself. Later, we started an affair. Plus, she was looking to terminate her own marriage and move to the spiritual sanctuary of Santa Fe to start a whole new life. She sounded like my kind of gal. Karen and I helped each other extricate ourselves from our lives in New York and planned a combined western trip.

Karen helped me select an RV trailer, and I moved into a mobile home park in Bayshore, NY. Then, in February, I spent another couple of weeks at RSE. However, I got a severe case of bronchitis upon my return to New York and crawled back to parental care. In the meantime, Karen used the time to wrap things up in her marriage.

By April, we were ready to move west. However, a few days before we were scheduled to depart, I got a call from Jeff. He had started a newsletter for Ramtha students, and asked me to attend a major UFO conference in Trenton, New Jersey and interview one of the speakers, the author Zecharia Sitchin. Sitchin had written a very popular book, *The Twelfth Planet*, in which he described how Extra-Terrestrials named "the Nephilim" had come to Earth 250,000 years ago and had genetically modified *Homo erectus* into the modern humans of *Homo sapiens*.

"Sounds like your cup of tea," Jeff said with his usual smirky tone. I agreed, and Karen and I went to Trenton.

However, the highlight of the conference was not Sitchin. Rather, it was the ufologist Budd Hopkins. Hopkins specialized in alien abduction cases and he told a riveting story of a young man who had come to his door the prior week claiming he had been abducted by Grays for the purpose of having sex. As Hopkins described his conversation with this lad, I collapsed to the floor, writhing. Karen reached down and tried to comfort me, or at least steer me away from any of the surrounding chairs.

Slowly, I composed myself and was able to sit up. Karen put her arms around me. I rocked into her torso, unable to speak. She just held me as best she could.

Something in me had just been triggered by Hopkins' words. However, I had no clear understanding of what that might be—only that he'd confirmed for me that my sexual encounters with aliens were real.

By the time Hopkins concluded his presentation, I was able to function. I walked up to him at the podium and described what had just happened to me. He offered to help, suggesting a visit in his office the following week. I declined because of my plans to leave for Yelm. He countered by giving me the names of several hypnotherapists in the Pacific Northwest who worked with abductees.

"They might be able to give you some relief," he said.

I thanked him, then left with Karen. I was still shaken, but began to consciously accept that I had had sex with aliens.

Before Karen and I left New York, I had one last session with Sally. I told her about the Trenton episode with Budd Hopkins, and added all the theories I had heard regarding aliens rebuilding their genetic pool. It was a lengthy treatise, and Sally listened quietly. When I finished, she took a deep breath, then looked at me wearily. I filled in her silence.

"You don't think I'm gonna make it, do you, Sally? You think you're gonna get a call from some doctor in a hospital emergency room out there in Nebraska somewhere, asking for a clinical consultation on me."

"Yes, I do," she said.

But our time together was up, and I thanked Sally for all of her hard work with me over the years—400 sessions or so. As

I walked out of her office, Sally called out, "Bruce, wait." She walked toward me and extended her hand. We shook. "Good luck," she said.

The next day, I ended my relationship with Karen, too. There was no particular reason. I only felt deep inside that I needed to make my trip to Yelm unfettered. Karen was furious, but I left New York alone. As I crossed the George Washington Bridge and entered New Jersey, I looked in my rear-view mirror and knew there was no one back there who wanted me to ring their doorbell.

I didn't drive directly to Yelm, but took a meandering course through America. First, I toured the Serpent Mounds in Ohio, and then explored the Cahokia Ruins outside of St. Louis. Weeks later I was in New Mexico, the Land of Enchantment. It has always been a special place to me since I had spent 10 days at the Philmont Boy Scout Ranch. After getting a new belt to replace the original one, I spent some time in Santa Fe. Just north of the city, I parked my RV in the Pojoaque Pueblo campground, and one night the aliens visited again.

As I was settling comfortably in my RV bunk, I felt the aliens come in the front door. I tensed up, but then I saw my father's face at the foot of my bed. "Relax, Bruce," he said.

Calmed, I eased. Then I realized that it couldn't be my dad, and it was really the aliens playing with my mind. Instantly, I said telepathically, "Don't put me under. Don't mess with me. I can handle this. I want to be conscious. I want to know what is happening."

They ignored me. I was paralyzed just as I had been during that evening in Yelm the year before. But I could hear things. I heard the crunch of car wheels on a gravel road pulling away from my RV. I just accepted what was to come, and rested.

Later, in hypnosis, I recalled a lot of details from the Pojoaque abduction. First, I was transported in a blue van, one that looked like a Navy vehicle. I was unloaded at a shipping dock similar to what might be found at a large medical facility, such as a VA. My vehicle was one of several, with each van depositing an abducted fellow. We were all teleported out of our vans horizontally by a device stuck under our left armpit. As such, I floated along in the company of three other guys down a series of hallways that reminded me of the architecture I had seen during my work at the Northport VAMC.

Later, I was attended by beings who looked like human-sized praying mantis insects. One was tall, about 6', with a long protruding proboscis and spindly legs and arms. He wore a white lab coat and seemed to be in charge. He acted like a physician and appeared to be very concerned with my abdomen, but I have never been able to ascertain what procedures he might have been conducting.

In hypnosis, I recalled being at the "hospital" for a long period of time, often left unattended. Regardless, when I awoke in Pojoaque the next morning I felt refreshed.

Later that day, I visited the nearby Bandolier National Monument, a sacred site of kivas and cliff-dwelling ruins from the ancestral Pueblo Indians. As I walked up the trail to the first set of kivas, I heard a voice in my head.

"We will help you." It was the aliens.

I knew they were trying to make a deal for sex.

"How will you help me? I countered.

"We will help you survive the earth changes. If you help us, we will help you survive the cataclysms coming to this planet."

I knew plenty about global climate change, even though most of the world had never heard of the term. My work in New York managing a beachcleaning company had exposed me to the reality of sea-level rise. Further, I had seen vast ecological changes since I had been a kid learning how to swim at Point Lookout Beach on Long Island, and now the jetties were getting swamped with water at high tide. Plus, Ramtha had thoroughly educated me on the apocalyptic environmental changes that were destined for Earth due to pollution, a warming planet, and the collapse of the global food supply.

"So, you'll help me survive the End Times, eh?" I asked the aliens.

"Yes."

"Hmmm," I pondered. It was a good deal, kind of. On one hand, I didn't know exactly how devastating the Earth Changes would be, so having a bunch of Space Brothers watching my back sounded useful.

Nevertheless, I didn't want to be a guinea pig in somebody else's regeneration program, particularly since I had no control over the experience. I loved the sex, and I especially loved feeling special—being one of the Chosen Ones for a cross-breeding project—but I hated being paralyzed and rendered unconscious by the aliens. It just didn't seem right.

"No thanks," I said, finally.

The voices quickly left and I spent the rest of my time at Bandolier unencumbered. However, a week later something else happened that was bizarre and made me think the aliens were looking to impress me in a different fashion. By then I was cruising north of the Hopi Reservation in Arizona and passing through Utah on my way to Yelm. North of Moab my eyes began to burn, as if the sunlight was too strong for my sunglasses. I stopped at a gas station and bought the darkest sunglasses they had. They were insufficient, though, so I wore both pairs as I drove. By the time I entered the outskirts of Salt Lake City, though, my eyes were stinging so badly I had to stop and rest my eyeballs. I chose a Pizza Hut as refuge. Relaxing in the shaded environs, everything returned to normal. But when I got back on the road, I was forced to squint hard through the two pairs of sunglasses. Within an hour, I couldn't take any more sun and pulled into a KOA campground north of Salt Lake City. Several other travelers had pulled in at the same time and we all lined up at the receptionist's desk. One guy had a heavy-duty looking pair of sunglasses, and I asked him if the glare had affected him.

"Nope," he said, adding that he had just come down from Boise and hadn't experienced any difficulty with the sunlight.

However, another camper overheard our conversation. Later, when no one else was listening, he told me that he, too, had difficulty with the sun. Surprisingly, he had also just driven down from Boise.

"Yikes. What do you think is going on?" I asked.

"I have no idea," the quiet camper replied.

Nor did I. Nor did I know if it has anything to do with aliens, other than the circumstantial timing of the phenomenon.

Days later I was in Yelm and pulled my trailer next to Jeff's house in McKenna. Over glasses of wine, I recounted my travels and alien encounters. Jeff smiled, knowing that he was going to receive a bunch of stories for his newsletter.

A week or so later, I contacted one of the hypnotherapists Budd Hopkins had recommended to me, but we couldn't connect for scheduling reasons. In turn, they referred me to a local gal, Linda, who did hypnotherapy with alien abductees for free as part of her support of the UFO community. I made an appointment with Linda for the next week, and thus began a new chapter in my UFO saga.

I expected a deep hypnosis session like the ones I'd seen in videos, where the abductees were clearly out of their bodies and talking about strange and unworldly experiences. Instead, my hypnosis sessions with Linda were a form of guided-imagery experiences. Nevertheless, they were useful. Plus, my physical responses to the hypnosis told me something important was happening. I got very cold during the sessions and, even though it was June, Linda had to ply me with every blanket and comforter she possessed.

Linda helped me clarify many of the clouded memories I had of my experiences. We began with Suzy Wong, and I learned she was a Gray and not any kind of human being. Further, Suzy was able to project a "female" image onto my senses. What I had assumed was her vagina was not any kind of genitalia into which I ejaculated, but rather was a metal, box-like device.

Next, Linda helped me refine all the details of the Pojoaque abduction, assisting me in recovering the details I have described previously.

In addition, I learned that I had many abductions before 1989, being teleported aboard the Grays' spaceships for medical-like examinations and procedures. However, the exact nature of them is still a mystery to me. I also met lots of other abductees aboard these craft, and I witnessed other Extra-Terrestrials besides the Grays and Mantis People, such as tall "Nordics," who are statuesque, blonde-haired fellows.

Surprisingly, Linda couldn't help with the sunglass phenomenon in Salt Lake City.

I had six two-hour sessions with Linda, and even though I appreciated her assistance, I had to stop. These sessions sexed me up; for relief, I had to stop at a strip club on the way home and have a beer and watch the show. I also had a growing awareness that Linda was becoming aroused as well, and by the end of my last session I felt she wanted to jump my bones.

But we stayed friends. In fact, I became part of her outreach work in the UFO community. In particular, I began attending her support groups for other people abducted for sex. I was shocked to see so many women who claimed that they had had mysterious pregnancies, and also instantaneous-but-bloodless miscarriages. Linda invited me to speak at a number of UFO conferences that she hosted, and I spoke at gatherings in Seattle and British Columbia. Linda also recommended that other groups invite me. One was MUFON of Portland, Oregon, commonly known as PUFON.

In early 1991, PUFON invited me to talk before a group of 400 aficionados on the campus of the Multnomah County Community College. The talk was also filmed by the college's video crew and later broadcasted on Multnomah County Public Access TV. I understand that it was their most-requested re-broadcasted show for the year.

One exchange with an audience member stands out. As the gathering was finishing and folks were leaving the auditorium, a young man approached me, trembling.

"Your talk really touched me," he said quietly.

I stepped toward him and whispered, "Have you been having these kinds of experiences, too?"

He nodded in the affirmative and began to weep. I embraced him gently and he sobbed quietly in my arms. I held him for several moments. Eventually, he composed himself and pulled away.

"Thanks," he said.

"All the best to you, buddy," I replied. He slowly walked away, and I have never heard from him since. However, it is for him and others like us that I write these words. It's been a kind of slog, though, one that I have put off for years, even decades. I'm not sure why, but it is hard to tell this story. It's not guilt or remorse; it's more like PTSD exhaustion—the exertion of mental energy wrestling with the idea: *Is this real? Did I really have sex with aliens? What do I do about it?*

Eventually, I ended all contact with the aliens in 1992, but not before a final series of confrontations with the Grays. Simply, I figured if I was having sex with these aliens then I probably had kids somewhere in outer space or on a space craft. *What a lousy place to grow up, even if they're only half human.* As a good father, or at least a good Scoutmaster, I wanted to see my kids and see how they were doing. Maybe help them out a little. Hence, I asked the aliens telepathically to arrange a visit with my kids. They never complied.

Incensed, I decided to go looking on my own. "They're my kids, too, dammit!" I shouted in consciousness. In deep meditation I eventually found them, at least in my mind.

My kids were a mess. They were frail and sickly—imagine an unkempt detox center for impoverished teenage drug addicts. I never questioned if these youths were my offspring or not, as they clearly needed help. The teens could barely talk, grunting or only uttering a single word. They had trouble walking or standing up straight, and the Grays telepathically told me they wanted me to dance with the kids. Apparently, they had no sense of rhythm, either. Previously, I had done years of music therapy with my psychiatric patients, and now drum music sprang into my head and I formed a circle.

"Just feel the music," I said to them, as I knew they were telepathically connected to what I was hearing. "Feel the deep tones of the drums. Move your hips and shoulders to the beat." I had to demonstrate so they could understand what I was asking them to do.

Our drum session was modestly successful, and when I left the kids had a spark of life in their otherwise dull eyes.

I returned in consciousness a few days later, and the kids were swimming in a pool. Or rather walking in chest-deep water, which was something they could do more easily than moving on land. I sat poolside and watched. Soon, I was joined by a Gray whom I had seen at the drum session. He was a Yoda-like character — wise-looking and old. He indicated that he was in charge of the hybrid program. Telepathically, I asked what he thought of his project.

It has problems, he replied.

It sure does, I retorted. We sat in silence. I wasn't angry with him for abducting me, nor for creating a bunch of troubled youth. Rather, I sent him the thought that I understood his intentions. Then I left.

The next day, I decided my relationship with the Grays had to end. I realized that if I had done anything like what they were doing to me, I would be facing the death penalty. Kidnapping and paralyzing me, taking my sperm — along with stealing the ova and fetuses from the women in Linda's groups — all this was conducted against our will and without any consent. The aliens simply could not do this. It was worse than immoral. For anyone, any race of beings, no matter how technologically advanced they may be, such behavior is utterly unacceptable. The Grays needed more than human chromosomes for emotional vitality. They needed psychotherapy. Or jail.

So, I simply said out loud, "No more."

I haven't had a visitation from the ETs since.

That is, until three decades later. Then, I met an Extra-Terrestrial, sort of, when I went to his website. The ET was named Bashar, who channels through a gentleman from Los Angeles named Darryl Anka. As I understand Bashar's linage, he is a Gray that has traveled back from our distant future to help us prepare for direct, physical contact with Extra-Terrestrials. Now, if you can't wait to read the next part of my alien saga, go ahead and leap-frog to Chapter 58, "Revisiting the Aliens: Seeking Direct Contact with Extra-Terrestrials."

Or read the stories from the next 30 years of my life and learn more fully why I wanted contact, and how I got myself ready for such a remarkable encounter.

Either way, the next page awaits you.

19

Nice Guys
Learning I'm not as nice as I thought I was

I did not see the three Colorado cowboys enter the Steamboat Springs tavern. Nor did I hear my friend mumble, "Who let those damn cowboys in?"

But the cowboys heard it, and the lead of the three walked up behind me and put a large hand on my shoulder. With a firm grip he pulled me around and out of my chair. I straightened my knees and stood.

"Are you the guy bad-mouthin' cowboys?" he asked.

"No, buddy. I don't know what you're talking about," I replied.

"You didn't say something about 'damn cowboys' when I walked in here?"

"Nope, and I didn't hear anybody else say anything about cowboys." The blank, naive look on my face convinced him I was telling the truth.

The cowboy put his face whisker-close to mine and said, "Whoever did ain't got no right to be talking about cowboys that way, and I'm gonna see to it that they don't." Then, tapping me on the chest with the back of his knuckles, he smiled and said, "I wanna fight so bad my teeth are chattering."

I smiled back and put my hand on his shoulder. "You must want to fight pretty bad," I said, chuckling.

He continued grinning for a moment, but then lost his smile. He squeezed his mouth tight and said, "Shoot, I can't fight you, you're a nice guy."

Yes, I'm a nice guy. I'm a former altar boy, peace-nik, force-for-love-and-righteousness-in-the-world type of nice guy. I've been a Boy Scout, environmental activist, and a healer-in-a-psychiatric-hospital. I've helped raise other men's children. My stepdaughters tell me I'm the role model for the kind of guy they'd like to spend the rest of their lives with.

Still, when I'd left BJ—the mother of those stepchildren—she and several of her daughters had exploded with a rage I didn't know was possible by civilized human beings.

When I ended my relationship with Karen on the day we were to leave New York, I'd spoken for her as she flumed and flustered. "I'm not a very nice guy, am I?"

"You certainly are not, BUSTER!"

Later, when I got a job at another psych facility, I learned that several of my female colleagues refused to work with me because my large physical size and "masculine-presence" triggered flashbacks of sexual assault.

Further, our charge nurse told me that my arrogance "terrified" her, and I hadn't even *known* I was arrogant.

For a nice guy I'm triggering a lot of havoc, and I wonder how much trouble has that cowboy caused in his life? More than mine? Less?

Is his simply more blatant and mine more veiled, hidden by a New Age sanctimony?

20

A Full Moon and Fig Newtons
Satisfying my hungers on the road to enlightenment

I saw her for the first time at the Chaco Canyon Ranger Station in New Mexico — lean, dark-haired, and replete with a cleft lip. Her visage cut to my deepest longings. My knees went weak and I clutched the ranger's counter for stability. *Why haven't I ever known a woman like her?*

Later that night, a full moon drew us to the same Anasazi ruins. We talked, and then, sitting on the rim of an ancient kiva, I asked her for a kiss. It was sweet and soft, like fireweed honey, and it touched my soul. The ease of our connection was as luscious as the lunar glow, as strong and pervasive as the moonbeams blanketing the New Mexican desert around us. Making love in my RV was an afterthought.

The next day, she was off to the Garden of the Gods, and afterward, her home in San Diego. For reasons I cannot fathom, I rejoiced in not traveling with her. Instead, I headed toward Monument Valley, Arizona. I guess relationships overwhelm me, or maybe I need lots of lunar energy to sustain them.

Once in Monument Valley, home of the only scenery in the world that can stand up to John Wayne's swagger, I moved on from the Kiva Kiss and developed a craving for Fig Newtons.

At first it was a simple late-night snack attack, the kind a quick trip to a convenience store can satisfy. However, the camp store at my RV park did not stock Fig Newtons. Instead, they carried a local brand called Fig Bars, from a bakery in Farmington, New Mexico. I love eating native cuisine and I bought a box.

They tasted horrible.

The next morning, I didn't want my regular breakfast of muesli. I wanted Fig Newtons. *Must be the desert air or that Kiva Kiss hits deeper than I realized.*

I surveyed my RV neighbors. They were either Pop Tart freaks or rock-solid Americans eating scrambled eggs and bacon. But they all assured me that Chenle, the nearby hub of the Navajo Nation, would be big enough to have a supermarket carrying Fig Newtons.

Normally I wouldn't burn $20 worth of gas just for cookies, but since I also needed to find an ATM and Chenle is next to Canyon de Chelly, the site of the Navajo's last stand against Kit Carson, it became my next destination.

Canyon de Chelly was majestic, but Chenle did not have an ATM. Worse, it only had more Fig Bars from Farmington.

So, short on cash and longing for Fig Newtons, I headed north toward Utah and onto my new home of Yelm.

The first big town I came to was Blanding, Utah. There I found an ATM and got more cash. But in their grocery store's Nabisco section there was only an empty gap on the cookie shelf where Fig Newtons should have been. As a result, the good people of Blanding were treated to a royal New-York-style hissy-fit.

"Please mister, calm down," said the manager, as customers peered from both ends of the aisle. "We'll have a new shipment tomorrow, or the next day for sure. We have some local Fig Bars, from Farmington. Maybe you'd like to try them?"

"Arrrgh!" I groaned in primal disgust. My hands and eyes grappled with the empty space above me, trying to make Fig Newtons appear from thin air. Grunting incomprehensible wailings, I rushed from the store. Outside, my karmic metabolism surged and roared. I took deep breaths. I saw myself as master of my reality—calm and focused. I settled down, at least enough to drive.

I continued north. The 80 miles of desert highway to Moab soothed my tortured soul, and there in the city that rhymes with Ahab, I found cookie nirvana in a Safeway.

Funny, sometimes it's the love that comes easy and not the cookie...*OM*....

Note: Fig Newtons™ is a registered trademark of the National Biscuit Company, I think.

21

Philmont Belts
Celebrating the synchronicities

Besides memories, one of the most cherished things I carried with me when I left Philmont in 1966 was my Philmont belt. It was a thick leather affair, best described as a "cowboy belt." It had PHILMONT stenciled into the leather, along with cattle-branding signage and other western flourishes.

But the best part was the buckle, a large brass plate engraved with a famous rock formation symbolic of Philmont, known as the "Tooth of Time." I wore that belt every day until the mid-1980s when the brass clasp broke from the backing of the buckle. After that, the belt and buckle lay curled in my souvenir box of Boy Scout patches and neckerchief slides. It was a sad day putting away my belt, not dissimilar to when "Woody the Sheriff" was placed in a cardboard box in the *Toy Story* movie.

So, when I was driving cross-country on my relocation to Yelm, I decided to swing past Santa Fe and head to Philmont. *Maybe I can buy a new belt. It's April, perhaps there will be a few staff around getting ready for the season.*

I pulled into camp on that cool and cloudy spring day. Even though the 200 wooden platforms of Tent City looked like the skeletons of beached whales, there were a few cars parked at the administration building. I walked in and was greeted by a cheerful receptionist.

"Hi there, can I help you?"

"Hello," I answered. "I was a former camper here, back in the...um, sixties. Ah, ...I was wondering if I could buy a new belt. My buckle broke a few years ago and I'd like to replace it."

"No problem. The Ranger is around back unloading a UPS delivery, and he should be able to help you." She picked up her phone, made a quick call, and within seconds a short, friendly guy came to the receptionist desk.

"This guy would like to buy a belt," she told the Ranger.

"No problem, if you're willing to help me load up the UPS stuff and take it to the commissary," said the Ranger.

"Of course," I replied.

As we drove along in his pickup, I felt like I was riding with Johnnie Jones at Wauwepex all over again. Sweet and bouncy. But I realized I was asking for a favor—perhaps a big one—so I spoke: "I want to thank you for letting me buy a belt. I hope I'm not putting you out too much. But I wore my belt every day from 1966 until the day it broke, so I'd really like to get a new one."

"No problem, fella. We get a couple guys like you every day, coming here and asking to buy a new belt."

"You're kidding me!" I exclaimed. *Two a day?*

"Yup. "Every day, 'cept for Christmas and Thanksgiving. Sometimes the buckle is broken like yours, but most of the times it's because they've gained weight and their old belt doesn't fit any more."

"I never realized that Philmont meant so much to so many other guys, too," I murmured.

The Ranger just looked at me and smiled.

The commissary looked much different from the way it looked 25 years prior. Back in my day it was a cubby-hole of a place to buy memorabilia and postcards. But in 1990, it was a well-equipped camping store with backpacks, boots, polar fleece coats, and all the other things modern backpackers need on the trail.

"Wow, it sure has changed," I said to the Ranger.

"We have a lot of new programs in the spring and fall, too," he replied, "so the Scouts need a lot more gear. It's a pretty decent shop," he said proudly.

I got my new belt—a couple sizes bigger than when I was 16 years old and a size 32. I put it on right there in the shop. It felt good.

Cost a lot more than it did in 1966, too. But I had the money, and I felt proud being able to buy it and not having to count pennies as I had when I was younger.

Ten years later, I told this story to an RSE schoolmate, Dave. We were sitting in his kitchen in the town of Eatonville, Washington. I had been helping Dave on a few tree-felling jobs and we were relaxing and drinking some red wine. We started telling each other about our journeys to Ramtha, and I mentioned that I had made a big detour from I-90 to head south to Santa Fe and Philmont.

Dave smiled. "Yeah, I was at Philmont, too. Worth the extra miles for sure," he said.

"When were you there?

"1966," he replied.

"1966! Really? Me, too!" I shouted. "I was in group 716-I. How about you?" The designation 716-I meant I was the 8th group to arrive on July 16, 1966.

"Heh, heh," Dave chuckled. "I left on July 16."

"My Gawd, Dave, you left Tent City on the morning of the day I arrived. I could have slept in the same bunk you did the night before."

Tent City was indeed a city of tents, with 200 8x12 wooden platforms covering dozens of acres, and all topped by 8-foot-high, two-man tents. Approximately 800 Boy Scouts tromped through Tent City every day: 400 in the morning waiting to board their buses and head home, and 400 just arriving, eager for their Philmont adventure.

"I've got a Philmont belt story for you, too," Dave said. "When I got out of the Navy, I didn't know what to do with myself, so I went on a road trip down south with some Navy buddies. We stopped in Kitty Hawk to see the sights and go swimming. After coming back from a swim in the ocean, I was shocked to see that my car had been broken into. But what was worse than anything—even worse than having my wallet stolen or even my camera—they took the cutoffs that had my Philmont belt on it."

The next day I called Philmont and ordered a new belt for Dave. "An early Christmas present," I told him when it arrived.

Over the months that followed, I worked with Dave on occasion, and we formed a working man's friendship. When I returned from Nashville in 2000, Dave let me stay in his RV trailer until I found a more permanent home.

Over dinners and some more red wine, we shared a few more life stories and I was astonished to learn that our paths had crossed a couple times beyond our close encounter at Philmont. Dave's RV trailer had North Carolina license plates; he'd bought it when he was living near Asheville. During the time he was in Asheville, I was there as well, first picking rocks at the Western North Carolina Agricultural Center with my Sandsifter, and a few months later backpacking in the Pisgah National Forest. Dave and I were only a few miles apart during that time, and now I was living in the RV that took him from the Smokies to Yelm.

As we dove into more stories, I learned that Dave grew up in Quakertown, just on the outskirts of Bethlehem, Pennsylvania and home to Lehigh University. Hitchhiking south to Philly to see my first big-time girlfriend, Rachel, probably put me on the same roads Dave was driving on his 450 Norton.

For the next 20 years I lived in Dave's RV, and I wrote the bulk of this book in that abode. So now, dear reader, you're part of this connection, too.

Welcome.

22

Any Place Can Be a Home

A – D
I live in a cozy place, 18 by 8 feet long.

D – A – E
And I could stand up straight in it, if I was a leprechaun.

A – D
But my brother said I can see the loneliness

E
Etched in your face

A – D
So why don't you stay in the trailer

A – D – E
'til you get your own place.

Cause any place can be a home if the love's inside
Any place can warm the heart if the love is bona fide.
A mansion, a cardboard box, or a double-wide,
Any place can be a home if the love's inside.

I lived in a mansion, high above Santa Fe
Its walls were thick adobe, it was a real beau-ty.
But the lady of the house could not share respect,
So, two weeks after movin' in… I left.

One day I'm gonna build myself a home
Gonna build it strong, make it safe and warm
But no matter what it looks like, what'll be my biggest pride
Is knowing that I built it with lots of love inside.

All Bruce's music can be viewed on his youtube channel at https://www.youtube.com/@BruceASmith-hn4zq

23

On Becoming a Hunter
Self-reliance brings me to inter-dimensional realities

Of all the things I did when I left New York to study with Ramtha, the craziest thing—according to BJ—was not leaving *her*, selling Sandsifter, or attempting to turn water into wine. For her, I went off the deep end when I bought a rifle and became a hunter.

Her consternation was understandable because I shared her disgust seeing dead deer strapped to the hoods of sedans driving south on the New York Thruway from the Catskill Mountains. But here in Yelm, which is halfway between Seattle and the Cascade Mountains, lots of people hunt. During the season, many of the pickups at my local Safeway have guns in their cab racks as men stop to buy groceries on the way home from a hunt or a plinking session.

But I didn't buy a gun to bond with my new neighbors. Rather, I had decided to take greater responsibility for my life and become more self-reliant. That meant growing a garden, planting fruit trees, and getting a gun.

My weapon was not some kind of Rambo-type machine gun. Instead, it was an old-style musket, a single shot, black powder rifle—the type where you ram stuff down the barrel with a rod, just like Daniel Boone. In fact, my gun, known as a "Hawkins," was a replica of the rifle preferred by the Mountain Men of the 1840s—the guys who gave up on civilization, came west over the Rockies, and married local Indian women. My kind of guys, because I began to do something similar when I arrived in Yelm. I let my hair grow *really* long and lived deep in the woods. In season I hunted, and one year I hooked up with several other muzzle-loading fellows and hunted for a week on the western slopes of the Cascades near Mount Rainier. Although I had opportunities, I did not get my deer.

Still, I had many wonderful experiences, the best of which was seeing elk for the first time. While crossing a clear-cut in the Gifford Pinchot National Forest, I felt the ground shake from the pounding hooves of two dozen elk stampeding behind us. It was like an earthquake. I turned and saw these massive animals, taller than I was, galloping at 30 miles an hour across a huge clearing as if they were on a joy ride through Mother Nature. Until they caught our scent and stopped—fearing us more than whatever they had been escaping. Moments later they drifted silently into the bush.

During our hunt, I lived the essence of nature. Up before dawn I saw the sun rise, or at least the sky getting lighter and darkness leaving the woods. We hunted like a wolf pack, two or three guys flushing deer into clearings from their hiding places in "re-prod," the tangle of cut-down saplings common to timber country where foresters plant "reproduction," or second-growth seedlings to jump-start the growth of new timber. Our plan was to push the deer into the open, exposing them to the others who were waiting in predetermined firing zones.

We hunted with the weather, seeking snow and telltale tracks or moving in accordance with air temperature and wind. Most mornings the winds blew uphill as the upper slopes of Rainier warmed, so we hunted down-slope into the wind and away from our scent. In the afternoon, we reversed our movements, just as the wind did. Daily snow squalls and bitter breezes on the slopes gave way to warmth in the flats. Surprisingly, I always saw the sun at some point during the day.

When we got hungry, we stopped and ate sandwiches. Wrist watches became superfluous. What mattered most was dry boots and always knowing where the rest of the guys were. I knew keenly that I had killing power at the flick of my finger. I wore "hunter orange" on my hat and vest, and would smile when I spotted my buddy's orange hat 200 yards away in a salal thicket.

On the next to last day of the season we decided to bid goodbye to the daily rain, mud, and snow, and go back home to warm clothes and dry beds.

The following morning, I awoke at 5 a.m. and, while lying in bed, had a lucid vision. The walls of my room disappeared. I could see into the woods surrounding my home, yet I felt neither cold nor wind. From a distance I saw a cloud come toward me. As it neared, I saw four deer standing on the cloud, their legs wrapped by the mist. When the entourage got to within a few feet of me, the lead of the four asked, "Are you coming?"

"What do you mean?" I countered. "Coming where?"

"Are you hunting today?" the deer said.

"Me? Why do you ask? Yesterday, I was trying to kill you," I replied.

"Yes, we know. But that doesn't matter. You are one of us. You are not a tourist or a backpacker. You leave the trail and walk where we walk. You step in the same brush that we do, the same puddles. The rain falls on you like it falls upon us. The snow clings to your feet like it does to our hooves. You are one of us. Are you coming?"

I weighed the invitation, but moving my body seemed too much of a task.

"No, not today," I replied.

The leader looked straight at me, but did not speak or move in any acknowledgment. I sensed a profound neutrality, a blank response utterly devoid of any judgment on whether I stayed in bed or took up the gun. The cloud and deer receded. When they reached the horizon, my vision ended.

That was the last year I hunted with my mountain men, and other than one shot at a stump, I have not fired my Hawkins since. On occasion I have hunted with a modern rifle, and although I feel my greatest intimacy with the natural world when I am walking in the woods with a loaded weapon—greater even than Wauwepex—in hunting season I have never seen a deer since.

24

Of Mice and Men's Groups
I learn the glories and pitfalls of being a man

Shortly after my arrival in Yelm, Jeff telephoned in a rush to say, "You have to come over right now and watch this TV show." It was a telecast titled: "A Gathering of Men," a documentary on poet Robert Bly and his efforts to help men discover their manhood. I thoroughly enjoyed the broadcast.

"How do men learn to become men?" Bly asked. "Who teaches us, and do we learn everything we need to know? If not, why not, and what are the consequences of an incomplete upbringing in manhood?"

It is Bly's perspective—and mine—that most men know diddly-squat about being a man. I know I wasn't taught much, at least not directly. Our fathers should be the ones to teach us about manhood. However, my dad taught me very little about being a man, although I'd like to think he would have done if he himself had been schooled in such a manner.

This lack of specific male training has been going on for quite some time, I suspect, and I don't know how or when we lost it, but we did. Aboriginal tribes, like the ones I read about in anthropology texts, know more about teaching the skills of true manhood to their boys than our civilization.

One of the things I learned from Bly is that historically it has been the job of men to do the killing for the tribe. That means hunting and fishing for the meat, or providing protection. We still fight the wars, but nowadays men—along with women—provide a community with inner strength, too, leading the way with discipline, insights, or moral instructions. Bly links these aspects together by citing Celtic wisdom: *Don't teach a man the art of war until you've taught him how to dance.*

And so, what is a manly man? My definition, and I think Bly would concur, is: *A true man is a tender warrior who can express himself fully.*

A warrior can protect and provide for his loved ones—he brings home the bacon. A tender man has the compassion and self-awareness to guide his aggressiveness to a greater good. That means a real man has to be able to talk about his feelings.

Bly makes the simple observation that men don't talk about their feelings because they don't know what their feelings are. If we did, we would probably talk about them. So, it's not that we're hiding anything from anybody—our feelings are often hidden from us as well.

One encounter with my therapist, Sally, was particularly illuminating on this issue. After a discussion about one of my Sandsifter employees who quit without any notice, Sally asked if I was angry. I said, "No, he's just being unprofessional," to which she replied, "Well, you look angry."

Again, I stated that I was not angry, but she kept digging.

"Well, Bruce, *why* do you think you *look* angry, if you're not angry? Are you *sure* you're not really angry?"

"NO. I'm not angry. I'm just, well… frustrated, I guess. But if you keep pushing this anger thing, I'm gonna get angry!"

"Really?" she replied, and smiled slightly. "I think you *are* angry, but you aren't allowing yourself to truly feel it. What would you say to that?"

After more discussion I agreed with her. I was blind to my anger. That in turn opened up the whole field of what happens when we suppress our emotions because anger or some other feeling is too troubling for public consumption — such as being a kid in a family that didn't want to hear my thoughts or feelings. As a result, I shoved everything into a protected box. Not only anger, but also joy and intimacy.

Despite plenty of therapy and meditation, much is still hidden to me, particularity in the area of love and sexuality. Impotency has been a life-long issue for me, as are developing satisfying, meaningful friendships with men. One of the greatest lacks in my adult life is the absence of close male friends. When people talk about the diminished capacity of men to be intimate, they usually mean with women and sex. But many men have great difficulty being close with each other — of having the kind of friendship where they are comfortable telling a friend anything and everything, and expressing their feelings in ways other than physically acting out or getting drunk.

For decades, until I met Jeff, I'd never had a close male friend as an adult. Wonderfully, Jeff and I talked up a storm about being men. We took a close look at who our fathers were as men and what they taught us. Surprisingly, Jeff and I discovered that both of us had only begun to consider ourselves "men" in middle-age.

For me, turning 40 helped. Now, I figured, I should be old enough to be a man, and I began to feel somewhat a "man." Fortunately, as the 40s rolled into the 50s, then the 60s and 70s, that realization has deepened, and I see that it has come from my growth in personal fortitude. Moving to Yelm from my home in New York meant I needed to separate from BJ, sell Sandsifter, and relocate across the country, which took quite a bit of self-determination. I had to say in the face of a lot of adversity: *This is my desire. It is my life, my decision. End of discussion.* True men talk like that, and now I've accepted myself a man.

Following those insights, I thought other men would like to talk about their views of manhood. However, the process of starting a men's group was daunting. When I put up flyers announcing the formation of such a group, I heard from plenty of women stating *they* would like to attend, or that they wanted their husbands to participate. Only a handful of men actually came, though, and the initial discussion was so awkward and unsatisfying we never held a second meeting.

Regardless, back in the day when I thought about my dilemma of "no male friends," I thought about sports. *Why not? It could be a nifty way to have fun, connect with other men and makes friends.*

I've traveled this path a few times, particularly when I lived in New York. One experience is worth retelling.

When I cleaned beaches, I never had a day off in the summer, but my winters were free. I have had a life-long love of baseball, so the question for me was: Where can I find a baseball team that plays in the winter so that I can indulge my love of the sport and possibly make some male friends?

Fortuitously, enterprising baseball enthusiasts have converted a large warehouse in Commack, NY into indoor softball fields, and organized men's leagues. At the beginning of the 1988 winter season, I asked management if there were any teams that might need a solo player.

"Sure, a few teams need a couple of extra players. What position do you play?" the sports manager asked.

"I love to pitch," I replied.

"Great. We've got a team that is looking specifically for a pitcher. They call themselves the Long Island Mice. They're a good team, too, from what I've heard. But, they're from out of our area so they're new to the league. But I hear they're looking for an upgrade in the level of competition."

"Sounds fantastic. I'd love to join."

The guy took my money, and gave me the contact information and game schedules. Then he said, "By the way, the Mice are an all-women's team. I hope that's okay. They're one of the best in the country. In fact, they were ranked #2 in the nation last summer."

All women? How was I going to make male friends? Hmmm. But I wanted to play baseball and I wanted to pitch. Who else would give me a shot? So, I was ready to become a temporary "Mice."

At our first practice, I immediately saw how good they were. *They sure don't throw "like girls."* In fact, the Mice told me they had joined Commack's "B" league for the winter because none of the women's leagues in the Greater New York area could provide them with suitable competition. Although our men's league was at the "B" level, they were still very good. The Mice kicked some serious butt that season, although we just missed the playoffs.

I had fun playing with these "jocks," as the ladies called themselves. For their part, they enjoyed having me be part of their team. I was an "okay" player, but more importantly I was their spy in the men's locker room. They especially loved hearing my reports on the crumbling egos of the guys they had just beaten. I remember vividly a team composed of NYC toll booth operators screaming at each other because they had "lost to a bunch of girls!"

I also remember our first base woman, who had the largest hoop earrings I have ever seen, which made her a great throwing target. Plus, our shortstop had the best arm of any infielder I've ever played with. The Mice were truly formidable.

But they were also frail, or at least mentally vulnerable. If our opponent scored first, my gal-pals became deflated. You could see their energy and confidence drain from their faces, and only once did we rally from a deficit and win.

I had fun that season, but I obviously didn't make any new male friends.

All that is changing, though. As I reach inside to find my feelings and act on them, I become manlier. It's a process, and at 70-some years old I'm still at it. I've found it takes a lot of strength to be a man, but I am grateful for the rewards. Jeff and I keep in touch, and I leave no stone unturned with other men. With women I am better able to act on deeper stirrings, better prepared to resolve the fears and anxieties that come with newer levels of connection. Intimacy in any form can be frightening, but I tell myself: *Every warrior is frightened on the eve of battle.*

25

On Being a Santa Claus
Learning the power of myth

My first job after moving to Yelm was working as a shopping mall Santa Claus. Beginning the day after Thanksgiving, I pulled four-hour shifts at the Capitol Mall in Olympia, Washington posing for pictures and hearing what kids wanted for Christmas. Some days were grueling—try listening to endless Christmas carols—but some moments were sublime.

One of them was experiencing the deep mythos that Santa Claus has on people, especially kids aged five to eight—the core group who still believe. One kid stands out, and I think about him to this day.

He was about seven years old, and he came to Santaland with a contingent of three women and five or six children. He caught my eye because he hung back from the cluster. I assumed that one of the women was his mother and the other two adults were her friends bringing their own children. I soon learned that his reserved behavior was intentional.

As the group approached, the boy never looked at me directly, but just quietly let all the other kids sit on my lap, one at a time. The mothers took turns edging closer to Santa's chair so they could hear what their kids wanted for Christmas.

When it was his turn, the boy climbed on my knee and began to recite his memorized list of gifts—a GI Joe, LEGOs, and some other small stuff. His mother had leaned in to hear the recitation, but when she heard the usual list, she pulled away and turned to chat with the other moms. As she pulled away, the boy knew he had a few moments free from parental scrutiny. In a flash, he slid close to me and put his face to my ear.

"But Santa, what I really want is the Ark of the Covenant and the Holy Grail." Then he snapped back up, sitting straight on my knee. If you weren't looking closely, you would have missed it—just like his mother did.

I was stunned. *Whoa!* I wasn't sure I had heard correctly, and my mind scrambled to find a logical interpretation of what *I* thought he had intended to say.

"You, um... you'd like the... video of the Indiana Jones movie, *The Ark of the Covenant*?"

"Oh, Santa, noooooo...." The kid looked aghast, betrayed even. He pulled away and slid off my knee. He stood on quivering legs in front of me and began to turn away. I grabbed his shoulders.

"Wait a minute, kiddo. C'mere." I turned him around so he faced me directly. I knew this boy wanted the real thing and not some movie, but I didn't know what to say. Then the Magic of Christmas hit *me* and the following words just tumbled forth:

"What you're asking for is a very big gift. It may take years for me to get it to you, or for you to be ready to receive it. So, in the meantime, will a hug from someone who has seen the face of God do for this year, or until I can deliver such an important gift?"

"OH, YES! SANTA!" His face beamed and his eyes shone like crystals. He stepped forward and melted into my arms. We hugged tightly and he nuzzled his face into my beard. I held him firmly to my chest, and we breathed in rhythm.

After the third breath we both knew that his mother would be giving us the eye, so I released my arms and he pulled away. He rejoined his mom, and their entourage left Santaland. The boy never looked back, and his secret has been held sacred for the past 30 years.

But, kiddo, if you're out there and hear this story, Santa wants to know how you're doing. So, give me a call, will ya?

26

Hey, Granddad, Thanks for the Banjo

The following song is about my grandfather, and it's dedicated to a man I've never met—Rutherford "Rud" W. Smith, the original banjo player in the family. Rud was a renowned raconteur and, even though I never heard any of his tales directly, I've heard plenty about *how* he told his yarns.

Back in granddad's day, the family's tradition was for him to regale his family's guests at the dinner table after the main course, while my grandmother went off to make dessert—usually a couple of apple pies with a deliciously tangy lemon icing.

My grandfather had a second job besides entertaining guests, and that task was to make whipped cream from scratch for the pies. One Thanksgiving, he was telling a tale that was so good *and* so long that he whipped the cream into butter, and had to start all over again with a fresh bowl of cream—and a new story.

Rud died of a heart attack in 1947. He was 61. Dad was stationed in Germany at the time, and loved his tenure there as part of the post-WWII Allied occupation, and returned to Brooklyn reluctantly.

But like *his* father, my dad loved to tell stories—in his case, about his Army days. Dad put me to bed every night regaling me of his military time, and also about how his pop told his tales.

Hey Granddad, Thanks for the Banjo

C—F
Hey Granddad, thanks for the banjo

F—G
The first strings I ever played

F—C
Were ones that you put on.

C—F
I found it on Thanksgiving morn, when I was ten and three,

C—G—C
And since I never knew ya, it brings you close to me.

Verse 1
I found your banjo, long after you were gone,
Up in the attic of your old Brooklyn home.
I brought it downstairs, got Grandma's okay,
And even though the skins were cracked, I began to pluck away.

Chorus
A four-string Challenger, from the Paramount Company.
You were a sign painter and their employee.
But who had money then, it was 1903,
So they gave you this banjo as your month's salary.

Chorus
The family says I'm a lot like you, I like to sing a song.I
like to sit at the head of the table, and know what's going on.
I hope you can hear me, up in heaven a-playin' your banjo song,
I hope it puts a smile on your face to hear your banjo strong.

All Bruce's music can be viewed on his youtube channel at https://www.youtube.com/@BruceASmith-hn4zq

27

Don't Give Up Your Song
More manifestations

This story began in 1993 when the IRS audited me for the first year I was a professional storyteller. The IRS claimed that if I was doing everything I said I was doing in 1991, such as telling stories, singing songs, and even doing a little stand-up comedy, I should have made more than the $324 I declared on my income tax.

The truth of the matter was I had lied. I did not make $324. I made only $296, but I was too embarrassed to put that figure on my 1040, so I bloated the number up to $324. Knowing that I had filed a false claim added to the anxiety I already felt being grilled by government agents, so to soothe my paranoia I brought a tape recorder in case the government got cranky over the $324. To my surprise, when I entered the IRS office and the auditor saw my little Radio Shack tape recorder, she freaked out.

"Mr. Smith," she said shrilly, "If you're going to tape record these proceedings, we will be required to have a neutral third-party observer witness the proceedings." Then she left the office, presumably to find a neutral third-party observer somewhere in the Federal Office Building of Olympia, Washington.

Alone in the auditing chamber, I wondered what could be the problem. *If they're uptight about my tape recorder, they can pull out their tape recorder and my tape recorder can record their tape recorder and we'll be even-steven, right?* No.

The auditor came back in five minutes, followed by a second woman I suspected was another auditor because she was carrying several manila file folders, each an inch thick. I figured she was pulled off a case that was dealing with figures bigger than $324, like maybe Boeing.

They both sat down, facing me. The original auditor quizzed me about my business plan and the markets in which I was trying to establish myself. I figured that meant she wanted me to talk about myself, which I find easy to do. I donned my raconteur hat and gave them a storytelling tour of my performing life: My sing-alongs and storytelling programs at nursing homes, my day-camp storytelling in a few parks and community centers, and an occasional school assembly. On a good day I was making 40 bucks, and one week I even made $75.

As I was cruising along recounting my Life in Storytelling, the neutral third-party observer leaned over to the auditor, whispered something to her and then faced me, asking, "Mr. Smith, have you ever told stories at the Wolf Haven Wildlife Sanctuary in Tenino, Washington?"

"Why, yes, a couple of times at their weekend 'Howl-Ins.' It's a good gig. I get $35 a night."

"Marge," the observer said to the auditor, "I knew that voice was familiar. I've heard him tell stories at Wolf Haven, but it was at night so I didn't recognize him. He really is a storyteller, and a very good one." With that expert testimony, they let me go.

As I drove down I-5 and left the IRS in my dust, I heard a gleeful voice singing inside my head:

G–C
Don't give up your song, even though the night is long,

C–D
You don't know who is listening and needs you to go on.

G–C
Don't you give up your song, even though you're alone,

D–G
You don't know who is dancing, down deep in their soul.

C
Sometimes you give it your best,

G
Sometimes you give it a rest.

C
Sometimes you get ignored,

G
Other times, you hear a knock on the door.

C
And just like my Grammy said,

G
"Even if they take it all,

D
If you look down deep inside,

G
You know you'll find a song."

Figuring that dodging the IRS bullet was a sign from the Divine, I continued my efforts to develop my storytelling career. In the next two years I made more than $324, but not enough to live on, and for those basic living expenses I took cash advances off my credit cards. When I racked up $15,000 worth of debt, I decided I needed a real job, and for the next eight months I searched diligently. But to no avail.

In desperation, I dusted off my certification as a recreation therapist and made the rounds of psychiatric facilities in the Puget Sound area, even though when I had left the field 10 years prior I'd sworn I would never return. At St. Peter Hospital in Olympia, Washington my emotional state boiled over.

"Please, Mr. Smith, can you stop crying," said the Director of Human Resources who had been summoned by the receptionist when I collapsed at their front counter and sprawled across the carpeting.

The Director led me back to his office. "Please have a seat," he said motioning for me to sit in front of his desk. "We don't have any openings for a rec therapist. All I can offer you is a part-time job as the evening ward clerk in the Mother-Baby Unit. They need a male presence there at night at the front desk to provide a sense of security to the all-female staff. You'll just have to answer phones and take care of the visitors. Are you interested?"

"Sure, I'll take it."

"Whoa. You'll have to take an interview with the charge nurse, first. It'll be her say. I'll call her and see if she can meet with you right away." The HR guy made the call, and I went over to see the charge nurse.

During the interview the nurse's phone rang. She answered, but looked very puzzled when she heard the voice. "It's for you, Bruce," she announced.

The Director for Human Resources asking to speak with me. "Mr. Smith," he intoned. "Do you believe in miracles?"

"Why, yes I do," I replied.

"Well, you should, because one just happened. The recreation therapist on our psychiatric unit just resigned five minutes ago. Would you like a second interview today?"

"Yes," I said gleefully.

I got the rec job and went back to psychiatry.

For the next four years I rebuilt my financial stability and didn't perform professionally, although I told stories on a weekly basis at KAOS-FM, the public-access station at Evergreen State College.

One day out of the clear blue, I received an application from the National Storyteller-Of-The-Year organization in Black Lick, Ohio, inviting me to submit a story on the theme of perseverance.

Boy, have I got a story for you, I thought, and sent them this story. They loved it and invited me to be a finalist in the 1997 competition. I quit my job at St. Peter's, and with all my savings and the proceeds from selling my black-powder rifle, I had enough money to travel to Black Lick.

I placed third and received $150, which was enough to get me to New York to see Mom and Dad, whom I hadn't seen in several years. At dinner my second night with the folks, I announced I was heading to New York City that evening to play guitar and tell my IRS story at an open mic at the Fast Folk Café.

"Going by train, son?" my dad asked.

"Yeah, I'll take the 6:05," I replied.

"Well, I'll drive you up to the station," he offered.

"Dad, it's only two blocks. I'll be fine."

"No, I'll be happy to," he replied, and I could see he really wanted to do this act of kindness, which surprised me. In the past, he had not been very supportive of any of my leanings toward an artistic career. As a kid, every time I indicated a professional interest in the arts he would say, "There are 20,000 unemployed actors in New York City. What do you want to do, join that bunch? C'mon, get your head out of the clouds and get your feet on the ground."

Those words effectively shut down my inclinations as a youth, but my spirit was not to be denied and, now in my 40s, it led to storytelling.

When we got to the Long Island Rail Road station, my dad announced, "They've changed things a bit since you've been gone. There are no ticket counter people in the station any more. They only have machines selling tickets now, and this station's machine only takes $10 bills. Do you have one?"

I looked in my wallet, only to find a solitary $20. "No, Dad, I've only got a $20. Do you have change?"

"Ah, don't worry, I'll buy you a ticket." He placed a $10 bill in the machine and purchased a round-trip ticket to Penn Station. "Here you go," he said, handing it to me. "By the way, do you have any subway tokens? You're going to need them to get downtown."

I shrugged.

He reached into his pocket and dug out a fist full of coins and tokens. "Here you go," he said a second time. Then the train came into the station. I hugged my dad and picked up my guitar, but as I turned to get on the train, my dad grabbed my shoulder and turned me back to him.

"Is that $20 all you've got?"

"Yeah, Dad. That 150 bucks from Ohio didn't go far. Things mount up you know, like seven-dollar tolls on the Throgs Neck Bridge."

My dad lowered his arm and brought out his wallet again. He took out all the green he had—$68—and shoved them into my shirt's breast pocket.

"Go get 'em, kid," he said, patting me on the shoulder.

"Thanks, Dad." It was the first money he had ever given me to support my artistic dreams. But better than the money was the look in his eyes. They twinkled.

He's excited by my performing. He's cheering me on! My Gawd, if I can get my father's support, I can do anything. I'll never give up my song.

And I haven't.

All Bruce's music can be viewed on his youtube channel at https://www.youtube.com/@BruceASmith-hn4zq

28

Shoelaces
Untied and Unlimited

At first, I thought it was the rain. My new home of Yelm, Washington receives over 60 inches of rain per year, almost 50% more than my old abode on Long Island. As a result, things get a tad slippery around here. But whether it's my Clark walkabouts, hiking boots, or sneakers, none of my shoelaces stay tied. Since I've arrived in Yelm, I'm double-knotting for the first time since I was three years old.

For the first year or two, I didn't pay any attention to this odd nuisance. I just retied the darn things. However, in my new job as a recreation therapist on the psychiatric unit of St Peter's Hospital, my patients began pointing out that my shoelaces were chronically undone. So, I took a closer look at this phenomenon.

I was surprised to learn that none of my colleagues reported their shoes to be persistently untied, and more disturbingly, looked strangely at me when I asked. They, of course, joined with the patients on a steady surveillance of my shoelaces.

After a year's worth of unwanted scrutiny, however, a "shoelace" epiphany occurred at the barber shop. While viewing myself in the mirror, I pondered my rapidly expanding baldness. My hair loss is the typical, "premature, male-patterned balding," which is due, oddly, to an over-production of testosterone. According to experts, this increase stunts the growth of hair follicles on top of one's head. So, I wondered: *Might I be producing great gobs of testosterone, maybe not Superman levels, but sufficient amounts to leak out my finger tips and make everything I touched a little oily? Was I becoming a middle-aged, hormonal King Midas?*

These secretions might be so small that I didn't notice them in day-to-day encounters like shaking hands. But could something that I touched daily and never washed, like shoelaces, become supersaturated with testosterone and thus become too slippery to stay tied?

My friends thought I was nuts when I shared my biochemical hypothesis. But once the boundaries of "common sense" are passed, there is no turning back.

So, if it wasn't the testosterone, what could it be? *Could my shoelaces be influenced by something from a more esoteric realm? Forces more sublime than a hormonal oil slick?*

Searching for answers, my mind wandered in a blissful exploration of the Muse, and in a second epiphany I realized that my laces went south—not only when I started losing hair—but when I left BJ and moved across-country. In fact, my relocation to Yelm precipitated a great deal of change besides ending a relationship. I had sold my business and left family and friends to do something quite epic—coming to Yelm to study the science of consciousness—which burrows heavily into the world of quantum physics.

Since I had untied the knot of familial love and social convention, could my shoelaces have responded with a parallel expression of liberation in some kind of Quantum Resonance Effect? *Can my shoelaces be physically manifesting what my psyche is experiencing? Are my shoelaces rejoicing with my soul, shouting together: We are untied and unlimited, open to wondrous possibilities!?*

For years I never told this story because I didn't enjoy the blank stares of listeners. But I have come out of the closet because of a recent experience. During a performance at my community theater a few years ago, I noticed a fellow cast member triple-knotting his shoes before we went on stage. I asked him why.

"Damn things won't stay tied. Ever since I quit drinking six years ago, none of my shoelaces stay knotted. None of them—boots, dress shoes, golf shoes, nothing—not even my tennies. It's the strangest thing."

Now, whenever I have a dark night of the soul, I just look down at my shoelaces and know I'm not alone.

29

A Good Samaritan in Tucson
My family needed one, again...

Maybe it's our genetics, but my family and I go nuts whenever we drive into an airport. My mind scrambles trying to understand the signage:

Am I an "arrival" since I'm arriving at the airport, or am I a "departure" since I will be getting on an airplane shortly to fly somewhere else? No, I can't be an "arrival" because only people flying into this airport from another airport can be arrivals at this airport. So, when I depart here as a "departure" and arrive at my destination – then I'll be an "arrival" there, until I leave there to come home, here – which will then make me a "departure" there, but an "arrival" here!

Does this make any sense to you?

I navigate these mental corkscrews while trying to find my terminal and not wreck my car, and since all airport roads seem like slalom courses designed to train NASCAR drivers, I'm sweating by the time I actually show up to check my bags. In short, it's total *agita*, which is New Yorkese for a super-duper pain in the tuchus.

On top of this familial disability, my dad, born and raised in Brooklyn, apparently was never taught the purpose of directional signals when he learned how to drive. His rebuttal to years of chastisement over sudden lane changes has been to say, "But I've never had an accident in 62 years of driving."

His stubbornness was on full display one afternoon in Tucson.

Mom and Dad were in Tucson to see if they had any interest in moving to the Sun Belt. My dad was 80 and promising to "retire soon." They asked me to fly in from my home in Yelm to help drive them around since I had been in Tucson on business 10 years before, thereby qualifying me as a maven on Arizona. But, more importantly, as they said in their own words, "We're slowing down, and at our age we enjoy being driven around."

Due to my personal bankruptcy in 1993, however, I did not have a valid credit card. Therefore, their car rental company would not let me drive.

"I'm just driving the car," I shouted at the rental agent, "not renting the damn thing. Give me a break!"

"It's company policy, sir. Without a valid credit card, we can't authorize you to drive our vehicle," said the well-trained clerk.

But my dad had a valid credit card, of course, so he was accepted as the official driver.

Out in the parking lot I said to my *pater*, "C'mon, Dad, give me the keys; that's what I 'm here for."

"No, son, you're not authorized and I don't want to break the rules."

Why did I think he would start now?

So, I became the Grand Navigator of Tucson Roadways. Sitting next to my father in the front seat and giving directions, my mom, with her Macular Degeneration-based tunnel vision and 20/400 eyesight, reigned as the Royal Empress of the Back Seat, ready to aid in any way she might deem suitable.

For two days we toured the sights of Tucson and visited my parents' old college buddies who had preceded them down the Retirement Trail. At the end of our three-day weekend together, they drove me back to Tucson Airport for my return to Yelm. Driving off the Interstate, we encountered the mishmash of signs: Arrival—Departure—All Rental Cars. Family panic set in.

"Go left," shouted my mother. "Rental cars!"

"If we're driving a rental car, but not returning it, do we still have to drive in the rental car lanes???

I began to panic. *I'm a departure, correct?* I said to myself. I took deep breaths. *Yes, I'm a departure....*"Eh, Dad, I think we have to go right, for departures. Get in the right lane, Dad. It says 'departures.'"

My dad had his own ideas, however, and decided his best option on the three-lane access road was to weave in slow undulations from the middle and straddle sections of the right or left lanes until he could get the feel of where he wanted to go.

Approaching the right lane on his second arc, I braced myself for the impact I knew had to come. Inexplicably, I heard neither the screech of tires nor crunch of metal. I peeked in the right side-view mirror to see how close we had come. I didn't see any car alongside us, but I did see something magical happening behind us.

A white Pontiac had its emergency lights flashing and was driving slowly in a wide "S," echoing my father's swerve across the three lanes. The Pontiac's actions had effectively blocked traffic all the way out to the Interstate.

I watched this Good Samaritan make a couple of sweeps across the lanes. Then my father exclaimed joyfully, "Here we are!" and scooted up the departure ramp.

When we were clear of the highway, the white Pontiac turned off its flashers and accelerated to normal speed. The backed-up cars sped up as well, and quickly spread themselves out. It was over in just a few moments, and my parents had no idea what had happened.

I figure an off-duty cop must have seen us shouting and pointing in three different directions. A map of Arizona flailing in the air must have been a giveaway that they had another *"Out-Of-Towners-Rental-Runaway,"* and they did the right thing: Block Tucson traffic until we New Yorkers could figure out where the heck we were going.

Whoever you are, thanks. The Smith family owes you A Big One.

Note: After dropping me off, it took my parents two hours to find their way back to their motel, 10 miles away. My mother said later, "When I saw signs for Mexico, I knew we were in trouble."

They returned their rental two days later and flew home to New York. When I asked my dad if he liked Tucson he replied, "I like it here," which means in Brooklynese, "Dis boy ain't leaving!"

30

Miracle at the Crossroads
I find a partner to dance with in the mystic

When I left the stage after my three-song performance at the open mic in Bellevue's Crossroads Shopping Mall, my footsteps echoed louder than the audience's applause. In a daze, I found the table where I had camped for the previous two hours and sat down, then began packing my guitar. "Bombed again," I mumbled, and after gathering my coat I headed down a long corridor to the parking lot.

At the exit doors I stopped, paralyzed. I couldn't face the outside—the rain, the December cold, and the loneliness. My little encampment on an ex-girlfriend's property, where I had been parking my little homemade camper, was not welcoming. Plus, I had another case of bronchitis, and my living situation was no place to recover from a chronic affliction.

At the exit doors, however, a stack of *Seattle Weekly*s rose off the floor 5 feet high. Pausing, I fingered through the tabloid rather than wading into my life.

A few moments later I heard a loud voice booming directly behind me. "Do you know the name of the movie where Elvis smashed his guitar in the bathroom after bombing at the Grand Ole Opry?"

I hadn't heard anyone come up behind me, yet someone was obviously there. I felt confused and disoriented.

"Yeah," the voice said again, "do you know the name of that Elvis movie? I can't think of it and it's been bugging me all day."

I turned to find where the voice was coming from and banged into the torso of a very large man dressed in a bluish-gray work suit. *How did he get so close to me? I never heard him, or even sensed him!* My pivot forced him to back up a step, and he moved a dust mop to the side. *My Gawd, he's the shopping mall custodian!*

"I gotta remember the name of that movie," the janitor said with urgency. "It's been driving me crazy all day. Do you know it?"

"No, I don't know the name," I said. "I never even knew Elvis was in a movie smashing a guitar."

"Oh yeah, it was one of his first ones. He had just bombed really bad at the Opry. He walked into the men's room and figured he was all washed up. Took his guitar and smashed it on the sink. Don't you remember? C'mon, ya gotta remember! You've got a guitar. C'mon, I'm sure you know it!"

"No, sorry."

"Oh, man, I gotta remember that name."

He moved a few steps away from me and resumed pushing his dust mop. This bizarre encounter made me light-hearted and happy. I was almost laughing! My depressive mood had been broken, and I knew the cleaning guy was responsible.

His timing was perfect, too. *Wait a minute, too perfect. It feels divinely perfect. It must be, oh, my Gawd! I'm having an encounter with a divine being!*

"Hey mister, wait!" I called out.

The custodian stopped and turned. I continued, "How did you know to ask me that question at this exact moment?"

His eyes, which had been sparkling and clear, turned hazy and dull.

"Uh, I just wanted to know the name of that movie," he replied.

I asked him a few more questions, probing to see if he was actually an angel or some kind of inter-dimensional being. Plus, I wanted to thank him for brightening my mood.

But each question I asked made him squirm. He grunted or shrugged his answers. *He doesn't get it.*

He backed away from me, avoiding my eyes.

Then I became scared of him. *Maybe he's crazy.* I wanted to get away from him immediately, so I made a lame excuse about having a long drive home. I turned and strode to the door. But as I moved through the mall doors, I heard him call out.

"Hey, are you coming back next week?"

I stopped, and turning, I faced my benefactor. His eyes were bright and clear again.

"Yeah, sure. I'll be here." I gave him a big wave, hefted my guitar and walked into my future.

The next day, I called an old friend who ran a bed and breakfast. It was time for me to come in from the cold, and I asked if I could rent a room on credit. I had a deep, confident knowingness that the money would come from somewhere.

"Sure," my buddy replied. "It'll be great to have ya here. Sixty bucks a week. Pay me when you can."

I moved in immediately. The next day my dad wired me $200 to pay for a couple weeks of rent, food, and whatever I needed to nurse myself back to health. Later that week, he sent me a plane ticket to come home for Christmas, where I recuperated from the lingering fatigue and coughs. But before I left for New York, I returned to the Crossroads.

That night the audience enjoyed my music for the first time in my life. I jubilantly exited the stage and headed to the parking lot. Approaching the familiar exit doors, lined with a new stack of *Seattle Weekly*s," I saw my friend, the custodian.

"Hey, I'm back," I called out, and walked in his direction. He paused and looked up from his mop.

"Yeah, I feel so good," I continued. "Tonight's a big night. I really connected with the audience for the first time."

He looked at me blankly. I was surprised he didn't remember me.

"Did you ever find out the name of that Elvis movie?" I asked, trying to help him remember our encounter. He looked searchingly at me, then shook his head slightly from side-to-side. I couldn't tell if he was wincing or telling me, "No."

Gawd, he doesn't remember me at all. I'm not even sure he remembers asking about the Elvis movie. He seemed eager to break contact.

"Well, thanks," I said and stepped away.

He doesn't remember anything at all, I thought, walking to my truck. *The blank look on his face tonight is the same dazed look he had the last time we spoke when I started asking him questions.*

Then I heard a voice in my head. I didn't know if it was mine or someone else's. Ramtha? Regardless, I paused and listened closely. "He's a simple man."

I understood. The custodian was a vehicle, a channel, to make an intervention in my life. My thanks to all, whoever you are.

31

Flight 800 and the Blue Angel
My first encounter with an inter-dimensional being

TWA Flight 800 was a Paris-bound 747 that crashed on July 17, 1996 just minutes after take-off from JFK. I was deeply affected by the accident, perhaps because it plummeted into the waters off Long Island I knew from my beachcleaning days.

Driving to work at my recreation therapy job, I wept hearing the news on the radio. I followed the developments throughout the day, and in the evening I called my family to get the latest updates. My mother said that she, too, was deeply troubled by the tragedy, and we surmised that we were moved because it was an incident close to home when disasters of this magnitude usually occur far away. I agreed that this one felt personal, but I felt I was affected for reasons beyond mere geography. I sensed that something beyond mere tragedy was at work. Even the new Governor of New York, George Pataki, had waded into the surf to lead a memorial ceremony, and his actions seemed authentic to me, not politically contrived.

The facts of the case also tugged at my heart. Flight 800 exploded at 13,000 feet a few moments before sunset, and was only eight miles out to sea. As a result, many people strolling the beaches saw the plane break apart. Then wave after wave brought the wreckage onshore—bodies, shoes, clothing, seats, a baby doll—items that families might be carrying aboard a summertime flight to France. Local TV cameras captured all of the drama.

In addition, dozens of boaters and fishermen witnessed the demise of 800, and many offered disturbing clues. Over 200 eye witnesses told the cops they saw streaks of lights arching toward the plane, and some claimed they saw vapor trails coming from different directions. Many thought they were seeing missiles or rockets.

The FBI's investigation of the incident did not resolve much of the anxiety that lingered in the air. Especially unsettling was their conclusion that the crash was triggered by faulty fuel lines rubbing together, causing static electricity charges that ignited the empty fuel tank in the center of the plane.

I conducted my own investigation of Flight 800 using some of the techniques I had learned at RSE. In particular, I engaged an energetic form of focused meditation, and I sensed strange circumstances surrounding the crash. What I discovered changed my life dramatically, and it pushed me onto the path that has led to writing this book.

In my focus I saw two images. The first was a pipe or tube with bubbles streaming out one end, like someone blowing soda through a straw.

The second vision was a small girl holding her father's hand while she clutched a Raggedy-Ann type of doll. The girl appeared to be a seven-year-old version of Little Orphan Annie.

But I still didn't know why Flight 800 had impacted me so profoundly.

Tellingly, I was thrilled several months later when RSE invited David Morehouse, author of *Psychic Warrior*, to discuss his remote viewing activities in the 1980s as part of the US Army's Stargate program. Remote viewing is similar in some ways to a focused meditation, in that an individual can bypass time and space by shifting their consciousness. Despite its obvious value to intelligence agencies, remote viewing is highly controversial; reportedly, the Army shut down Stargate in the mid-1990s due to political pressures and professional skepticism. But Morehouse and his colleagues, such as Joe McMoneagle, the author of *Mind Trek: Exploring Consciousness, Time & Space through Remote Viewing*, continued their remote viewing activities privately. Both have acknowledged that their work is not absolute in terms of accuracy.

Regardless, Morehouse stunned me with his bold claim that Flight 800 had been intentionally shot down by particle beam weapons stationed at Brookhaven National Laboratory. From Morehouse I learned that the military was developing a kind of microwave space cannon that could blast targets via a laser-like beam of highly charged atomic particles. Morehouse also said that the US Congress had ordered the military to shut down its particle-beam program because they didn't want the world scrambling to build satellites capable of zapping the surface of the earth. But the military refused, and their weapons development simply went underground.

Morehouse's statements confirmed for me that the "bubbles coming down a straw" scenario I was seeing in my meditations might have been a representation of particle beam weaponry.

Morehouse also said that the downing of Flight 800 was a tragic error—the plane was simply in the wrong place at the wrong time, mistaken to be a drone by the flotilla of US Navy ships participating in a particle-beam test that was actually occurring about 100 miles further off-shore of Long Island.

Nevertheless, two years later, in the summer of 1998, I attended a retreat at RSE and the crash resurfaced from the recesses of my mind. It came in the form of visions and a song during a session of free-form dancing powered by lots of indigenous drum music. At first, I experienced an overwhelming fear—I felt incapable of providing myself with food, clothing and shelter despite my growing abilities as a professional entertainer. My dream of becoming a performer now felt like a monstrous nightmare of poverty, isolation, and vulnerability.

I attempted to dance a resolution to these anxieties, but the more I moved, the deeper I sank into a desperate state. It felt bigger than I could handle, and I released a mental SOS.

"Ramtha, please help me," I called out in consciousness.

Unbeknownst to me, he was standing right in front of me, seemingly just waiting for me to ask for assistance. He stepped up to my ear and said matter-of-factly, "You can do it."

I lifted my eye-blinders and saw my teacher stepping back and walking away.

I refocused on my dance. Instantly I was catapulted into a realm of consciousness that I had never experienced before. I felt "totally elsewhere."

I became wrapped in a sparkly blue swirl of consciousness, and an entity with a round, smiling face approached me. For the next several hours I experienced a stream of interactive visions with this entity, who instructed me, "When you tell people about me, just tell them I'm the 'Blue Angel.'"

The Blue Angel told me the full story of Flight 800. First, he said Morehouse only had part of the story correctly and, although particle beam weapons were used to destroy 800, the incident was actually an *intentional assassination* of a French family—particularly the father and his daughter—by global financiers, possibly by members of the group known as the Bilderbergers. This cabal had hired a private European commando team that used particle beam weapons to murder the father and daughter, and obliterate all the evidence by destroying the plane. The Blue Angel also said the assassins had positioned themselves inland on properties adjacent to Brookhaven National Laboratory and known locally as "Navy Land." In addition, their weapons left ionized moisture trails in the sky that mimicked missile launches. The Blue Angel told me that the targeted man was a powerful banker and part of a global elite, but he had strong liberal tendencies that disturbed the majority of this financial clique.

More troubling for the cabal was the daughter. They perceived her as the greater threat because she had the potential to become more popular than Princess Diana, and much more powerful—having the potential to achieve great political and financial positions—which she would use to thwart the efforts of this group to control the world through debt and financial obligations.

The Blue Angel told me that he wanted me to write a song based on what he was revealing.

"Why me, Blue Angel? I'm not a singer."

"Why not you? You're *becoming* a singer. Besides, who else should I ask? James Taylor or Jackson Browne? They'd never do it because they're wrapped up in their careers. You're open to the possibilities. With you, I've got a chance."

The purpose of the song, the Blue Angel announced, was to assuage the guilt of Boeing employees who felt they had built a "bad" plane. My angelic friend wanted to assure the good folks of Boeing their labors were not at fault—the 747 they had built for TWA was a good airplane—and Boeing was being unjustly blamed in this deadly international drama.

Further, the Blue Angel said that Flight 800 was purposefully shot down in US airspace to involve President Bill Clinton in the coverup. The Blue Angel said that the cabal was especially angry at Clinton for his efforts to end the civil wars in Kosovo, Serbia, and Croatia because those actions had made him the most popular politician in Europe. At that time, the bankers were planning their massive debt plans via the collapse of the US housing markets, and they knew Clinton would act to stop them. Hence, they wanted to neutralize him. So, they piggy-backed their attack onto his illegal particle beam testing so Clinton would be forced to add a second layer of coverup to protect his own administration.

Clinton followed the cabal's script and orchestrated a bogus FBI investigation to veil both the shoot-down and the illegal weapons testing. Next, he convinced Boeing to take responsibility for the "accident" by developing plausible scenarios for the crash. Clinton sweetened the deal for Boeing by arranging for several South Asian airlines from places such as the Emirates, Singapore, and Thailand, to order dozens of new 747s.

Over the course of the day, I had several sessions with the Blue Angel, interspersed by rest periods. Each session detailed a new part of the Blue Angel's plan; first came the details of the downing, then the song, and, finally, what he wanted me to do with the composition.

As we dove into this project, the Blue Angel established the background story for the song. Initially, I saw myself as the Blue Angel's commanding officer in Viet Nam, flying a B-52 bomber out of Guam. Then, Blue Angel morphed into a second entity, called Jimmie T. Rogers, and said he was my copilot. In my vision of the crash, Rogers was the captain of TWA 800. Although I have never flown a plane, let alone a B-52, the visions were fully lucid and I really felt like I was a bomber pilot.

The visions were straightforward, as if I were watching a video. But they also possessed a hyper-dimensional quality and often shifted reference points. Once, I felt I was both the Blue Angel and Captain Jimmie T. Rogers. As a result, I had the experience of watching myself be someone else, and through it all I felt the song come alive within me.

Lyrics came in full lines or odd chunks. In my head I heard the opening phrase, "Jimmie T. Rogers was a good man, he hailed from Tennessee," in one piece. Not only did it come complete, it became a talisman that I would return to mentally in other sessions whenever the visions dimmed. After my retreat when I was composing the song, it was where I started each writing set, and it felt like an old friend that reassured me that I could write the song even when the project seemed too big or too bizarre.

Immediately after my encounter with the Blue Angel, I debated whether I should research the veracity of the story. Always my knowingness said: *No, there will be time later. Right now, continue to drink from the well.* When I pushed to check the truth of the story, the Blue Angel returned mentally and said in my head: *Compose it as I gave it to you.*

After my retreat, I wrote "The Ballad of Flight 800" in six days while sitting on the tailgate of my pickup, camping in the woods near an old girlfriend's place. I also had the company of four bottles of red wine. But writing the song was only the first part of what I've termed, "The Flight 800 Project."

In the second phase, which the Blue Angel revealed in later trance-dancing sessions, I was to record the song and make sure it was heard by Boeing employees.

"I'd like to see the program director, please," I imagined myself saying as I walked into the reception area of a local radio station. "I've received a song from a spiritual entity who calls himself 'The Blue Angel' and he wants me to give it to your station in order to get air play in hopes that Boeing employees will hear it."

In my vision, an overworked, and highly skeptical middle-aged man would come out of an office. "You have a song that you want me to listen to?"

"Yes," I would reply. "It's titled, 'The Ballad of Flight 800' and it's about the crash of the TWA plane several years ago. An angel appeared to me and gave me a song about what happened. He wants me to get it air play in markets where Boeing employees might hear it. It's a song intended to heal the anxieties of the men and women at Boeing who feel they built a 'bad airplane.' I've written the song. That was my job." And then, handing him the tape, I would say, "Now, I give it to you. Please listen to it and decide if it meets your standards for air play. If it does, please play it. If you think this is all too crazy and you're just going to throw it in a trash can, then please give it back to me. I've spent all my money making a few dozen copies, so if you really don't want it, I'll take it back."

In my vision, the program director would hesitate, then a look in his eyes would tell me that he'd at least listen to it and I would know I'd gotten to first base. The song would receive some air play. Then, I would hand out copies to Boeing employees at entrance gates, and I would go to union offices to distribute copies to Boeing people there. Slowly the word would spread.

The third phase—direct healing—exploded like a dam bursting. There were multiple visions, but in the last phase the Blue Angel asked me to perform the song with Air Force personnel, especially B-52 bomber crews who fly nukes. In particular, he wanted me to share what I knew about particle beam weaponry and governmental cover-ups. The Blue Angel was especially concerned about these air crews because they take great pride in protecting us but also feel a double-bind as their work secures a government that often lies to us. "It's a rub that cuts deeply," said the Blue Angel. "They're risking their lives for people who don't deserve it, and who could betray them in an instant when political winds shift in another direction."

In my visions I met with these bomber crews and danced with them—circle dancing while holding hands, like old-fashioned country dancing. The purpose was to heal and build connections with each other, to dispel fear and isolation.

During all my sessions with the Blue Angel I wept profusely. In rest periods between sets, I lay flat on the floor and could hardly breathe. But something inside of me was shifting. I could feel it. A fear of embracing my deepest self—my most genuine parts of me no matter how wacky—was transmuting. I was accepting my outrageousness, my boldness, my unique individuality. I was discovering what I truly love, and finding how to love myself. With this knowingness came the understanding I could take any subject onto a stage and perform it with all my heart and soul. No fear. Complete joy.

After writing "The Ballad of Flight 800," I recorded it at a local studio. I sang the song at a few open mics and noticed my voice was opening up. I could finally sing the way I had always wanted. My greatest dream, to sing professionally, was beginning to unfold.

Within a few months I sang "The Ballad of Flight 800" at a New Age convention at the Boeing campus in Everett, WA, where the 747s are built. I gave away all my copies of "Flight 800," and I hoped some of the people were Boeing employees. I never found the courage to go into radio stations or union halls, however. Nor have I sung it for any flight crews. Those tasks still remain.

But in the spring of 1999, I took the song to Nashville, Tennessee, the "Music City," where I stayed for 15 months. I played "800" at a few open mics, but, more importantly, I learned a lot about singing and songwriting. Eventually I became a stagehand to pay the bills, and loved working on the stages of the music world and being 30 feet from the microphone. Quietly, I dreamed of holding one myself.

After enduring two summers in Dixie, I had had enough of its heat, humidity, and suffocating religiosity, so I moved to Santa Fe. But after six weeks of New Age repose in the Land of Enchantment, I decided to move back to Yelm to continue my studies with Ramtha. By then I had realized I was a better storyteller than singer, and I applied myself whole-heartedly to writing. First, I wrote about my life in Nashville, and developed a collection of behind-the-scenes accounts of rock and roll, titled, "Stories from Backstage." Then I became a newspaper reporter and investigative journalist, first at the *Dispatch* in Eatonville, and later at the *Mountain News-WA*.

But I've always loved to tell stories, either on a stage or around a campfire. It is my deepest passion. So, here is the song that has helped me become the performer I am today, "The Ballad of Flight 800."

The Ballad of Flight 800

Bm—G—D
Jimmie T. Rogers was a good man, he hailed from Tennessee.

Bm—G—A
And he was my copilot over Nam in '73.

Bm—G—D
I hadn't seen him since that time but I saw him last night.

Em—G—D
I thought I was sleeping, so maybe this was a dream, all right.
But there he was in front of me as plain as daylight
He looked just like the old days; his eyes were clear and bright.
But all around him sparkled with electric blue light,
Then he gave me a friendly wink, let me know ev'rything's all right.

"Smitty, my man, come fly with me tonight.
I know how you like to fly in the hours past midnight.
I remember how you used to say on the Guam pre-dawn flights,
'Hey Jimmie T., it's just you and me and the angels up here tonight.' "

"Smitty, my man, I've come to you tonight
'Cause I was the skipper on 800's last flight.
I was sitting in the big chair the night that we went down
And now I've come to sing a song and let a healing truth resound."

"We'd just taken off from JFK,
300 on board, ev'rything was okay.
Hundred people on the ground saw us hit and go down,
On the beaches of Long Island, next day our remains were found."

"We were hit all right, but not by a rocket or grenade.
A ground-based laser put 800 in its grave.
The experts say they can't find a trace of explosives
(and it's true)
'Cause what put 800 down that night was a hi-tech microwave."

"We were gone in a second, no one suffered, there was no pain.
For the next few miles, on flew that glorious plane.
Then the 'lectromagnetics ignited up the fumes
In the empty belly fuel tank and down we went in
a fiery plume."

I'm here to tell the truth, not start a revolution.
Don't mean to rile people up, startin' investigations.
But I was a good Captain and proud to wear the blue.
And I want the world to know what happened to my passengers and crew."

Chorus:
D—G—D
"Tell the good people of Boeing there's no blood on their hands.

Bm—G—A
The '47 I flew that night was the finest in the land.

Bm—G—D
A particle beam weapon brought us down that night.

Em — G — D
So, tell the good people of Boeing, Blue Angel says to sleep real good tonight."
"Now don't go blaming the Navy or the scientists at Brookhaven.
We had been diverted so those boys could test their weapons.
An elite commando team used the Navy as a ruse
To take out a big money player who wasn't playing by the rules."

"I'm talking big money son, the kind that dictates the direction.
Of what a country can do or not, by its financial obligation.
Well, one of those bankers had a change of heart.
So they took him out over US soil to foil any more upstarts."

"Now, Smitty, my man, sing this 'cross the nation,
People gonna call you crazy, say you got too much 'magination."
…"You got that right, Jimmie T., I'm just a storyteller."
"…Well, Smitty, if ya catch any flak, just tell those folks the Blue Angel sent ya."

Then Jimmie T. smiled, and glided to my right.
Dozens more blue figures came forward in that light.
They stood beside me said, "Don't be afraid.
This is a healing song, many gonna be helped by what you say."

Chorus:

D – G – D
"'Specially tell the good people at Boeing

Bm – G – A
There ain't no blood on their hands.

Bm – G – D
The '47 Jimmie flew that night was the finest in the land.

Em – G – D

A particle-beam weapon took him down that night.
"And tell the good people of Everett, (vamp)…Washington, the Blue Angel says to get some sleep tonight.
A real good sleep, a long overdue sleep,
Sleeping-like-a-baby-all-through-the-night-kind-of-sleep,
Sleeping-with-an-angel-kind-of-sleep…,
Tonight."

All Bruce's music can be viewed on his youtube channel at https://www.youtube.com/@BruceASmith-hn4zq

32

Neil Diamond
Up-close glimpses of fame and power

When fans of Neil Diamond discover I've been a stagehand and have worked his show, they always ask me the same question: "Is Neil Diamond really the jerk that everybody says he is?"

"No, he isn't," I reply. "He's just idiosyncratic."

"How so?"

"Look," I say, "I think what you're asking about is Neil Diamond's extraordinary shyness. Yes, it's true Diamond has a reputation of forbidding anyone backstage from making direct eye contact with him. But I understand his concerns. Diamond, like most performers, are in a 'zone' when they leave the stage. They are so emotionally *elsewhere* that they have to be escorted, usually by the stage manager, who steers them down the steps and through the maze of cables, amps, and catering carts, and depositing them safely in their dressing room. When performers are exiting the stage, they do not look at anyone. Backstage, it is well understood never to talk with any performer, and especially *never* to ask for an autograph or pitch a song."

So, Diamond, as his crew calls him, takes his privacy one step further, maybe two. He asks the local stagehands to build him a tent-like tunnel that runs from the stage to the dressing area so that he can have total privacy and safety. At Diamond's Key Arena show, I was on a special detail that strung the interior lights through this 100-foot canvas structure.

That said, I do not think that Diamond is weird, nor the tunnel excessive. In fact, I think it's smart, and maybe essential in order to keep a high-profile career going for 30-plus years. The emotional energy required to be in the public eye and face their demands and expectations compels a performer to be wise in how exposed they get. I understand that.

But not everyone agrees.

One veteran stagehand told me that working for Diamond with his "no look" rule was a major irritation, and he remembers the days when Diamond required stagehands to sign contracts agreeing that they would not look at him at any time. This stagehand described it as, "working while you're walking on egg shells."

That's not fun, but touring is tough and I appreciate what Neil Diamond goes through.

Nevertheless, such sensitivity should never warp one's mind to the point where a performer does not trust their stagehands.

We're pros, too, Neil, and I'm glad you don't need us to sign those documents anymore.

33

Dixie Chicks
Observing power and grace

Chicks Rule! Yup, best concert I've ever seen, and I'm not alone in that assessment—the 12,000 screaming fans in the Key Arena, mostly women, came close to lifting the roof off.

Their ceiling-busting energy came from something deeper than fans appreciating a great show. The Key concert was held a few weeks after lead singer Natalie Maines told an audience in the UK she was "ashamed that President Bush was from Texas," or words to that effect, because of his decision to invade Iraq. In response, critics of the Chicks burned their CDs or crunched them under bulldozers. Worst of all, Nashville's hierarchy turned their backs on Country Music's number one act and sanctioned radio stations across the nation to pull Chicks tunes from airplay. This included the industry's number one hit, "Travelin' Soldier," a song about a scared Army guy who finds a true-hearted girl before he ships out to Vietnam.

In an unprecedented act of solidarity, Dixie Chicks fans, I was told by one of their roadies, sold out the entire USA tour in 48 hours. As a result, their Key Arena performance, one of the first on the American circuit, was humming. Security was cranked up several notches—first, because of 9/11 terrorist alerts, and secondly because of threats against the Chicks. I had to show my Key Arena ID twice just to get to the loading dock, let alone backstage.

So, the crew and fans were all jazzed before anyone took the stage. When they did, the Chicks took everyone higher when they opened with "Earl," a song about a woman who poisoned her abusive husband who had "walked right through the restraining orders." Before singing the last line of the chorus, the Chicks stopped. The band vamped for a few beats, and then with dramatic flourish all three Chicks thrust their microphones toward the audience, signaling them to finish the line.

"EARL'S GOTTA DIE!" they screamed, and folks, I wasn't really sure the building was going to hold together. Looking at the upper reaches of the building in my earthquake reflex, I noticed the Chicks had done something I had never seen before or since. The entire ceiling was used as a back drop, bathed delightfully with colored lights and designs from gizmos called *gobos*. It was extraordinarily inventive and, instead of the roof just keeping the rain out, the Dixie Chicks had turned it into an art gallery.

That level of innovation continued throughout the entire show. Above their stage-in-the-round, which was multilevel and wondrously lit, the Chicks flew three levels of truss that had curtains, scrim, and other hanging stuff that produced another splendid accent to their superb music. Creative, pricey, and again, singular in the industry.

As for the music, it was top notch. I love the Dixie Chicks sound—modern rockin' country, but rooted in banjo and fiddle. And the Chicks can play their axes, too; they're much more than three ladies who look good while singing.

Maines is their lead singer, and when she joined the two founding sisters of the original Chicks she made the Dixie Chicks what they are today. She has soul, grit, and a rock-y edge. Yet, she warmly embraces the country ethos: Be close to the earth and tell it like it is, which is exactly what she did with George W. Bush and Nashville's old guard.

In addition, the Chicks brought along a dozen of Nashville's finest for their backup band. Together, they were downright bodacious.

Unfortunately, on their next tour to the Pacific Northwest the Dixie Chicks chose not to play the Key, but instead went to the Tacoma Dome. Since the T-Dome is not a union house, and I consider the production company that has the stagehand contracts there too cheap to work for; i.e., they pay half the union rates, do not provide any health benefits, and generally never pay overtime, I don't work much at the T-Dome. Too bad, too, because I live just down the road.

But, more importantly, I think the City of Tacoma, which owns the Tacoma Dome and rents it out to the hosting production companies, should insist on living wages for all employees who work there. The T-Dome is a symbol of Tacoma Pride, and that emotion should be evident in the how the city pays its help.

Nevertheless, a union brother in the audience told me the show was great. Once again, he said, Natalie had something to say about President George W. Bush because his Pentagon chief, Donald Rumsfeld, had just resigned a few days prior. But Natalie and the Chicks did not utter a single political word until the very end, and then she chirped: "I guess you guys are wondering when I'm going to say something about the President and Secretary Rumsfeld." The T-Dome erupted like they did at the Key. Natalie smiled, and then launched into the next song.

She didn't have to say a word.

34

Cheap Mickey
Dealing with the foibles of others

"Disney on Ice," an ice-skating tour that features productions based upon recent kiddie movies such as *Finding Nemo*, is not really from the Disney folks or even Pixar, but another outfit called Feld Entertainment. Regardless of the origins of "Disney on Ice," in stagehand circles the show is called "Mickey," and in Seattle they have earned the reputation of being the cheapest road show because they are the only ones to charge stagehands for coffee during our breaks.

One might ask: Why don't you quit whining and simply go out to a local Starbucks, or better, have a coffee pot brewing in your crew lounge?

A little history is needed here. Two things: First, there isn't enough time in a 15-minute coffee break for 50 hands to leave the arena where the load-in is taking place and walk one, two, or five city blocks to the coffee shop, stand in line, get a coffee and get back.

Secondly, many, and certainly all of the large tours, especially the "rockers," travel with their own catering service. The big outfits have at least 30 to 40 people on the road crew — the Dixie Chicks had 120 on their national tour in 2004, which was matched by Brooks and Dunn, who brought their families along, so it is simply more efficient to feed them in-house than make them hunt and peck in a strange city every day for a place to eat and grab some joe. Thus, the tour caterers usually serve coffee to us locals along with their roadies. I think everyone views it as a professional courtesy.

But not Disney, apparently, or at least their surrogate Feld. To begin, their catering service for their 12 or so roadies and dozens of skaters is abysmal. I hope there's an explanation why "Disney on Ice" has such a poor chow program. Maybe they give out *per diems* and everyone goes to fancy restaurants, and I just don't know about it. All I can tell you is what I've observed during the load-ins, and that is a food service akin to a college student's pantry—a little cart with a rickety wooden cabinet that had a large assortment of Ramen noodle packets, bags of Famous Amos' chocolate chips, and herbal tea bags. Plus, a jar of self-serve instant coffee. Fifty cents got me a little eight-ounce Styrofoam cup of coffee complete with powdered creamer and sugar. Yuck.

But I drank it. Stagehand work—unloading heavy cases of lights, feeder cables, and enormous props, and then setting it up on a frozen surface—is hard work, and often dangerous. Coffee breaks are important. So, I paid Mickey his half a buck. Plus, another $0.65 for a tiny bag of Famous Amos'.

But that seems to be changing. The last few Mickeys I did, specifically at the Everett Event Center and Seattle's Key Arena, the Disney stage manager did us right, providing us with dozens of free donuts and a couple of pots of coffee, replete with fresh half-and-half. Paid for it out of his own money, a roadie told me later.

Now, that is one brother taking care of another. Whoever you are, dude, thanks.

35

On Being a Stagehand

One of the things I enjoy about being a stagehand in Seattle is emerging from the bowels of the Key Arena—since 2021 known as Climate Pledge Arena—after a rock show and smelling the salt air drifting in from the Puget Sound. It's a primal, haiku-kind-of-thing—the soft, immutable power of nature snaking through the cold, quiet concrete and steel of the city. The Space Needle is usually soaked in fog and clouds, too, giving the whole scene a *Lord of the Rings* glow. Into the freshness I stride like a Man of Rohan, but instead of a handcrafted sword I'm sporting a six-inch Crescent wrench attached to my hip with an OSHA-approved lanyard.

Then, there's the music. I cherish being 30 feet away from the microphone of great performers. Watching from the wings, I've savored a stream of celebrities taking their stage. I love sensing the power of their achievement. I know what it takes to get on stage because I've been in pursuit of that for years as a professional storyteller. I am the 1998 Storytelling Champion of the Year runner-up, but I still need a day job. Hence, stage work.

Perhaps because of that I feel free of any jadedness, even after years of humping 600-pound speakers from semi-trailer trucks. Hearing Sarah Brightman's voice washes any weariness away. Her voice is so transcendental and so sweet that it held me and a Standing Room Only crowd riveted during "Time to Say Goodbye."

One of my favorite performers is Rod Stewart. I've worked a few of Rod's concerts, and I've only grown in appreciation of his creativity and whimsy. During his songs he often teases his backup singers by flouncing their hair or tickling them with the back of his hand. It appears spontaneous and unexpected, and a welcomed relief from the canned stagecraft of some acts, like the Moody Blues.

Now, those guys suck. Not their music, which I love fervently, but their show. It is the most static piece of theater I have ever witnessed. Every song, joke, and stage bits are identical from show to show. Even their tech crew is bored out of their skulls. During the two shows I've worked, the sound guy read a book during the entire performance even when fans complained they couldn't hear "Tuesday Afternoon."

One of the things I've enjoyed learning about celebrities is how physically small they are. Sting is tiny, or at least he looked that way when he walked past me. Jackson Brown is a pip squeak. Yanni is short *and* skinny—I bet he doesn't weigh more than 120 pounds.

I've also learned to appreciate their showmanship. It takes a great deal of talent, determination, and perseverance to become a successful artist, and maintaining this through a lengthy career is a whole other dimension of effort. Elton John has performed over 6,000 concerts in 30-plus years of touring. He looks a bit weathered, hardly moving about the stage. But his music certainly isn't boring, and he puts something special into each performance. His piano entrances are lengthy and mysterious, and a delightful tease—*Gee, I wonder what famous hit song he is going to sing next?* His magic is real, and I had tears in my eyes when EJ, as his crew calls him, tilted his head back and crooned, "I can see Daniel waving goodbye...."

But, other great artists, like Eric Clapton, offer little on stage physically. Eric's music is great and his show at the Key was wonderfully produced, but close your eyes and it could have been a CD playing on a really huge sound system. Plus, I didn't hear Eric say one word to the audience. Maybe after 50 years of concerts he doesn't have anything left to say to virtual strangers.

Plus, as they say in Nashville, *It's all about the music, man.*

Mark Knopfler, lead of Dire Straits, is the same way. His quiet, expressionless face camouflages the musicianship that can vaporize the varnish off a guitar. On stage he appears exhausted, and I asked his crew about it. All they could say was, "Yeah, he's old."

So what? Knopfler is still considered the best guitarist of his generation by many stagehands and other pros of the industry.

Fortunately, some performers excel in playing to the audience. The Indigo Girls create magic at every show — everyone sings along, the *Bics* get flicked, and enchantment exudes from even tired stagehands who dance backstage with a cup of coffee in their hand. Meet-and-Greets with the Girls look lively, as if Emily and Amy are actually having fun with their fans. Plus, the Indigo stage set is elegantly simple, small enough to fit into only a couple of semis. Hence, the load-out is quick and I still get my four-hour minimum. Less is more! Thanks, ladies.

Yes, the Dixie Chicks are my favorites and Diamond needs his darkness. Yet, I savor Seattle's after-the-show glow of radiant 3 a.m. blackness borne of a job-well-done coupled with heartfelt goodbyes to my brothers and sisters of IATSE Local 15.

36

Arlo Guthrie
A new chapter opens

An icon of the 1960s, Arlo Guthrie made a one-night stop in Seattle in 2008, replete with graying hair and tons o' stories peppered throughout each set.

Reflecting my own evolution, Arlo's performance was the first one I saw from a seat in the house after 10 years of watching from the wings. Yup, I'm not a stagehand anymore — too many years of dust, dirt, and fumes for my lungs to handle, so I had to dig up a new line of work. In 2006, I became a newspaper reporter, and Arlo's show was my first gig at an old stagehand haunt, the Paramount Theater.

Not that Arlo needed many stagehands, only requiring a handful of guys to push his guitar rack on stage and position his grand piano. Less is more, and Arlo had all he needed.

Besides the cushy seat and breathing clean air, I was able to cross a threshold forbidden to stagehands: Talking to the performers. Paramount graced me with a 30-minute phone interview and my first question had to do with my biggest surprise from his concert.

"Your audience was filled with young'uns, Arlo! Where are all the gray-haired hippies?" I asked.

"Yeah, my audiences are really changing. And just in the past eight months, too," Arlo said, chuckling. "I've been discovered on YouTube! Now a whole new generation wants to hear 'Alice's Restaurant'."

Arlo, the consummate storyteller, continued. "I hadn't played it for years, but when its 40th anniversary came around in 2005, I figured I ought to bring it back. Took me three days to re-learn it! Then the young people started coming, so now I sing it every night."

Arlo estimates about a third of his audiences nationwide are now under 30.

"There's a very wide range of interests because of that," he said. "You don't see that very often at concerts these days."

Arlo says it brings a magical component to his performances.

"I can hear the impact. It's not the songs — they're little vehicles. It's the feeling of: 'We're in it together' that comes out. Young and old, rich and poor, all in a room together listening to music. So many people on so many sides of things, so many sides of life…they get to go beyond the cheesy and get to the soul of things."

I asked Arlo about his famous father, Woody Guthrie, the extraordinary songwriter and folk singer from the Dust Bowl and McCarthy eras.

"Woody is present, he's all around," Arlo replied. "He's physically present, he's there in all of us. What's especially nice is that his quiet feelings are there — present in my life, my kids' life, and my grandkids' life… Now, he didn't start the thing — these feelings, they come from so far back. But when I feel the continuity, I begin to relax."

Arlo tours throughout the year, taking only eight weeks off in the summertime. Often, he performs with his kids, one of whom, Annie Guthrie, has teamed up with Amy Nelson, daughter of Willie.

As for the Paramount stagehands, Arlo praised my old crew from the IA-15:

"One of the Paramount crew gave me a big hug when I came off stage," he recalled. "Just walked up to me and wrapped his big arms around me. He had tears in his eyes. I love that—when the crew is with ya."

37

The Bus Driver
Realizing the depth of my emotions

I met the bus driver in the summer of 2003 at Ramtha's School of Enlightenment. She was my partner for a week-long retreat, and it was a stirring occasion for me because that was the time I decided to run for the presidency of the United States.

"Why not be great?" Ramtha had challenged us previously. In response, my political juices flowed, first with disgust at George W. Bush and the Iraq War, then with excitement as I envisioned being the president.

As a result of such a powerful vision of myself, when I learned my partner was a school bus driver for the nearby suburb of Tumwater, Washington, I felt disappointment. A part of me said, quietly, *Is that all you dream yourself to be, a school bus driver?*

But that judgmental part of me was only that—a part. Another side of me enjoyed the bus driver's quiet acceptance of my dream. When the rest of my friends were telling me openly that I was crazy—*president of the United States? Bruce, you've gone too far this time!*—and even my former psychotherapist called to say she was concerned about my "grandiosity," the bus driver just kept cruising down the highway of our friendship. She didn't even suggest that I first run for mayor. *Thank Gawd!*

Another part of me connected with her openness. In quiet spurts of conversation, she told me about her childhood in Canada, a mysterious weight gain in young adulthood, and her difficulties with money and debt. It was an easy back-and-forth. I'd tell her my plans for Iraq, and she told me how she dealt with bullies on her bus.

Beginning with that event at RSE, we formed an acquaintanceship comprised of a couple of emails a week, occasional phone calls, and a barbecue every now and then. She and her friend Linda even came out to my little hideaway in the hills of Eatonville, a 16-foot RV trailer that required guests to sit outside and brave the cold and rain — or heat and mosquitoes. The bus driver was one of a few social contacts that made the trek. Plus, when she partook of that evening's red wine and chicken roasted over a wood fire, she allowed me to vent about my lonely, impoverished life.

Sometimes weeks or months would go by without a word exchanged between us, and then an email would pop up from her saying, "So, what's new?" and our friendship would be re-nourished. I began to be regularly invited to her shindigs — birthday parties at her house, or a jaunt to a Christmas gathering with friends.

But my judgmental nature broke the connection. I remember it clearly: Eating pizza at the Casa Mia café in Yelm after seeing the movie *Fahrenheit 911*. I had enjoyed the movie and was still ranting against the stupidities of Bush and Company as we munched our pizza. The bus driver was strangely still, though.

"Why are you so quiet?" I parried.

She told me she disliked the movie and disapproved of Michael Moore's trashing of the president.

My Gawd, she's a Republican! I screamed inside. I couldn't handle it, and I cooled toward the bus driver. We rarely spoke after that.

When I heard that the bus driver had died of a heart attack several years later, I was surprised. *Wow, another RSE schoolmate gone. That's the third this month. What is wrong with us students? We're supposed to be learning how to be masters of our bodies! Healing with a touch! Walking on water! Fabulously wealthy!* As a result, I drove to the commemoration ceremony with a numb mind.

When I turned the corner on Tumwater's North Street and saw the big yellow school bus parked in front of the funeral home, I burst into tears.

Shaken, I walked into the ceremony room and found an empty seat. I didn't recognize a soul. *Must be all the school bus drivers.* I had met a few of them when I helped the bus driver move out of her house and resettle in an apartment to get her finances under control. Having met her buds from work, I knew how important they were to each other, and I was not surprised to see a room full of what I assumed were other bus drivers.

By a hidden knowingness, however, I had sat directly in front of a small crew of RSE students, who gave me warm hellos, even though I hadn't seen them as I entered. I knew I'd picked the right spot and settled in.

But I was not ready for what happened next. As fellow bus driver after bus driver spoke, my tears fell in torrents.

The drivers told of their love for our friend, of how she had helped them in their own personal dramas — how she encouraged one driver to become a gospel singer and to partner with another driver to make their singing dreams come true. *Just like she had encouraged me to run for president, or tell stories at her dinner parties.*

They told of her love for her kids on the bus, and how she started a "Books on the Bus" project, now a national program that earned her both professional recognition and a $2,000 honorarium from the school district.

I realized what a difference a school bus driver can make in the world, just by being a caring part of her kids' lives as she took them to and from school.

I sniffled back the tears, but they overran my plumbing. At one point, my breath shot a stream of teary mist out from my mouth. *That's never happened before. The death of the driver is hitting me deeper than I had imagined possible.*

Then I remembered the two jackets the bus driver had given me shortly after I had helped her move from her house. During the move, I had worn a ragged rain jacket, duct-taped together at the seams. It was a pitiful garment, and a few weeks later the bus driver quietly handed me a brown paper bag at a coffee rendezvous, saying, "I found these in the move and I thought you could use them."

They were used rain jackets yet in good shape, one a Gore-Tex and then other a Helly Heck job that would have cost hundreds brand-new. I realized even then that the bus driver had gone shopping for me and that these weren't just "left-overs." I hadn't worn them to the memorial instinctively knowing they would trigger a teary response.

Nevertheless, a family member strode to the front of the room and asked the assembled to call out one word that encapsulated the bus driver. I wanted to shout out "generous," but my lack of composure prevented me from speaking, a strange state for a storyteller.

Afterward, he asked us to come to the dais, pluck a rose from a bouquet and place it into a commemorative glass jar that would accompany the bus driver's body to its final resting place. My RSE pals invited me to join their little group in line.

"I'll meet you in a minute," I replied, "I have to go the bathroom." I had to pee, but more importantly I needed to pull myself together.

In a toilet stall I wailed. I blew my nose over and over, triggering a massive sinus headache. When it receded I returned to the group.

I blubbered again on the family's receiving line. I became confused. They were so dry-eyed, and I was so wet. *How does this happen? They're family, and I'm just a friend who hasn't even seen her in two years.* I realized then how much she'd really taught me about the beauty of the simple life.

I've also come to realize that I have been impacted by the bus driver just as much as her school kids. I suppose I was on a bus ride with her for years and never knew it.

These days I'm a newspaper reporter and talk to politicians and community leaders every day, wading through their spin, half-truths, and bull. But none of the powerful and mighty folks have touched me like the bus driver from Tumwater. What a ride she could give: a story or a smile, mile after mile, through every curve in the road.

In Memoriam:
Toni Earles, a student of the Ram, and my friend.

38

The Flute Player
Engaging a schoolmate stuck in his anger

I met the flute player in 1991, shortly after he had arrived from New Zealand to study at RSE. Our fledgling performance careers echoed each other from that day.

One of my first manifestations in those early days was finding venues to tell my stories, and I was hungry to find places to perform.

One day, I received an invitation to tell a few stories at a house concert in McKenna, WA. My then-girlfriend had a friend who was an emerging opera singer, and he was going to perform at this event. By his grace, I was invited to be part of the show.

Before I told my stories, though, the hostess brought forward another student, the flute player. The owner of the house stood beside him and announced that since he was new to performing, he would not be playing directly in front of the audience.

It sounded cryptic, and I was unsure what was going to happen. The audience was seated in the living room, which was open to a kitchen area and delineated by a couch placed across the unfettered space.

Apparently too frightened to perform in the open, the flute player blew a few opening notes from behind a kitchen door. This first song, an instrumental, was brief, more like an introductory piece. When he finished, the flute player moved behind the couch, sat down on the floor and began again. It was weird hearing the flute player but not being able to see him. However, the general tone in the room was one of acceptance: *Let the shy brother do his thing.*

The tunes the flute player offered were original compositions, and I found them uneven. Some movements touched me, others did not.

Over the next few years our paths crossed again, either shopping in town or at an occasional open mic, and I enjoyed our artists' camaraderie. He had also created an affordable recording studio that I used to make some storytelling tapes and songs. In fact, I recorded "The Ballad of Flight 800" there.

Nine years after first meeting the flute player, I took the next step in my entertaining career and moved to Nashville, Tennessee. On my way out of Yelm, I stopped at my ex-girlfriend's New Age store to say goodbye to friends. There, I discovered the flute player had just released a new composition, which I bought. It proved later to be a providential purchase when I arrived in Nashville.

Nashville, the Music City, was a grand gift I gave to myself, and I reveled in spending 15 months in the company of committed artists. But it was also a lonely time, particularly since Nashville prides itself in being the Buckle of the Bible Belt. To weather the storms in my spirit, I listened to the flute player's new CD. It was light and transcendental, but it also had substance and guts. Best, it had vocals from singers back in Yelm whom I knew. It featured my friend on his flute, and it calmed me to remember my fellow "masters," the term Ramtha uses to describe his students.

But now, years later, I've come to learn that the flute player was angry. He claimed that the teachings of the school didn't work, and that he had been deceived. He also publicly stated that RSE was a fraud because he could not do "the extraordinary," as was promised. He couldn't heal with a thought. He couldn't walk on water.

As a result, he rose against Ramtha and RSE, and publicly denounced them. The flute player's actions were covered in the newspapers as far away as New Zealand, drawing other disenchanted students to his side.

Yet, I remember when the flute player hid behind a couch to give voice to his soul. In Nashville, I held tangible proof in my hands of his evolution as a master of music. Upon my return to Yelm, I gave him thanks for helping me get through some tough times in the Music City. Now, I'd like to return the favor. Perhaps this story can soothe the discontent in his soul like his flute playing did for me.

Oh, Flute Player! I have seen you create great music and I have benefited from it. But never once have I forgotten who you were at the beginning—the frightened, courageous musician.

May you remember, as well.

39

Pink Sky and Red Wine
Learning not to tarry as aging and death approaches

The last time I saw my friend, Flo Edmundson, was in the winter of 2008, a week before she died from pulmonary disease. As I approached her hospital bed, she was gazing quietly through her window at the sunset. Suddenly, she punctured her reverie with a loud exclamation: "It's going pink…it's going pink… the sky is going pink." Sure enough, the setting sun had produced an alpine glow across the sky.

Her outburst was striking because Flo could hardly breathe, needing to focus on every breath. In fact, Flo struggled to breathe in *and* out. Every action was an effort, and Flo, in her tough, cranky manner, had been doing so for months.

As a result, her lighthearted delight at a pink sunset was sweet. It was an even bigger treat knowing that a few minutes earlier she had shown her grumpy, unforgiving side to a nurse's aide when Flo asked for her bottle of red wine.

That was Flo—Tough Broad and Sweetie-Pie. Judgmental and bitchy, yet insightful and compassionate. Flo was a really good mirror to me, helping me see my narcissistic arrogance.

I first met Flo in the early 1990s at St. Peter's psych ward, known as One-South. I was the recreation therapist and Flo was a clinical specialist in out-patient services. We never talked too much back then, just part of the half dozen or so Ramtha students working One-South, floating through the charged atmosphere of schizophrenia, slashed wrists, and administrators wondering where their souls had wandered once they'd entered management. Flo and the rest of us offered each other quiet support in all that *mishigas*.

But I got to know Flo much better after One-South when we were working at Charlie's Restaurant, a private hamburger concession that operated at Ramtha's school. Charlie's crew were like family to each other, and I even married one of my co-workers, Jen.

Flo was the primary dishwasher, and I still hear her mantra: "NO slop, NO sharps! (knives)" ringing in my head when I wash my dishes. So, it was natural for us to help Flo when her strength ebbed and her lung disease required her to tote oxygen tanks. At one event, I was part of the spontaneous group who took down her tent, packed her van, and got her home. Over the following year she was still attending events, but her health then required a heated RV with an accessible toilet, and I became one of her RV attendants.

She wanted to cook me a dinner to thank me for these services, but I never had the wherewithal to accept the offer. So, I was pleased when Flo called a few weeks before Christmas in 2008 and gave me another chance to connect. On the phone she sounded weak, but when I actually saw her in her hospital rehab on Christmas Eve, she was a basket-case. Lying on her side, her belly was profoundly distended and she only had the strength for a word or two between breaths.

"I guess I'm going to have to do all the talking," I said.

She nodded and uttered a weak, "Yup."

So, I told her Christmas stories, school gossip, and brought her up-to-date on my life's happenings. She downed two glasses of red wine as I sipped between tales. It was Gawd-awful stuff.

"Flo, you gotta start drinking better wine," I admonished.

"*I* like it," she spit back.

For once, I didn't take offense to a woman's zinger. Our mutual pissiness told me we were real friends. In addition, toward the end of our visit, she pieced together half-sentences describing her thoughts on the attitudes that had put her in a hospital bed. That's when I realized what I wanted from Flo —communion on our deepest attitudes—the ones that have given us poverty, ill health, and death. The Nittus-Grittus as the Big Guy says, and Flo looked like she was up for it, even if she was lying horribly still.

I don't remember exactly what we said beyond acknowledging our arrogance, but at least we had opened the discussion on why our lives were so troubled. After a few moments of tortured conversation, her strength was fully depleted. I stood up to leave and said, "Flo, you look like you're in pretty rough shape. What do you think is going to happen?"

"I'm not... going to die!" she barked. "I've come... too far... to let that... happen."

I gave her a little squeeze on her shoulder, smiled, and said, "So Be That! I'll see you soon."

At my next visit a couple of days later, Flo looked a little stronger. She was able to tell me that her health issues had commenced, ironically, at a summer retreat at RSE. She had to be transported directly to St. Pete's, and the prevailing medical opinion was that Flo was having an acute reaction to the long-term usage of the steroid prednisone, which had been helping her breathe. But six months of detoxification from the steroids had left her gasping for air, physically crumpled, and aching to watch the alpine glow for a few minutes at the end of her day. Even though she seemed to be healthier on that last visit, she succumbed to death two days later.

Death is very close to me these days. The veils between the world of the living and those who have passed seem to be at a razor-thin edge in our Ramtha community. Toni Earles is gone, as is my former best man Bruce Haney, and fellow thespian Linda Groulx.

Serious health issues abound in my life, too. In 2005, I had to quit my work as a stagehand due to "industrial asthma" brought on by excessive dust, fumes, and diesel exhaust. But it was a catalyst to become a newspaper reporter in 2006 at the *Dispatch* in my hometown of Eatonville, WA. Nevertheless, in 2012, I had a heart attack, which required me to have a stent inserted. Clearly, we are pressed to become God-Realized. To me, all these experiences are reflections of the truth of our lives. Witnessing the deterioration of Flo's health was a major wake-up call. Imagine if she and I had started our "attitude conversation" a few years ago instead of at the 11th hour. In retrospect, though, all the bumps on my road have made me humbler, more forgiving, and more allowing. I take that as a worthy trade.

So, enjoy your new journey, Flo. Go with grace and courage, and of course your trademark fierceness and determination. And thanks for being my friend, inspiring me in death not to tarry with my adventure into God-awakened consciousness.

However, Flo, when we meet again *I'm* bringing the wine.

40

Love Letter to You All
Thanks for saving my life

The voice answered on the first ring. "9-1-1," the woman said, calmly.

"I'm having chest pains," I said. "I'm 62 years old and overweight."

"Please stay on the line," she replied. "I'm going to bring on a medical technician."

A male voice entered the conversation immediately. "You're having chest pains?" asked the tech.

"Yes."

"What kind of pain? What does it feel like?"

"It feels like a hand grenade just went off in my chest. I have sharp, radiating pains all over my torso."

"Do they go all the way into your arms?"

"Yes."

"Where else? Your neck?"

"Yes. The pain is up in my neck and jaw, and it's even ringing in my teeth. The cavities in my teeth are singing."

"...Medical units have been alerted — they are on their way...." the 9-1-1 voice said over our conversation.

I took a breath and listened for the sirens of the South Pierce Fire Department ambulance coming from their station house two miles away. But I didn't hear them.

They must just be getting dispatched. I'll give 'em a few minutes....

"Any trouble breathing?" the med guy continued. "Shortness of breath?"

"No, I can breathe."

"Okay. The medical unit should be there shortly. Is there anyone with you?"

"No, I'm alone, but I can call a neighbor to come help me. He's just on the other side of the driveway."

"Is there anything else we need to know right now, do you think?"

"No, I think I'll be okay. I'll just wait.... The gate's locked, though."

"Would it be okay if we cut it?" said the female voice, jumping back into the conversation.

"Sure, but I can get my neighbor to open it."

"...Medical units have just confirmed they are on their way," the woman interjected. "Good luck, sir."

"Thanks," I replied.

"Yeah, good luck," the male voice said.

They hung up, and I waited. Soon, I heard the faint drone of a siren coming down Mountain Highway. I called my neighbor, Dave, and told him what was happening. Without hysterics he confirmed that he would unlock the gate and direct the paramedics when they arrived.

"Hear those sirens, Dave?" I asked. "That's my ambulance." I was slowly going into shock and spoke the obvious to keep me grounded and prevent a total freak-out.

As I listened, I realized there were two sirens. Two vehicles. An ambulance and—as is customary in rural areas—a fire engine with firefighters aboard to provide backup. Nevertheless, I savored the quiet drama of life and death flowing around me. I entered a Zen-like stillness. Then I realized I had to pee. I stood up and walked outside to the garden to urinate. *Gawd, I don't want to do this with a bunch of paramedics standing around me. Better do it now before they get here.* But my chest ached. *Maybe this isn't too smart of an idea.* Nevertheless, I leaned against a post supporting a roof over my little 16-foot RV trailer. As I relieved myself, I heard the sirens getting closer. They sounded insistent as if they were screaming through a red light.

They're coming for me! I've never had an ambulance come for me, before. WOW.

It all felt new and incredibly vital.

I went back inside and sat down. I tried to follow their approach. *Are they coming down the Eatonville Cut-Off Road or coming the back way, down 78th Street? I couldn't tell.*

They got a little louder. *Must be the Cut-Off Road.* Then, silence. I waited for another round of siren whining, but it never came. *Where are they?*

I waited quietly for several moments, maybe minutes. *Who can tell time when you're waiting for an ambulance?*

Suddenly, out of the corner of my eye I saw movement. I turned and looked out the window. I saw three blue uniforms.

Thank Gawd!

My neighbor Dave was leading them, and they marched through my garden gate to my trailer's door. Three strange faces crowded around the entrance and peered inside. Wait— one of the faces I knew! Paramedic Cindy Worden, the woman I had interviewed two weeks prior for the Mountain News on a piece on the health impacts of wood smoke.

"Hi, Cindy, it sure is good to see a familiar face right now."

"I bet it is," she said with a smile. Then she took charge and directed traffic. She sent in one of her colleagues, a firefighter, toting a blood pressure monitor and an EKG machine.

Must be the $50,000 portable rig the firefighters were telling me about that they keep on the engine truck.

The firefighter told me his name, but I can't recall it. Much of what was happening became wrapped in a blur of anxiety and drama. Another paramedic placed EKG pads on my chest and legs, and Cindy attached monitoring wires.

Then the first firefighter put the blood pressure cuff on my right arm and pumped it up. As he released the air he looked frustrated, and tried again.

"It's 160-something, but I can't get the low number," he called out. He tried a third time.

"Still can't get it."

Cindy traded places with him and re-positioned the pressure cuff. She pumped up the bladder until I screamed. "You're killing me, Cindy!" I shouted.

"I've got to pump it up to get the reading, Bruce. It'll only be for a second or two."

"It feels like you're amputating my arm," I said weakly, trying to complain and make a joke at the same time.

Cindy pumped the blood pressure cuff up a second time and called out: "169 is the low number. I'm having trouble getting the systolic!" She pumped past the original pain and kept going. Then, she backed it off again, and then re-pumped even tighter.

"It's at least 219. I can't get it exactly. It's in the 230s, probably 238." She quickly unwrapped the cuff and grabbed my shoulder.

"Bruce," she said, "we're taking you to the hospital. Is Good Sam okay?"

"Sure, Cindy. Good Sam's fine with me."

Cindy barked more orders, and while the outside firefighter turned the ambulance around, another readied the gurney and a third brought a "stair chair" to my door.

"Do you think you can walk down your steps to the chair?" Cindy asked. "We'll wheel you out from there."

"Sure."

She held my arm and steadied me as I descended the two steps to the outside. There, I plopped down on a skinny, metal-framed chair with small, hard wheels.

They haven't changed these chairs in the 40 years since I was an ambulance orderly at Meadowbrook Hospital in New York.

I was rolled through my garden and sympathized with the firefighter panting to pull me over the blue-chip stones that filled the pathway.

"I could have walked to the bus," I said, using the slang of New York medics for an ambulance. *But why take a chance? These guys are strong.*

At the "bus," I was unstrapped from the chair and transferred to the gurney. Then I was re-secured with a harness over my shoulders, waist, and legs. Then they slid me into the back of the bus just as I had done for hundreds of patients back in my day.

Cindy joined me and re-connected the monitors. She also gave me a shot of nitroglycerin. "It'll dilate your arteries and help bring down your blood pressure."

Next, she prepped an IV. I insisted that she stick me before we started moving even though she assured me that she could insert it while we swayed on the road. "Thanks for doing it my way, Cindy," I said. I also asked that we not roll with lights and sirens, and that the driver move slowly and carefully, flowing normally with traffic.

"When I was an ambulance orderly," I told Cindy, "I often thought that the use of lights and sirens was overused. I think it's contraindicated, medically. I really don't want to bang around back here as we bump our way up Meridian Avenue."

Cindy smiled wanly. As we crept down the driveway and began our journey through rural Eatonville, Cindy and I debated the finer points of medical transport.

"If you stop breathing, Bruce, or your heart stops, we're going full-tilt boogie with lights and sirens," she commanded.

"I agree. When someone's not breathing or is bleeding—anything that is absolutely life-threatening—ya gotta run."

She smiled a little more supportively. As we drove up Meridian toward the hospital 30 miles away in Puyallup, Washington, Cindy gave me a couple more hits of nitro, and we watched my BP come down to 185/110. She took notes and got all my vital information, including next of kin, and explained "Do Not Resuscitate" protocols.

This is getting serious.

I hesitated on the DNR, and we agreed that I could do the signing later, with a doctor around to explain the finer details. She also assured me that since the voters of the South Pierce Fire District had approved the latest EMT Levy, my ride was pre-paid if I didn't have insurance.

"I don't have money or insurance, Cindy," I announced.

"Then, don't worry."

It was the first of many wonderful gifts I was to receive from taxpayers.

Cindy called the Good Samaritan Emergency Room on her cell phone and gave them the details of my condition.

After a 40-minute ride, Cindy and the boys in blue were wheeling me through the ER doors past a monitoring board indicating which room was reserved for me. They whisked me directly into a private chamber. It was unlike most ERs I had been in where gurneys were parked end-to-end in the hallways awaiting a triage nurse.

Instead, my room had a nurse and cardiac tech waiting for me, and I was transferred to the hospital bed immediately. More monitors and wires, and a new IV in my other arm. As the hospital team took a blood draw, Cindy and her crew bid *adieu.*

Thanks, I mouthed as they left the room. I was sorry to see them go. *They probably saved my life.*

The Good Sam team took over. An ER doc arrived, then a cardiac specialist. The nurses gave me more meds—pain killers, anti-anxiety medications and vascular dilators—and they began to work ever so gently. My mental acuity began to fade. I soon learned that my heart had experienced a 95% blockage in the rear circumflex coronary artery, and some heart tissue had been deprived of oxygenated blood. In turn, the heart was sending out distress enzymes, which the blood tests quickly discovered. With that finding, I was zoomed down to cardiac surgery, a large room called the Cath Lab, short for Cardiac Catheter Laboratory.

*This is getting **really** serious.*

But it all felt surreal since I had no pain unless I tried to move. How could I be so ill and not have any symptoms? Whenever I had been in a hospital before, like for my broken leg, I *knew* I belonged there. I summoned my courage to ask a tech for a straight answer on my medical condition.

"Would it be fair to say that I've had a heart attack?" I asked. "No one has actually said that out loud to me, yet. The words 'heart attack.'"

"Dude, it could have been fatal," the tech replied.

WOW.

I was prepped for an angioplasty to determine the size of the blockage and possible stent placements. That meant more drugs, having the hair shaved off my legs, and signing releases. My last coherent statement was an announcement to the three or four technicians buzzing around me, "I can still understand English!" I shouted. I felt very proud that I could still comprehend what was being said even though my ability to reply was quickly evaporating into a pharmaceutical haze.

Nevertheless, here is what I understand happened next.

Over the course of several hours, two physicians and the technicians opened up my right leg to access my right femoral artery. They then built a quasi "work-station" there so that several tiny instruments could be inserted into the femoral artery, and eventually snaked into my heart. This portal included a four-inch plastic liner that was placed inside the femoral artery, and connected to a kind of plastic manhole cover placed temporarily on the surface of my leg.

Inside this portal a camera and a balloon, plus a small metal stent, a kind of flex-pipe for the artery, were wiggled toward my heart.

The balloon was inflated at the site of the blockage, which was caused by plaque—a hardened lipid residue that takes years to build up. When the balloon was inflated, the arterial tissue expanded and cracked loose its plaque. Then the balloon was retracted and the stent positioned in the artery to secure the newly opened blood vessel. The stent is about the size of the spring found inside old-fashioned ballpoint pens, but smaller.

The docs woke me during the procedure and told me that I had a 30% blockage in another coronary artery, but the chamber that it served, one of four—two ventricles and two atria—was still "ejecting" about 60% of the blood volume of a normal heart beat. Since a 65% ejection rate is the sign of a healthy heart, they decided to leave it alone.

Afterward, I didn't remember a thing until I woke up in a cardiac recovery unit that evening.

"Hi, my name is Catherine and I'll be your nurse for the next twelve hours or so," said a slim woman standing by the side of my bed. "I just came on at 7."

I laid back on my pillow and mumbled, "Okay."

Catherine explained all of the procedures that would follow in my immediate recovery—blood pressure checks every 15 minutes, hourly inspections of my leg to assess swelling or bleeding in the portal area, and monitoring of my heart's EKG. Plus, they were going to pull the portal device in a special bedside procedure at 4 a.m.

I nodded.

An aide came in and asked if I wanted any dinner.

"Sure."

A turkey platter soon arrived.

Catherine swirled about, taking care of me and three other patients—all of us in adjoining single rooms. She was one of the busiest nurses I have ever seen, even during my 14 years of hospital work.

My room was spacious—bigger than my trailer! No-nonsense looking monitors straddled both sides of my bed. It looked like the kind of place a really sick guy could be found. But I didn't feel sick—actually I felt pretty good—just a little woozy.

After dinner, I was more alert. Then I got tired and dozed, as Catherine came in regularly to do her latest medical chore.

On some level I didn't fully comprehend that I had had a heart attack. Intellectually, yes. Emotionally, no. It was too foreign a concept. I guess you could call it the "shock of reality."

About 11 p.m. Catherine began working on my psycho-social history. It felt like she was asking me about somebody I knew really well but who wasn't me—a fellow who used my name and birth date, but came from another world.

"Married?"

"Ahhh...no, divorced."

"Do you live with any significant other?"

"Ahhh...no."

"Is there anyone you would like us to call?"

"Hmmm. No." *Really? There is no one I want to let know that I had a heart attack? Am I that estranged from everyone I've ever known?*

But as she plowed through the paperwork and tested my blood pressure, it began to dawn on me that I was recovering from a heart attack and I pondered what that meant, at least pragmatically.

Two things happened instantaneously. I decided NEVER to eat any fatty foods ever again—it was an immediate revulsion of anything that would harm me and plug my arteries. No ice cream, butter, or beef. None.

The other was a realization that I would need to change my life. I had to fix the love situation of my life besides healing the blockages in my heart. Love and hearts—the two go together like peanut butter and jelly.

Okay, cool, I thought. *I've been working on those issues for a long time. Now, I've really got to make some changes for the better.* It felt like good news to my soul.

So, when Catherine asked me about my next of kin, my embarrassment and resistance crumbled.

"Okay, Catherine!" I called out. "I admit it. I'm a lonely guy and I don't have anyone in my life. Yes, I live alone—it makes me a good investigative reporter—but I don't have any friends, no one who I can talk to about how I really feel down deep. I know I've got to change that. I need to create better connections with people, build stronger relationships. Be less judgmental, more open and loving—and be open to receiving love. Love in all its forms, not just romantic or sexual stuff, but friendships and social connections. Especially the love of life."

I was on a roll. Catherine let me rant.

"I really am a 'stop and smell the roses' kind of guy," I continued. "I've just got to do a better job of it. I really appreciate the beauty of life. And I've got to learn how to really love my life. I haven't up to now."

Through Catherine's remaining hours I deepened my awareness of how my heart attack had arrived—too many fatty foods and not enough exercise, and not enough love, expressed or felt.

Katie, the day nurse, came on at 7 a.m. and, after my mid-day nap, preached the virtues of salmon and veggies. I told her that I already ate as much salmon as my food stamp budget would allow.

"What else besides salmon is good for the heart? How about whole grains?" I asked.

Katie searched her diet guide book for an answer, but found nothing that satisfied me. I resolved to call Ray, the guy I had interviewed the prior year for the *Mountain News*. He had lost 160 pounds eating the way I now needed to eat.

With my new insights I launched the first steps of change.

First, I called everyone I knew. I wasn't going to be stoic, suffering in silence or isolation. That had been my tendency, and it was often punctuated with sharp bursts of whining. No, this time I would be emotionally healthy.

I called Dave and thanked him for his help with the paramedics, and gave him the good news of my successful surgery. I also called my writing friend Judy Spiers for a ride home upon discharge. As stalwart a buddy as Dave has been—watching my back and making sure I had a roof over my head—I decided that I didn't want to ride home in his pickup truck with a leaky door and iffy heat. Instead, I opted for some self-love and asked Judy for a ride in her Lexus. Judy complied.

Next, I called Carol Wright, perhaps my most kindred of spirits in Eatonville, and she came to visit.

I called New York and spoke with Mom, Sis, and BJ. I savored the scene as I watched the energies of love from back home swirl around and seek to gather me to its bosom. I shaped it as it grew—Mom said she would send me some money to take care of things as I recovered—but I had to buffer some family dynamics when it grew testy, such as my mother questioning how I was going to spend the money. Even BJ began chastising me for being "cavalier" with my health, although what she was really saying was, "Don't you dare die on me, you sonovabitch." *Ah, love comes in so many forms.*

I got more love from the folks at Good Sam, too. A social worker visited and gave me my prescriptions and tips on aftercare. She also set me up for cheap meds at Walmart. In addition, she completed all the paperwork that arranged for charity care to cover the stent operation and for Medicaid to secure all my followup.

So, I survived the crisis. All it took was one phone call to a 9-1-1 operator who picked up on the first ring. Say what you will about national health care, we have certainly created a system to take care of people when they have a heart attack, even for guys who are broke. I am very grateful, and I thank each and every one of you since all of you have paid some taxes along the way, which is the source of all this help. For me, there was nary a delay anywhere, and I received Cadillac health care every step of the way.

So, I thank you for voting for the common good, paying your taxes, and sending me your healing thoughts. It's good to be alive.

41

Yuchi and Me, and Donald Trump
Following my heart's desires

I asked Yuchi Tamaguchi, the Olympic figure skating champion and later a Hollywood fixture in Kung Fu movies, for a date in 2003. Specifically, I invited her to accompany me to the Christmas Ball at Ramtha's School of Enlightenment. In addition, I was stunned to learn that, in 2016 when he was elected president, Donald Trump had tried to date Yuchi as well. Before Melania, I think.

As for my dating Yuchi, I had asked her in a letter, not face-to-face. The truth was I didn't know who Yuchi was, exactly. I had never met her or even seen her. I knew she was gorgeous — after all, she was a famous actress and had been on the cover of Sports Today magazine — but that, and the fact that she had just started attending RSE, was the total sum of my knowledge. However, this information was coupled with an intriguing tidbit I'd read in Modern American Life magazine. When the reporter asked Yuchi why, at 42, she had never been married, her answer exploded inside me with unbounded excitement.

"I haven't found my match," she told the shocked journalist.

Yuchi's words thoroughly enraptured me because I hadn't found my match, either. This dynamic had become acutely self-evident via another quirky connection I had with The Donald. In August 2003, I had decided to run for the presidency of the United States.

For the following six weeks, I became immersed in the business of running a legitimate political campaign: fund raising, organizing a team, and completing the filing applications for all 50 states. In addition, I composed positions on the pressing issues of the day, such as Iraq and Afghanistan, which was a fairly straightforward plan of removing all of our troops from those countries.

I admit that I was surprised when I discovered how my presidential declarations would eradicate my social life. Everyone thought I was nuts. No one wanted anything to do with me. Except for my sister, who stayed by my side, probably because she had a friend whose brother had also run for president years before, so she wasn't too fazed by my behavior.

Overnight, I found myself alone in the world. Certainly, no one in my life was my match. I couldn't even keep a friend, let alone attract a wife. In some ways I was like Yuchi, a Japanese immigrant in Hollywood who couldn't speak English when she first arrived. Fortunately, she could dazzle a film camera along with an entire Olympic ice arena.

Shortly after my social world collapsed, it re-blossomed in strange and marvelous ways. On one occasion, a complete stranger walked up to me in a parking lot and said, "I hear you're running for president. Can I help?" We talked for a bit, and I learned she was a tax accountant. I asked her to be my campaign treasurer. She agreed.

A few days later, another woman walked up to me and handed me a $50 bill, whispering, "You're probably gonna need this." I did. I went out and had a great steak dinner, and bought gas with the leftover money.

A month later, Ramtha announced that he was going to host RSE's first annual Christmas Ball. I immediately thought of Yuchi and started inquiring if any of my classmates could introduce me to her. No one offered, or dared. I'm not sure why, but I was frozen out.

Frustrated, I Googled "Yuchi Tamaguchi" and discovered that she had a fan club, a press agent, and a manager. I wrote them all and explained my situation, asking if they would kindly pass on my offer of a Christmas date. I heard nothing back. Approaching complete desperation, I Googled further and discovered Yuchi had a father who had just followed her to the United States and was living in Palm Springs, California. Even though I didn't speak a word of Japanese, I wrote her dad — in English — and asked for his help in getting a date with his daughter. Again, I never heard anything.

The Christmas Ball came and went and I never got my date with Yuchi. Nonetheless, six months later I attended a week-long retreat at RSE, and when I entered the Great Hall where Ramtha addressed us, a cute Asian-looking woman was exiting. She spotted me and our eyes locked. We stopped for a split second, but she turned away and scurried on.

That has got to be Yuchi.

It was.

Ironically, I sat a couple seats behind her during the retreat, and spent days gawking her. Eventually, I decided I needed to spend my time in a more productive manner, so I gave up on Yuchi and shifted my attention back to Ramtha.

When the retreat ended, I stopped in the school bookstore before heading home. I slowly wandered the aisles and, rounding a corner, spied a diminutive woman browsing alone in the music department. It was Yuchi. In an unprecedented display of courage, I walked up to her.

"Excuse me, Yuchi," I said. "Do you have a minute? I need to ask you to do a favor for me. Actually, I have an apology to give you. Really, um, the favor is to deliver an apology...to your father."

"My father?"

"Yes. Last October, I wrote him asking for his help in getting me a date with you. I was trying to go to the Christmas Ball with you. But I've come to realize that I went too far. I never should have involved your family in my, um, fantasy or desire, or whatever it was; the crossing-over, you know, between the celebrity stuff and your family's privacy…."

"Yeah, he was pissed." Yuchi said over my words.

"…Will you please tell him I'm sorry for invading his privacy?"

Without looking at me directly, Yuchi raised her arm and offered her hand. "Apology accepted, sir."

We shook on it.

I was hoping she would ask me to be her friend, or offer some other gesture of connection, but none came. After a second of hesitation, I said, "Thanks." Then left.

I've never seen Yuchi after that, even though we both attended RSE for years. But I take great solace in knowing I had the chops to ask a famous actress for a date.

Also, I hear that she turned down The Donald, too. Heh, heh.

42

TJ Doyle, Bill O'Reilly, and 50th Reunions
I see beauty and ugliness entwined

I received an invitation to my high school's 50th reunion at the same time our most famous alumnus got fired from his job at *Fox News* for sexual harassment. Yup, Bill O'Reilly and I are former classmates, Chaminade High School, Class of 1967.

Bill was just as big a jerk then as he is now, except these days he seems to have expanded his repertoire to include terrorizing women. But he scared me back in school, too.

I didn't know Bill very well, then — we were never friends — but he did cast a large shadow. In our junior and senior years, Chaminade, a private, all-boys Catholic school in Mineola, New York, made an adjustment in teaching style that brought Bill to my attention. Initially very strict and formal, our school began to implement a more Socratic method of teaching, and that meant there were more open-ended discussions in the classroom on topics of the day. In fact, one English teacher spent the first 10 minutes of every class reading to us from the *New York Times*, usually the Russell Baker op-ed piece. Another teacher, Brother Thomas J. Doyle, even had us turn our desks toward the center of the room to form a kind of circular debating hall, where we would argue on themes such as the Vietnam War or the nature of God.

Brother Doyle, aka "TJ" for Thomas John, was my favorite teacher and I thrived in his classes. By senior year he often gave me passes to skip the classes of other teachers and join him and other selected students in advanced discussion groups. These gatherings were extraordinary and very exciting, morphing into field trips to New York City to meet TJ's colleagues who were involved in social action activities, such as the Catholic Worker Center or the International Youth Hostel.

Some of these expanded discussions happened in combined classroom settings, and that is when I saw Bill O'Reilly in action. He was a fringe element, but loud. His perspectives were not mainstream with the rest of the student body, and I was surprised to hear how exceptionally conservative and strident he was. It was bizarre seeing a young man during the height of the 1960s cultural revolution espouse 1930s perspectives. In fact, some of Bill's sidekicks, one fellow in particular named Mac, sounded like a Nazi youth. I remember Mac declaring that Adolf Hitler had accomplished a lot of good for Germany before he destroyed his country and much of Europe.

My fellow students and I were aghast, and Bill didn't repudiate it, as I recall. But his own comments often seemed as if he was in his own world, one filled with unreasonable fears and strife.

I don't remember any of his specific pronouncements, but I do remember talking *about* him to my mother at the dinner table, and her response has stayed with me all my life: "That boy can't see the forest for the trees."

For weeks I debated with myself whether I should return to Chaminade for my 50th. I wasn't sure if Bill would attend, and, if he did, I'm not sure if I would want to talk with him or wade through the throng that would be sure to surround him. I wouldn't want to argue with him about anything, for that would certainly seem to be a waste of time, but asking Bill to comment on how he became the Bill O'Reilly of Fox News fame might be worthwhile.

It would also be an opportunity to ask him and my other alums about sexual predators at Chaminade. As I write this, the former president of Chaminade, Father James Williams, is being investigated on charges of sexually assaulting students during his administration from 1999 until 2011. The *Associated Press* reported in 2016 that Williams was thought to be hiding in the Vatican to avoid capture and extradition back to the United States. Here, he would most certainly face stiff interrogation from the Nassau County DA's office, given the current political climate surrounding these issues.

But Bill O'Reilly did not investigate nor report these developments, and the *New York Times* didn't either, which is a greater tragedy in my view. The alums of Chaminade pepper many levels of New York's law enforcement and politics—the current and past Nassau County Executives are alumni—but I suspect they don't have the *cajones* to go up against the Church or their school.

But I do.

43

Tenney House
Embracing the wisdom of my mother's friends

One of the remarkable attributes of my parents was their ability to maintain their childhood friendships throughout their lives. For my mother, her group was the women from Tenney House, a small sorority-like residence at Smith College. My mom was a "Smithie," class of 1946, and the 16 women of Tenney House were like sisters. Not only did they live together for their last three years of college, they helped each other survive the tough times of World War II and afterward.

My mom never used her first name, "Olveria," in life, choosing to be called by her middle name, "Frances." However, Tenney House had another woman named Frances, so my mom needed a nickname. Her last name was Zizis, so she used the moniker that had developed in her old neighborhood of Worcester, Massachusetts, "ZZ."

Besides a cool nickname, my mother's ethnicity stood out as well; she was first-generation Lithuanian, hailing from the three-story, working-class, wooden structures of Worcester known as "triple-deckers." Plus, she and her family lived up the hill from a huge US Steel plant and her own mother's place of work, American Optical.

Mom's brainpower distinguished her from her working-class origins, but all Smithies understand they are smart. However, the Tenney Girls also knew they were "tough cookies." They were all on scholarships and worked hard — both on their academics and in school jobs to pay the bills.

My mom's academic prowess as a math major was odd, especially for its time. Even today, I don't know any women who have majored in mathematics, so my mother's accomplishment was quite singular.

But for all their moxie, my mother and her Tenney Girls seemed to have been trapped by forces beyond their control. My mother graduated in 1946 just as millions of soldiers from World War II were returning home and looking for jobs, wives, and normality.

Nevertheless, after graduation, my mom and a trio of her Tenney sisters moved to New York City to look for work. Mom found employment at AT&T, the big phone company. She earned $35 per week, and was proud for it, especially since she only had to work five days a week, while one of the Tenney gals had to work a half day on Saturday to earn her weekly pay. Initially, my mom worked in accounting and was able to apply her math skills to reconciling billing disputes. But soon the pressures of the world moved in. Within a few months of her arrival at AT&T, the all-female crew of telephone operators went on strike. Instead of settling with their union, the bosses gathered all the women from the administrative offices and trained them to work the boards. Hence, my mother became an "overseas" phone operator. She seemed satisfied with that work, too, but she never commented on her impact as a strike breaker. I'm not even sure she realized the harsh realities her actions supported. Maybe she didn't have much of a choice — she still needed a job, and they were getting harder to obtain as more men returned to the work force.

So, my mom carried on, commuting every day to Manhattan from her Tenney enclave in Point Lookout, NY, a seaside village near Long Beach. There, she lived with three

Tenney sisters: Irene LaPan, Barb Treml, and Florence Morley. They rented an apartment from Irene's stepfather, a gregarious fisherman named "Governor" Doxsee whom everyone in town seemed to love. At least that seemed to be the case many years later when my mother took my sister and me to visit the Doxsees. I can still remember how she admired Governor's obvious bravado, and also his vast sea of white, broken clam shells carpeting the parking lot at his wholesale fish market.

After settling into their employment, the Tenney Girls then went about the business of dating and finding husbands. I've heard many stories about this period of courtship—from both my mother and father—and they seemed to have gone about meeting the opposite sex in similar fashion: group dating.

My father had his own sizable crew of buddies, beginning with friends from his boyhood neighborhood of Avenue "I" in Flatbush, coupled with his considerable group of Army pals. As I understand their dating process, when one Tenney Girl, or conversely one of my father's band of brothers, had a girlfriend or even a date, he invited a buddy or two to join him on his next date where his lady friend would bring along dates for the gentlemen. Hence, my father met my mother on a blind date arranged by somebody in their social circle. Their first date was a Yale football game in New Haven, Connecticut.

"Yes," exclaimed my mother when I asked her about it, "and Columbia won on a field goal at the last second. I remember! The kicker's name was Jablonski and he lived at the bottom of the hill from us in Worcester."

New Haven seemed like a long way to go on a blind date for a guy from Brooklyn and a woman from the seashore of Long Island, but love conquers all, I suppose. Regardless, my parents had a great time. Soon my father asked my mother for a New Year's Eve date, but she replied that she had already promised that night to another.

"Well, how about a date for the following New Year's?" my father replied.

Mom said, "Yes," and the rest is romantic history. My parents married in January, 1948 during a New England blizzard, and I was born in the midst of the Baby Boom, in September, 1949.

I'm not sure my mother gave a great deal of thought regarding motherhood. My sense is that she was doing what everyone else was doing—certainly all of her Tenney sisters—which was to go on a blind date with the gang, have some fun, get a little serious with a guy you really liked, and then, well...? It wasn't very clear. The clarity that has come from the Women's Movement of the 1960s and the #MeToo Revolution had yet to happen, so for a woman in the 1940s, what options did she really have? Getting married and having a couple of babies seemed like a default position. Hence, I arrived on the scene, and my sister, Barbsie, followed in 1953. By the way, Sis is a Smithie, too—Class of '75, Dawes House.

For me, growing up in the suburbs of New York in the 1950s and 1960s also included the Tenney Girls. Besides visiting the Doxsees, my family and I went sailing with Barb Treml and her husband, George Buck. First, we sailed aboard *Trumpeter I*," a good-sized sailboat called a yawl, and I learned a lot about sailing from Mr. Buck, such as how to tie a cleat hitch or the difference between a rope and a sheet. In addition, I was impressed knowing that this craft was named after the destroyer Mr. Buck had skippered in the Navy during WWII. Later, as the Bucks' fortunes grew, we sailed aboard Trumpeter II, a 56-foot ketch.

My favorite Tenney Girl was Kay Reese, who became an agent for professional photographers in New York City. Kay was also the black sheep of the Tenney clan because in 1943 she took $40 of her scholarship money and purchased private flying lessons, a decision my mother never forgave nor forgot. Also, Kay missed the last few months of senior year—a man was rumored to be involved—so she missed graduation in 1946. But I loved Kay, and she was the first person to whom I ever showed my writing.

I remember her feedback, too. She typed me a little note—the usual form of correspondence in the days before emails and computers—and said that my stories were some of the worst-written missives she had ever read. But, later, she added a handwritten note at the bottom—penned in fountain ink—to say that there was something about my stories that had merit, for she was still thinking about them hours later. That carried great weight with me and sealed my fondness for her.

I'm pleased to see that Tenney House still lives. Since I wasn't sure how to spell Tenney House when I began writing this essay, I went to the Smith College website and read about the history of this place that has played such a large part in my mother's life and mine.

It seems very fitting that Tenney House is still home to 14 Smithies and now specializes in vegetarian cooking. I was particularly struck by the quote that each student in Tenney House is a "good cook by the time they leave." That was not the case for my mother, for she never really invested in domesticity.

Also fitting, I read that Tenney House is situated across the street from the home of the Smith College president, and I'm sure my mother reveled in living that close to influence. At her core, my mother was a woman who yearned for power. She was certainly the Boss of the Family, but she lived as a traditional suburban housewife. Despite all that Smith and Tenney House gave her, she did not rule the world.

But I got a dynamic mother who busted my *tuchus* nearly every day of my life.

Such may be one of the conundrums for my mother and her Tenney sisters—how do they feel about the lives they have lived? Perhaps one day, we'll learn of their inner journey—from graduation in 1946 to the World of Work, swirling through the suburbs of the 1950s and 1960s with expectations that others showered upon them. Then struggling in the 1970s and 1980s as their children grew up and defied much of their advice. Then facing loneliness and physical decline in their later years.... Were they content?

What I do know is that my mother and her Tenney sisters began a serious discussion about their health in the 1990s as their bodies manifested the obvious frailties of age. One day out of the blue, my mother announced that the Tenney Girls were discussing the notion of buying a residence where they could all live for mutual support, medical care, and camaraderie. It would be like Tenney House II—a self-directed, assisted-living residence for all these ladies who still wanted to be close to each other.

However, a few weeks later my mother manifested a look of true surprise and a ton of disappointment when she announced that *all* the husbands of the other Tenney Girls had shot down the idea of Tenney House II.

Not only was I sad for my mom, I was wistful. Tenney II would have been a kick-ass place to go for Thanksgiving, Chanukah, or Christmas.

This story would not be complete without a bow to the ladies my mother loved. The Tenney Girls of 1946 are: Marion Bronson (Bron) Strahan, Barbara (Barb) Treml Buck Stenard, Kay Powell Daub, Ruth Wood Pardoe, Irene LaPan Moss, Helen Sanger, Elsie Taylor Conly, Ruth Kraeling Day, Florence "Morely" Louden, and of course, Olveria Frances Zizis ("ZZ") Smith.

Lastly, Mom penned a brief memoir of her Tenney days, as below:

> Tenney House, home during our college years, offered a unique living experience. We were a unit unto ourselves. With a system of rotating pairs, the entire house was maintained completely—including the preparation of meals—by a total of 16 girls: two sophomores, four juniors, and 10 seniors. It was perhaps the cohesiveness of working and studying together that has enriched our friendships with each other through the years.

Immediately after college, four of us found employment in New York City. Since no apartments were available after World War II, Irene LaPan's parents graciously opened their doors to us in Point Lookout, Long Island. How we looked forward to a swim in the Atlantic after a hot day in the Big Apple!

Since 1946, countless mini-reunions have taken place among our housemates. Glowing hearths and savory culinary meals have welcomed us wherever and whenever we have met.

For our climatic 50th reunion, Ruth Wood Pardoe will again hostess all of us Tenneyites at her hilltop farm in Huntington (Massachusetts), appropriately named, "Joy Hill." The cooperative spirit lives on.

Knights have come a-riding to steal us maids away, but on this firm foundation our Tenney will always stay.

Note 1: In the spring of 2022, I returned to New York to join with my sister and care for our mom, who was failing health-wise at 97 years of age. At that time, I thought she was the last Tenney Girl of 1946 still alive. As she faded toward death, my sister Barbsie and I found the courage to talk to Mom about her inevitable passing, and not surprisingly she proclaimed: "I'm not afraid of dying. It's what happens after that, that has me concerned."

In response, Sis and I told her stories about Near-Death Experiences, especially the ones where the departed are greeted by loved ones and cherished friends. I even told Mom that she might be met by a coterie of Tenney Girls, and that heaven could feel like Tenney House II.

"Hmmmm," was all she could say.

Note 2: Mom passed away on July 14, 2022. When I called her "Tenney List" to deliver the news, I was surprised to hear from the daughter of Marion Bronson Strahan that her mother, "Bron," was still alive. However, several weeks later,

Ms. Strahan called to say that her mother had passed away, as well. So, all the Tenney Girls are gone, as far as I know.

Note 3: As mom declined, my sister and I would read aloud to her from books that reflected her life in Worcester or New York. One book dealt with young women from Worcester my mother remembered, which triggered Google searches for more information on these ladies and their friends. In that process, my sister found a "lost" Tenney Girl, Alice Gilman. Alice had befriended my mother in her first year at Tenney House, and had tutored her in science and mathematics. Alice left Tenney House in 1944 to marry her high-school sweetheart who was shipping out to Navy duty in the Pacific, but she left my mom with many warm and precious memories.

44

A Last, Great Lesson from my Father
Alan W. Smith, July 18, 1916-January 20, 2007

My father died as he lived—no muss, no fuss. He lived a simple, straightforward life, with little drama at the end, dying quietly hours after a heart attack.

But by simple I do not mean he was a simple man; far from it. Rather, he loved life in a simple way. He was a rare man, one who truly loved living, especially those moments of good company, family times, or swimming at his favorite summer spot on Squam Lake in New Hampshire. He understood nuance, but rarely practiced it. What you saw was what you got.

As for the details of my father's passing, it began innocently. On a Friday afternoon he announced that he wasn't feeling well and, although 90 years old and somewhat frail, he was in reasonably good health. Therefore, he and my mother planned to go on their regular Friday night dinner with my surrogate brother, Richard, my best friend in the old days and someone my parents had adopted when his parents had passed away. By the time Richard had arrived for their dinner date, Dad was nauseous, weak, and having chest pains. So, instead of driving to their favorite Italian restaurant, Umberto's, Richard raced to St. Francis Hospital. That night Dad received three stents to open blocked arteries, but by morning he was gone. Ironically, he died in the very hospital where my sister Barbsie had been saved 50 years earlier.

As a father, he was a mixed bag. He had trouble embracing my spiritually or creative passions, but he was certainly a generous and dependable man. Looking back, I see much that I cherish about the guy.

Dad was one of the regular drivers to Camp Wauwepex, taking me and a car full of Boy Scouts from Troop 166 on our monthly camping trips. At home, he was always ready to throw the ball around, and he surprised everyone at his 90th birthday when BJ asked him what his greatest experience was in his nine decades of life. "Being a Little League coach," he replied immediately.

It shocked us because he was supposed to say, "Being married to Fran," my mother, but he didn't. That was Dad. As proof, he wore his Garden City Babe Ruth League coach's hat nearly every day for 40 years. It's probably the one piece of clothing he never lost or misplaced. At his funeral viewing, I even saw *two* pictures of him wearing it.

I remember so sweetly how he put me to bed every night, giving me "back-squatches" as he ran his fingertips up and down my back and told me stories about his life—mostly his memories of WWII, but also the tales of his "chums" back on Avenue "I" in Brooklyn, playing street hockey or touch football.

Those moments continued in his last years as we sat around the kitchen table eating peach ice cream late at night after Mom had gone to bed. His stories would include his Sunday afternoons in Brussels in 1945 with his Aunt Alice and cousin Marthe, visiting from his Army base in Fontaine L'Eveque. Or his trip to Yellowstone National Park in 1939 with his cousin Donald, when gas was $.08 cents a gallon and they busted an axle in Illinois.

I benefited from his generosity, particularly during my efforts to develop a performing career. My move to Nashville was funded by Dad, who pumped over 10 grand into that effort, a gift all that much sweeter knowing how he had changed to become closer to me. I had changed, too. I no longer hoped he would engage me in deep conversations about the meaning of life or wrestle with the problems of the world. Rather, I accepted him as he was.

Now that he is gone, it's obvious to me that he was always around when I was a kid. Immediately after he passed, my sister and I realized it was the first time dad hadn't been a daily presence in our lives since 1960 when he went on a three-day business trip to Fond Du Lac, Wisconsin.

Yet, he wasn't a homebody, at least in the strict sense. He traveled with mom to Japan and all through Europe, from the Arctic Circle to Rome. But he enjoyed home best, especially summer evenings on the porch with family, barbecuing sirloin steaks, or going for a swim at the Garden City pool.

Yes, he is gone. Yet, his leaving has taught me one more powerful truth. He's gifted me one last time, from beyond the grave, if you will.

When I looked at his body at the wake, it was clear to me that his spirit was gone. I could see the essence that had made him who he was, had left. That awareness tells me that life is bigger than our bodies or what we experience in this human life. Our spirits are so powerful that when they leave the body, they are *required* to leave this plane of existence and go to another realm, one that is equal to its beauty and power.

Thanks, Dad.

45

Remembering Marty
Learning to drink beer, shoot pool, and date women

Marty was my best friend during our college days. We did a lot of things together, such as camping and taking regular trips to Florida to go shell collecting. We worked together at Boy Scout camp, too, and I later discovered we even had sex with some of the same women.

But Marty dropped off my radar screen after he got married in the 1970s and went to live in Florida. I hadn't talked with him for about 30 years until recently, when I called to get the number of an old girlfriend. Surprisingly, Marty died just a few weeks later of complications during surgery. He was 67.

Marty was a mixed bag. He was a good friend on one hand and a cold fish on the other, which is why I faded from his life.

I had met Marty at Camp Wauwepex in 1969. He was fresh from Florida and attending college at Hofstra University. Over the next three years we circled in each other's orbit, and eventually grew to be friends. After Wauwepex, I followed him to Hofstra where we became best friends.

One year, he lived in my dorm room until the school administration kicked him out for being a freeloader. But we had a lot of good times—smoking pot together, hanging out with the guys on our floor, and walking the sands of Jones Beach.

Fundamentally, Marty taught me how to be a guy's guy, like drinking beer, shooting pool, and courting women. In particular, he showed me the intricacies of 8-ball—how to make a cue ball curve or hop over another ball. More importantly, Marty helped me find the courage to ask a woman for a date. Later, he counseled me on how to keep a romance functioning, such as reminding me to give my girlfriend a Christmas present.

Marty also once convinced me to let him have sex with that girlfriend, to which she agreed. Afterward, the whole affair didn't sit right with me, and I attempted to apologize. Not surprisingly, she wanted nothing to do with me.

She was a gal that I had met during the time Marty and I traveled to Smith College on many weekends to hang with my sister. Over time, Marty and I dated a bunch of Sis' housemates. We also traveled to Frenchtown, New Jersey, an idyllic spot along the Delaware River, to visit with some friends of mine who were trance channelers and palm readers.

But in many ways Marty and I were like Mutt and Jeff. He was a traditionally masculine guy in most ways, and I was a New Age hippie-dreamer. But we were both isolated and lonely, and we loved one thing with a passion—Mother Nature.

One summer, we worked 16 weeks at Wauwepex. First it was "pre-camp," a small, specialized crew who worked with the Ranger to prepare the infrastructure for the arrival of the full camp staff, who in turn prepared the place for the kids.

The actual summer camp was eight weeks long, and that one summer we also closed down the place when the campers left, after which we worked on a week-long BSA fund-raiser. In essence, we both wanted to be away from our parents, so we were grateful for a May-to-September stretch under canvas with the Scouts.

Ironically, Marty had come north from Florida to reconnect with his father, a guy named Martin, Sr., whom I found to be a hard man to like. I only spoke with Martin Sr. a few times and found him sullen, tight-fisted, and angry. But Marty wanted family desperately, and had moved north to be with his dad.

Marty's mother had dumped him as a kid, and since she and Martin Sr. had already divorced, Marty lived with his grandparents in Miami. There he wandered the beaches and collected sea shells. As an adult, his collection grew to become world class. But Marty had a tough time gathering love to his bosom.

During our time together Marty tried to reconnect with his mother, and in 1970 we traveled to her new home in Maryland for Thanksgiving where we met her new husband.

The next year they relocated to Boca Raton, and Marty and I visited them again over our spring break. They all seemed to have a decent time together, but it was not an overly warm reunion. I would call it pleasant, and certainly not what Marty was craving.

Marty even spent time with his grandparents again, and I accompanied him to their home for a week or so. But they were elderly and on their last legs, headed shortly to a senior-living facility. In fact, Marty and I spent most of the time cleaning out *schmutz* from their kitchen cabinets, bathrooms, and cubbyholes.

With his own family a dead-end, Marty turned on the romantic burners and dreamed of starting his own. Marty became a joke—he usually proposed marriage to any woman that he dated more than twice. I constantly ribbed him about his "fiancé of the week."

Oddly, his real marriage developed under very spiritual circumstances. During one of our trips to Frenchtown, we participated in a séance with a "high-level spirit" who came to us through the auspices of our channeling friends, Carol and Roy. This spirit caused a tizzy because it told Marty that he would be married that year, and to a woman whom he already knew.

"Yikes!" we exclaimed, and gathered around Marty to query him on whom the lucky lady might be.

For the next month Marty puzzled whom he might marry — Rae, the gal from Hawaii who was my sister's first roommate and Marty's first Smithie love? Nope. Jennifer, her best friend? Nope. The cutie from his Hofstra English class that we still saw on campus? Nada.

After a month or so, we forgot about Marty's marital mystery and got ready for another trip to Florida. We stayed with his grandparents again, who were always glad to see him. After we arrived, they casually mentioned that they had met an old friend of Marty's in a grocery store, who had told them that another wayward stranger from Up North, Julie, was also visiting the old neighborhood.

"Wow, old Julie. We should call her, Bruce. She'd be fun to hang out with," Marty called out.

Julie was a friend from high school with whom Marty had worked at Woolworth's about 10 years prior. Marty called her parents' home and spoke with Julie's father, who invited us to join a family BBQ already in progress. Julie was there, along with a few of her friends from her new neighborhood in Boston.

I still remember the joyous scene at Julie's family home — drinking some kind of beer with a blue label that I had never seen before and hearing Julie's father cracking jokes and telling stories. Later, Julie and her Boston friends joined Marty and me for a walk along the beach.

About 10 minutes into our stroll, I stopped and turned around. Marty and Julie were about 75 feet behind us, smooching.

The rest is romantic history, and I was Marty's best man at their wedding that summer. By then, Marty had moved in with Julie, and I had begun hitchhiking regularly to see them.

Eventually, Julie got a teaching job in Florida and resigned her position in Boston. Once they headed south, I didn't see them for about 10 years. But in the fall of 1982, I called Marty and told him I was coming to Florida on business. Since I had last seen them I had started a beachcleaning business in New York, and I was looking to expand my operations into the Sunshine State, at least for the winter time.

Marty welcomed me and helped me get settled with old friends who operated a lobster business out of Boca Raton and had an apartment to rent. Plus, they had space for me to park my beachcleaning equipment.

I spent four months in Boca. During that time my own lady, BJ, joined me for a long weekend once a month. On her first visit we had dinner with Marty and Julie, and we had a good time. After I put BJ on a plane back to New York, I stopped by Marty and Julie's and asked them what they thought of her.

"Oh, she's great!" exclaimed Julie. "I really loved her."

Marty slid deeply into his lounger and mumbled something about BJ not being his cup of tea.

"What do you mean," I asked. "You didn't like BJ?"

"No, not really," he replied. "Sorry, I know you really like her."

"Marty, if we're going to have a real friendship like you always said we were going to have for our entire lives—then I need to be able to trust you and to talk to you about things that really matter to me," I said firmly.

"Okay, so what do you want?" he replied a bit too sarcastically for my taste. "You want me to say that I like your girlfriend? Well, I'm not too crazy about her. That's the truth. Isn't that what you want, the truth?"

"That's not the point, Marty. At least you're honest with me on that. Yeah, I'm disappointed that you don't like her much, but there are other things that I need to cleanup with you. Like the acid trip when you walked away from me when I was hurting, and the wacky phone call thing when I was going crazy at Hofstra. Or the wild stuff you told me about your life in Florida, growing up. I need you to be straight with me. Did you really hit a home run off of Tom Seaver as a minor leaguer for the Yankees? Or is that just bullshit? Or how about the time you said you shot an arrow 250 yards and hit the bullseye at that Boy Scout camp in Plainfield, New Jersey. Is that bullshit, too?"

"What are you so hung up on?" Marty countered. "I never said that I hit a home run off of anybody."

"Of course you did. Don't you remember that night we were sitting around at Wauwepex during pre-camp?" I argued.

"No, I don't remember it," Marty snorted.

"So, I suppose you also don't remember you telling me that you hit the target at 250 yards when you got your Archery merit badge?"

"Arggh," Marty growled.

"See, that's my point, Marty. I don't need you to hit home runs or archery targets. I just need you to be honest with me and care about me. I want to be able to trust you, and right now I don't think I can."

Marty looked very uncomfortable, and I knew the conversation wasn't going any further.

"Well, just think about it," I said. Soon I made my goodbyes, and left.

Two months later, BJ came down for New Year's Eve. We had dinner again with Marty and Julie, and it was pleasant enough, even though Marty and I had not resumed our discussion.

The next day, BJ and I went to the movies. When we came out of the theater my pickup truck was missing. I called Marty. He came right over, picked us up, and drove us all over Palm Beach County looking for it. I knew it was a fruitless effort, but I had to do something. Nevertheless, the truck was gone. I had to assume it was stolen and I would have to buy a new one.

With that realization I decided to throw in the towel on my Florida beachcleaning operation. My father had gifted me $5,000 for Christmas—"no strings attached"—and I used that money to buy a new pickup. Within days I had loaded up my beachcleaning equipment, and with BJ's daughter, Laura, I headed back to Long Island.

I didn't speak with Marty until I had another Sandsifter job in Florida—this time picking rocks at an equine training facility. I called him while I was in Florida, but we didn't meet and Marty sounded very distant on the phone.

I was done.

Thirty years went by without any contact. However, in 2012 a friend of mine, Cate Montana, wrote a book about being a woman in a man's world. It's called *Unearthing Venus*, her tale of maintaining her femininity while working as a top-notch videographer in the male-dominated world of sports television.

As a prelude to those experiences, Cate wrote a stirring account of a date rape she experienced in college. It reminded me of a comparable and troubling evening I had had many years earlier with a friend of Julie's—back when she and Marty were just getting together and I was with them often.

I called Marty to see if he and Julie remembered my date's name, because I wanted to apologize for my aggressive behavior back in the day. Marty picked up on the first ring.

"I thought I should answer this when I saw the caller ID," he said. He was pleasant, but not overly enthused to hear from me. I explained the nature of my call.

"Well, I don't remember the girl exactly, but I think her name was Theresa."

"Yeah, that's it!" I exclaimed.

"Well, I don't have her number, but I can give you Julie's. We're divorced."

"Wow, divorced."

"Yup, and it was horrible. She was a real bitch. She got the house and took me for everything she could get. You wouldn't believe how mean she got," Marty explained.

Marty continued ranting, and I realized he wanted me to join him in a Hate Fest. I declined, as I knew Julie was a decent woman and Marty was the guy with issues. I paused for a few minutes and allowed Marty get rid of his bile. Then I refocused him on giving me Julie's number. It was the last time I ever spoke with Marty.

When I called Julie, we had a wonderful reunion. I explained my quest to do right by my old fling, and Julie neither laughed nor scolded me. She offered to pass my message of conciliation to Theresa, and then we talked about our lives.

I told her of my 20 years with Ramtha, and leaving BJ after 14 years of living together.

I also told her of my difficulties with Marty, and she commiserated. She also added her own complaints, such as Marty's womanizing. Julie told me that Marty had sexually hit upon Theresa just a few years before. That tidbit loosened my lips and I told her about two other girlfriends of mine that I knew Marty had slept with.

That was Marty—good times and really lousy ones.

Julie called a few weeks later to tell me that she had passed on my apology to Theresa.

She gave me a second call two months later to tell me that Marty had died. He had succumbed to complications during a supposedly routine gall bladder surgery.

Julie was distraught, which surprised me since they had been divorced for over 10 years. In contrast, I was calm. I knew that Marty was not a happy man, at least in his deep places. Yes, he'd given many people a lot of joy, and I hear that his grandkids loved him and he was a great dad to his second wife's kids. But Marty's anger continued past his death when his widow forbade Julie from attending the funeral. That's classic Marty: *I can't love you if you don't hate the people I do.*

This behavior has to stop. I'm writing this story to show how a best friend can become a ghost. I don't blame Marty—and I thank him for befriending me when I was adrift—but I do kick his ass in the Great Beyond to get his act together now. Maybe he can make an intervention and convince his widow to do the right thing. Let the people who have loved him grieve their loss together.

Isn't that all we really want from life? To laugh and cry together? To get pissed off at the people who hurt us, and then find a way to forgive them? Well, I'll go first.

Marty, I forgive you.

46

On Becoming a Presidential Candidate
My transformation into greatness

The seed of my decision to seek the office of president of the United States germinated in the quiet moments following a retreat at RSE in the spring of 2003. Ramtha had extolled us to "become great," and afterward I became very ill with recurring fevers, bronchial congestion, and unrelenting fatigue. It laid me flat in my bed for weeks. I was unable to do my usual power-breath exercises in the morning and didn't have the energy to focus on mind-over-matter issues like healing myself. Rather, I struggled to sit up. When I did, I played endless rounds of solitaire while listening to jazz on the radio. When that exhausted me, I laid back on the pillows or ate gallons of Breyer's peach ice cream.

I was able, however, to read a few hours each day, and I slowly absorbed the novel, *The Nine Faces of Christ*. I felt like I was reading a training manual for God-Realization. I identified completely with Jeshua Ben Joseph—the Aramaic name for Jesus Christ—particularly his 46 days in the Persian wilderness. There, reportedly, he experienced a physical transformation through an illness similar to mine—a feverish malaise—that fostered a realignment of his molecular structure and molded his body into a state ready for a higher consciousness. Then, from the wilderness of my Eatonville sickbed, I briefly heard a voice that reassuringly said: *Don't worry. Just weather the storm.* I knew intuitively I was changing, transforming in order to become greater. But to what, specifically, I had no clue.

The next month, Ramtha called another event, a two-night affair. I knew intuitively that I had to be there, so I whipped out my near-maxed credit card and dragged my feverish and hallucinating body to school.

Ramtha spoke about being active in society, and finding our greatness within — challenging us to become dynamic forces in the world. He spoke extensively of Henry VIII and his daughter Elizabeth I, and how they had changed England for the better, setting the stage for the development of our American democracy.

At first, I took his statements more broadly and pondered: *How do I use these teachings in my life? Do I serve my own self-interest, or do I serve others?* I felt I wanted to serve humanity, and had often done so in the past, as in my work as a recreation therapist. After St. Peter's, I had spent another year as a youth counselor for a Tacoma-based community health organization, specializing in the treatment of teenaged male sexual offenders.

On the way home that night, my teacher's call to greatness struck home. I remembered Washington's governor, Gary Locke, was not going to seek re-election. Then, a kernel of thought just popped into my head, *Why not run for governor?*

I became electrified. *Yes! What a great idea!*

I buzzed with ecstasy as my mind flooded with ideas: *I can form a transportation district for the Puget Sound area and erase the traffic jams — bypassing eastern Washington's conservative Republican opposition to the taxes needed to get western Washington rolling again. I can turn the schools into wonderful places of mentored, cooperative education instead of fact-factories that have 30% drop-out rates, and high school grads who read at a first-grade level. Yippee!*

As I stopped for a red light in downtown Yelm, a second thought popped into my head: *Why not run for president of the United States?*

YEAH! I felt more energy flow into my body; more excitement, more buzz and tingle, more euphoria. "YES!" I said out loud. "Why not? Of course, yes!"

I buzzed the entire way home. When I got into bed, I trembled with such excitement I couldn't sleep. I could only lay flat, seemingly levitating inches above the mattress. I don't remember covering myself with blankets, and I pulsated all night.

Thoughts poured into me about what I could do—how things could be different for this country. No travesties like Iraq. No obscenities like the Patriot Act. No regressive thinking. No neo-conservative, reactionary, militaristic power-tripping. Honest CEOs. No Enron scandals. Healthcare for all. A new consciousness where everyone knows that God is within, and acts accordingly. Helping people learn how to heal themselves. A better balance with Mother Nature with no more clear-cuts and piles of timber slash and stumps. *That* world looked beautiful, and I felt great.

Birds started chirping as the sun came up, and a voice in my head said: *You'd better get some sleep, you've been up all night. You're sick, you know.* I turned over and slept until 2 p.m.

The presidential dream faded after that, however. I didn't make any focus cards on it, nor did I give it much attention during my morning meditations. Too sick and too broke to go to the next retreat at school, I turned my attention to returning to work as a union stagehand.

My first call back at work was a carpentry gig at the Seattle Opera Shop in Renton, WA. *It sure is a tough way to get back in the saddle...those shops are the dirtiest places in the world.* But I swirled my arms and spun my energy bands when no one was looking, and did some power-breathing in the washroom during breaks to build my energy. I also made $1,400 for the week, which helped my energy and attitude immensely.

Throughout the summer I received additional union calls. I rebuilt my physical health and finances, which was important since I had already asked my parents for $1,000 when I had been sick. By the time the next retreat came around in late July, I was ready.

Not on the first day and not on the second day, but I think on the third day my presidential dream came back. I had placed a card on our focus field titled: "I Have Never Been Afraid of My Power."

That card dealt with a limitation I had felt ever since I was 10 years old. At that time I had freaked out over hitting a home run in a little League game and, ever since, been a guy with lots of potential and only an occasional glimpse of greatness, like being the *runner-up* in the 1997 National Storyteller-of-the-Year competition. Simply, I felt I had never fully accepted my power, nor experienced it.

Wanting to address that fear I made a focus card that said, "I Swing Away." Surprisingly, while walking the focus field my mind shifted from regaining my power as a 10-year-old Little Leaguer to envisioning being president of the United States. When that happened, I left the field and made another card: "I Have Always Been president of the United States." However, when I considered placing it on the fence in the field, I was too scared to put it up and let the world see. Instead, I put it in my note book and focused on it privately, slowly nursing the dream forward into reality.

Not that day and maybe not the next, but definitely by the third day I told my retreat partner, Toni Earles—the bus driver—what I was doing.

"I'm focusing on being president of the United States."

"Really?"

"Yes."

"Cool."

"Yes, it is cool."

That was the extent of my first presidential announcement. As I've described earlier, Toni and I continued to talk about my presidential dream, and when I left the retreat I focused on it extensively. I also envisioned that I won the lottery in every state, running the table so to speak, as I crossed the country campaigning. As a result, I gathered the money I needed, along with the recognition that I was a legitimate candidate who possessed a great mind.

However, a voice inside reminded me: *Don't tie the two dreams together. You don't have to win the lottery to be president.* I listened and agreed somewhat, as I continued to link the two together silently.

After several weeks of focus and no lottery winnings, I lost heart. I stopped focusing on becoming president. In fact, I didn't think of it at all when I began my next retreat in September, 2003.

Again, not on the first day and probably not on the second day, but definitely by the third day my presidential dream came forward yet again. This time I made a new card and placed it on the fence surrounding the focus field. All through the retreat I focused intensely on my refined vision: "I Have Always Been President of the United States." I walked as president, letting the realization sink in that everyone I passed comprised the citizenry for whom I would have responsibility. I absorbed the fact that I had a duty to them — to care for them and always act in their best interest. It was a profound and sobering realization.

My quiet meditations were filled with new thoughts, too, with more ideas about Iraq and an immediate withdrawal of US military forces. I crafted a sojourn to Iraq to learn first-hand what needed to be done, which I called: "The Bus to Baghdad Program." During my free time, I drafted a "Salaam Aleichem" program, which would build bridges to the Islamic World via sports and interactive art groups. In other meditations I envisioned federal scholarships and cultural exchange programs for the best and the brightest of the Islamic World, so they could learn our ways, take our best ideas, and apply them in their own countries in ways that best suited them. Further, I reinstated the visas for the 12,000 Arabic men deported in the post 9/11 hysteria. In general, I devised plans to build new relationships with the Middle East so that mutual trust would be fostered, thereby reducing the need for military interventions.

One afternoon, I went into the woods along the southern edge of the campus and wrote down my ideas. They formed the basis of my presidential platform. However, my leading theme was helping America shift its consciousness. I wanted to change how America thinks. I wanted us to move away from the fear-based thinking that dominates our culture and evolve to a more mature, discerning consciousness. One that knows we are all expressions of the divine and that every American can envision the face of God in everyone, including the person they see when they look in the mirror.

Over time, those thoughts evolved into a simple political mantra: "The Greatest Good for the Greatest Number."

For the next six weeks, I actively campaigned to be president of the United States. I started to learn the ropes of what it would take. I contacted the secretaries of state in every state to learn their application procedures, and I was surprised to learn that the president actually has to run in 50 different elections. In truth, our national presidential election is a collection of 50 state contests.

I learned about federal financial campaign regulations and began to set up the proper checking accounts. I found people who could handle the monies that I knew would come.

I made flyers and designed a large sign for my pickup truck—the one I was planning to drive to New Hampshire in mid-October to begin a formal campaign in the country's initial primary.

Before then, though, I attended a weekend event that put the brakes on my presidential journey. There, I heard Ramtha talk about how best to apply one's dreams, and my take-away from that teaching was that until I could actually manifest physical changes with the power of my mind, all I really had were hopeful stories. True, I had a powerful dream and I was excited, but I couldn't actually manifest anything miraculous, like money or health.

Which is why I've suspended my candidacy until I can.

47

The Home Run
My fear of being powerful surfaces

When I hit that home run in a Little League baseball game, it was a solid shot that soared past the pitcher's head and arched over center field. I didn't watch its full flight because my father, who was also my coach, told me not to look at the ball after I hit it, but only to run to first base.

"When you're at first, turn your head and see where the ball has gone," he instructed. "If it's still in play and you think you can make it, run toward second base."

So when I reached first base and saw that the ball was still rolling away from the center fielder into the adjoining baseball field, I headed toward second. On the way, I saw the umpire running out from home plate and swinging his arm in the air, signaling a home run. *Okay, home run!*

In a daze I circled the bases and touched home plate. When I got to my team's bench, I got a bunch of back slaps from my teammates, and then a league official came over and presented me with a bat, a gift in recognition of what I had done.

I had never hit a home run before, nor did I know anyone who had, certainly not any 10-year-olds. I had heard in the prior year that a couple of the older boys, 11- and 12-year-olds, had hit home runs and got their bats, too, but I didn't know any of them personally.

On the bench my teammates described the home run in detail, relating how it was a high-arcing blast that flew over the center fielder's head and landed well past the chalk line circled in the outfield to signify a home run. My Little League was too poor to have outfield fences, or even a dedicated baseball field, so we played on diamonds laid over an elementary school's large grassy playground in a catty-corner fashion. As a result, our two center fields overlapped one another, and I had hit my home run into the other ballfield.

I soaked all of this in, but didn't rejoice in any dramatic way that I can remember. What I do recall is shrugging it off as if it was something that happened, but wasn't that big a deal. When the other team came to bat I took my regular position at second base, never thinking about the home run.

Two innings later, though, I came to bat again. Instead of swinging away, I bunted. It was an immediate, unconscious decision, one that I made without thinking. I tapped the ball weakly into foul territory.

"What are you doing?" my father shouted as he ran over to me.

"I figured they'd never think I'd bunt after hitting the home run," I replied.

"Well, they'd know now, so swing away. You're swinging good tonight, too. You hit that home run beautifully."

After my father left and the next pitch came in, I squared away to bunt, again, and hit the ball foul down the first-base line.

My father ran over a second time, now flustered and upset, maybe even angry. "What are you doing!?"

Once again, I explained my strategy. "Oh c'mon," my father exclaimed, "you're not going to fool anyone now, so swing away. Besides you have two strikes."

But even with the two strikes I bunted a third time, again fouling it off, which was an automatic out. I wasn't reproached by my teammates on the bench, but one did ask, "Why'd you bunt?"

"I thought I could fool 'em," I replied. My teammate shrugged and said nothing.

When the other team came to bat, I again returned to my position at second base and didn't think about the home run, nor the bunting.

Two innings later I came to bat a third time. Again, I tried bunting and my father was exasperated, running over to me at home plate and almost begging me to swing away.

"But Dad, they'll never think I'll continue to bunt!" I argued.

I had fouled off the first pitch, and on the second I was determined to bunt the ball fair. I gripped the barrel of the bat solidly with my right hand as I squared around to meet the pitch. But this time the ball hit my ring-finger—squishing it painfully. I screamed, dropped the bat, and held my stinging hand. My dad rushed over and escorted me back to the bench. After a few minutes of examination and seeing the swelling taking place, the assistant coach called another player to pinch-hit for me and I was removed from the game.

I could barely wiggle my fingers, and my father was uncertain what to do with me. "You should get an X-Ray, Alan," said one of the fathers, "just to make sure Bruce's finger isn't broken." Eventually, my father agreed and we trudged off to the car. But instead of driving to the local emergency room, my father drove home and picked up my mother, which reflected the odd nature of decisive thinking in my family. Then we headed to Nassau Hospital at the other end of town.

I sat in the back seat and whimpered. "Go ahead, Bruce," my mother intoned. "Cry if you want. It'll help with the pain." I continued to cry, but gradually the pain subsided. By the time I saw a doctor it didn't hurt much at all.

The X-Rays were negative, and the doc said my finger was just badly bruised. In a few days my finger was back to normal.

But in various ways this incident has stayed with me my entire life. First, I never hit another home run in my life and, in fact, only hit one fly ball to the outfield in Little League. But I hit lots of grounders and, since I ran faster than most kids, I could beat most throws from the infielders. In general, I was considered a good player with a batting average that was one of the highest on the team.

Occasionally, my father offered an interpretation on teenage growth patterns and uneven swings, which was a consolation in a veiled kind of way. Also, he worked on changing my batting stance and encouraged me to step into the ball like a slugger. "Swing like you're Mickey Mantle," he said, invoking my baseball hero.

It didn't work. I loved playing baseball, but I never hit well. After Little League I joined the local Babe Ruth League and memorably struck out five times in one game as the clean-up hitter, a role I was given because I was the tallest kid on the team. After that I was demoted to the bottom of the line-up.

In adulthood, I joined softball teams, and again hit meekly. At one point I started going to batting cages to practice, and even took a hitting lesson from a professional baseball player. Not much changed, but I did hit one soaring fly ball to left field in a pickup game between patients and staff at the Northport VA.

I started psychotherapy, too, and eventually joined RSE, so I was definitely exploring my inner world. Then one day in my 50s, during a deep meditation exploring the incompleteness of my life, I became awash with memories of the home run. I saw my blast and the subsequent decision to bunt repeatedly, and I realized it was the definitive essence of my life. I was afraid of being powerful.

Further, this fear was so unconscious it was like a quiet monster. It had no face nor a name, and it never spoke. It was like a fog that was always present.

I've come to learn that this fear has warped much of my life. I "bunt" everywhere, in all facets of my life. I have had a slew of jobs that have left me underpaid, undervalued, and unfulfilled, and when I focus on what I want, such as becoming a professional storyteller or an author, I've found that I sabotage my efforts. Mindlessly and unconsciously, my stage time as a storyteller oozes with snarky arrogance, or I spill coffee on the query envelope to an editor. One friend in the literary business told me that the publishing house where I had sent my promotional material thought the packet has been run over by a truck.

But that unbridled, unconscious derailment of my life is coming to an end. After that meditation I made focus cards that I've posted on my wall: "I Swing Away." "I Hit Home Runs." "I Am Not Afraid of My Power."

Over time I have made progress. I triple-check my letters to editors. I am mindful of my time on a stage. Increasingly, I view rejections from literary agents as more a form of critique than the obliteration of my soul. Fear is no longer a stranger popping into my life with surprise and sabotage, for I know it's been around for a long time.

I continue to meditate daily, becoming ever more mindful. I ask the fear in various ways: "Who are you? Where do you come from? Why are you so strong?"

I don't have much in the way of definitive answers, but I sense the source is a mix of fears—fear of failure, of being different, of being alone. I've come to realize that seeking what I most truly desire in life also makes me vulnerable—hence timid and clumsy—which diminishes my chances for success. It's hard to hit a home run when you're looking over your shoulder.

Becoming a storyteller is what I most passionately want to be. Yet the fear is still real and I can feel its presence. Sometimes it distorts me into a schitck-meister—a guy looking for a cheap laugh. Or a procrastinator. It took me days to build the courage to write this piece.

But I know I need to tell my story, and there is a growing hunger in the world for stories that are substantive and inspiring. I want to embrace that desire, and those audiences.

Along those lines, I sense that connection with others is what I long for most, and I've come to realize that my craving for real intimacy leads me to the company of folks who reside in the World of True Stories.

So, now I'm stepping up to the new home plates in my life, and when those pitches come in, I'm swinging away.

I hope you're swinging away in your life, too.

48

Peering into the In-Between
The mystical becomes visible

On occasion, I have been able to see what's in the "in-between." By that I mean I have glimpsed the energy forms and beings that live in the space between solid objects, such as in the air that exists between two people.

Of course, I learned how to do this from Ramtha. His guidance over many months of training was critical. The start was simple, but the learning didn't come easily.

At first it was tough. While sitting outside in an unused horse paddock, I looked at the sky, trying not to focus on the clouds or trees. Instead, I attempted to see the space between me and them. My eyes stung and I squinted fiercely to lessen the pain. However, after six day-long sessions over the course of a few months, I began to perceive some phenomena. First, there were orbs. I saw a round object suspended in the air, kind of like a ping-pong ball floating over the house of Ramtha's channel, JZ Knight. This orb fluttered downwards and circled back up into the air, its path forming a giant "J." Intriguingly, the orb flickered in and out of view as it moved, as if an illuminating light within it was being turned on and off every half second or so.

Excited, I tried to see more but nothing came. The next day I was back on our little field, and this time I was facing toward a forest of evergreen trees. Again, I saw an orb, but it didn't move and I was able to perceive it for only a moment. Then I saw a second orb, but it looked misshapen, a crescent-shaped object that blinked out before I could see it clearly or observe it for long.

At the same time, staff members from the school were photographing the skies around us to see if anything would show up on their digital cameras. They did. Their cameras had digital shutter speeds approaching 1/50,000th of a second, which was fast enough, apparently, to catch inter-dimensional beings or energy forms popping in and out of existence during their vibratory oscillations. It is my understanding that everything physical on the earthly plane vibrates in and out of physical reality, including our bodies, and these oscillations are something along the lines of 14 times a second. Too quick for us to perceive visually, so everything in our reality appears to be smooth and seamless. But it isn't. Therefore, to see the "in-between" we have to train our brains to perceive objects fluctuating at much higher speeds, and digital cameras can do that.

The orb phenomena recorded at RSE is extraordinary, and many pictures are available for public viewing. Oddly, though, most of the phenomena that I have seen have not been recorded by my school's photographers.

Over the next 18 months, I began to observe inter-dimensional phenomena on both regular and impromptu occasions. After an intense three-day manifestation workshop RSE, I came home and sat in my driveway to enjoy the stillness. Around midnight, I saw an amazing series of phenomena. First to appear were shimmery curtains of light that undulated across the sky between me and a grove of trees. These lights were bands of purple, blue, yellow, and red, much like miniature northern lights, but concentrated and very solid, not as shimmer-y as the Aurora Borealis.

My "light curtains" didn't last long in my perception—only a few seconds. But they reappeared a few more times in the next 20 minutes. Accompanying them were what I call the "Flying Vs," solid black objects that were much smaller than the curtains. The "Vs" opened and closed rhythmically and slowly as they moved across my vision, much like a bird flapping its wings. At first, I thought they might be bats flying through the night sky, but the "Vs" I saw flew more deliberately than the darting movements of bats.

Over the next few months, I saw these phenomena frequently while watching the nighttime sky.

During this time, I did a walking meditation along my driveway and saw a field of soft, tiny lights surrounding me, like a cloud of glitter. It was not a glow, *per se*, but more like a quiet emanation of light. It was similar to how light might reflect off leaves or the mist in the air when a light is shone upon it. But my glitter was all around me—omni-directional—and disappeared when my mind drifted from the trance state I was in. Although my skeptical mind searched for "reasonable" explanations and I tried to discern what light source from neighboring street lamps or homes might be causing a reflection, I saw none. Everything seemed to be tuned to my state of consciousness. When I was in a trance, I saw the glowing lights. When I wasn't, I didn't.

Later, I learned that many of my fellow students were also seeing glitter when they did their meditations.

But one illuminative phenomenon has only been observed by a handful of other people, something we call "spermy lights" or "the squigglies." These lights are a more pronounced version of the glitter, but seem to exist within a tube or tunnel that I do not perceive under normal conditions. The sensation is like looking down a large tube placed into a body of water to observe aquatic life more clearly. Through my tube-in-the-sky I could see squirming lights moving toward me rapidly.

So, there are really two interrelated phenomena here—the lights and the tube. These lights move directly toward me in a wiggly fashion and look like miniature tadpoles or spermatozoa. Hence, I call them "spermy lights." Additionally, these lights linger only for a split second before blinking out, but they illuminate back again in a kind of flux. Viewing this phenomenon at length, I've seen thousands of squiggly lights swimming toward me in an endless stream, so there seem to be a nearly infinite array of particles fluxing at any one time.

When my focus was strong, I could watch the spermy lights for long periods of time, certainly for many minutes, perhaps 15 or 20. When I was single-minded about watching them — and I had to be, because if my mind wandered they would disappear — I could watch them for so long that I got bored. On two occasions I remember thinking, *Okay, I've seen these lights, but what do I do with it? I'm still broke.*

Nevertheless, I did want to know what I was witnessing.

Fortunately, my "in-between" sessions were accompanied by many teachings from Ramtha on quantum physics, especially a unique phenomenon called Zero Point Energy (ZPE). This is a bizarre type of energy that is still active at Zero Point Kelvin, about 452 degrees below zero Celsius. At those temperatures light energy is static, electricity is frozen, and no other forms of traditional energy function.

But Zero Point Energy (ZPE) is observable and always pulsing. It seems to be a kind of energetic flux, where particles flip from positive to negative at rapid speeds, and this energy field is believed to exist everywhere. It is as if everything, including space, is filled with ZPE.

So perhaps my spermy lights are manifestations of ZPE.

Two years after I first saw the spermy lights, I glimpsed a fairy-like being during an evening's focus in my garden. I was endeavoring to see the spirits of the garden, particularly around the kale. After a short focus, a glow emanated around me and I saw a figure hovering about three feet away. The being possessed a masculine feel, and I've always thought of the entity as a "him." He was about 18 inches long, and positioned upright. He had two sets of wings attached to his back, similar to the configuration on a dragonfly. The wings were beating steadily, like a hummingbird's, but made no sound. Other than the movement of the wings, the being was motionless.

His dress struck me as unusual, too. He looked like a miniature Roman centurion, adorned with a tight-fitting but thick, leather tunic. He had similar protective clothing on his arms and legs. The look on his face was stern, which gave me the feeling that he was a guard on duty. Although it's easy to call him a fairy, he didn't look like the traditional image of Tinkerbell.

Also, I could only observe him out of the corner of my eye. When I turned my head to look at him straight-on, he disappeared from my perception, only returning when I resumed glancing at him sideways. I continued my observation for several minutes, then tried to communicate telepathically.

"Who are you?" I asked in thought, but received no reply. Still, I got a feeling that this moment was not the time for questioning, so I ceased asking.

The next night, I tried again to see my winged friend. I saw him briefly, but my focus was not strong and the encounter was over in a few seconds. I've never seen him again despite repeated efforts.

During this time, I also engaged in a candle focus. Similar to the fairy experience, I began to see a bright glow radiating in my peripheral vision. Again, when I turned to see what was shining so brightly, the phenomenon stopped. However, when I returned to a deep focus, the brilliant glow returned. I sensed I was seeing some kind of energy field around me when I entered a trance-like state, and it was reassuring knowing I was passing through a grand gateway into a deeper meditation.

Nevertheless, these experiences haunted me. *Even though I can see fairies, glitter, curtains of light, flying Vs, and the spermy things, what use is it in my regular life?* I had no answer, but accepted them as corollary phenomena as I engaged more passionately in my meditations to manifest what I did want in life—enough money to live comfortably, heal my body, and have meaningful relationships with others.

With this shift in intention, I experienced a transformation in my physical life. I became a full-time stagehand in theater, and I later became a newspaper reporter for a local weekly. I thoroughly loved these jobs, and I appreciated the regular monies I earned as well. During this time, I also observed another "inter-dimensional" phenomena, something I call "white mist."

I first saw this misty vapor after playing my guitar during a particularly satisfying jam. As I lay back in my chair, I noticed wisps of thin, white clouds emanating from my arms.

Condensation from sweat? The mist was reminiscent of seeing one's breath on a chilly night. But I was indoors, and it wasn't cold. Plus, I wasn't really sweating—I was more ablaze with passion. Further, I've seen the mist emanate from others. Vividly, I have seen white mist swirl off of the arms of other students at school after a session of power-breath meditation or trance-dancing. Again, I doubt that it is sweat condensing because the temperature in the arena after one of these sessions is plenty warm.

Plus, I've continued to see white mist lift from my body, especially my arms and shoulders, on numerous occasions, and when the phenomenon occurs, I smile. I know I'm engaging my soul's desires, and expressing myself deeply and authentically. That ability is perhaps the greatest gift I have received from Ramtha—learning how to dream my deepest dreams and having some tools, like meditation, to cope with any resulting anxieties.

Currently, my journey continues in the new direction of integrating what I've learned from Ramtha with my personal passions in life. I am writing and telling stories, and developing a career as a stage performer. Although my ability to manifest tangible objects like a $20 bill remains modest, I am proud of being able to peer into the in-between.

So, I offer my greetings to all those who have fluttered before my eyes, and I thank you for allowing me to see you. I wish you well on your journey, wherever and whatever you are.

49

Endings and Beginnings
Leaving Ramtha's School of Enlightenment

I ceased being an active student at RSE in 2009, and my decision to leave was not particularly dramatic. I had simply run out of money.

However, there was an underlying dynamic that steered me away from school besides the lack of funds. After two decades of trying to learn how to create my own reality, I still couldn't manifest much with the power of my mind. The thousand bucks I needed to attend my week-long retreats usually came from borrowing the money, hocking my car, or scrimping painfully for months to gather the necessary monies. But there was an even bigger issue. Did I really want to continue? I felt fatigued. Part of it was from the financial struggle, but there was more, although undefined.

My friend René was in the same boat. "I feel like I'm chasing the bus with a fist full of dollars in my hand, and I'm just *tired*," she said. "I'm just tired of chasing the bus to make everything happen in my life."

When she told me her feelings, a wave of exhaustion enveloped me. Not only was I tired of chasing the money, I was exhausted trying to make my life "remarkable," as Ramtha often extolled us to be. Everything borne of my dreams, like healing myself or levitating, seemed overwhelming. I felt like I needed to take a break, so I decided not to chase the RSE bus any longer.

Soon after that decision, my life fell apart. First, asthma attacks prevented me from working as a stagehand. Then, my teeth started falling out and I needed five of them yanked to prevent more infection. After that, I had a heart attack. Plus, I was impoverished and months behind on the rent. My health issues coupled with the despair of not being able to heal myself and pushed me into a deep depression. By the fall of 2012, there were days when I just couldn't get out of bed, and didn't. Sometimes I'd stay under the blankets for days. In those stupors I began thinking about jumping off the Tacoma Narrows Bridge, only stopping when I realized that if I actually killed myself, it would tear the heart out of my two nieces, both of whom were emotionally fragile and dealing with their own demons.

Even after my heart attack, my body still triggered lots of chest pains, which led to numerous runs to Good Samaritan hospital. Finally, one ER doc said, "Bruce, your problems aren't your heart. You need to see a psychotherapist and work on your life."

That stung like a slap in the face. Not only was I a former therapist, but I had been in therapy much of my adult life. In fact, I had received over 800 psychotherapy sessions. Now, I needed more? Yikes! But I took my doctor's referral and headed to MultiCare's Behavioral Health Clinic in downtown Puyallup, WA.

Soon I was seeing a therapist named Trista, who was a really sharp cookie. I began to dig into my despair. Working with Trista gave me the strength to begin writing a book based on my investigative reporting of the DB Cooper skyjacking. The result was the publication in 2016 of *DB Cooper and the FBI – A Case Study of America's Only Unsolved Skyjacking*.

While in therapy, I became liberated from RSE as I realized I had been living in a Ramtha bubble that I didn't even know existed. RSE had been my sanctuary for two decades—home to my friends, and a refuge from the criticisms of family and skeptics. It was the place where I had built my identity as a Christ-in-training. At RSE, I had focus and a schedule. I had high hopes and dreams. I had felt protected and purposeful in my quest to be God Realized—to walk on water, heal with a touch, and know the future.

Outside the bubble, I felt vulnerable, but I also felt clean, as if I were really on my own. I was going to find out exactly what constituted *me*. I smiled, realizing I was finally growing up. I was finally going to stand on my own two feet and be, if not God-Realized, then certainly a man.

I felt I was starting a new life; fortunately, I had Trista for support. I was taking all that I had learned—from Ramtha and 60-odd years of living—and creating a new life. Something bigger, grander, and more authentic began to arise within me. As the wise ones say: *When one door closes another one opens.*

I had to surrender my theater work due to my asthma, but my writings about being a stagehand earned me a full-time job in 2006, reporting for the *Dispatch* newspaper in Eatonville, WA. That gig lasted several years until the owners decided to retire. Shortly afterward I was out in the cold, again, as the new editors had no taste for my bold writing, nor my insistence on timely pay checks. When I left, I started my own on-line news magazine, *The Mountain News-WA*, which has been my journalistic platform ever since.

However, the *Mountain News* didn't make any money, and I had to sell my pickup truck because I didn't have the funds to keep it running. As a result, I didn't have any personal transportation for the first time in my life. I was living in the woods on six acres owned by a friend, but I was 12 miles from the nearest bus stop. I became dependent on others beyond any degree I had ever experienced before. I needed rides for everything—grocery shopping, laundry, or getting to doctors.

Fortunately, by 2012, I was 62, so I began collecting my social security, and that paid the rent. Then I qualified for food stamps, which kept me fed. Lastly, I qualified for full-scale Medicaid that arranged for Paratransit services so I could get a ride to the doctors. Plus, Mom agreed to pay for the dental bills that Medicaid didn't cover, so my teeth returned to good health.

My DB Cooper book garnered the attention of a few documentary film producers, and my appearance in several broadcasts helped sell a couple hundred books, all of which put a few bucks in my pocket.

Then, in the summer of 2017, I got pneumonia and was sick for two months. Much of the time I lay in bed, bored and restless. But I listened to NPR radio and heard numerous "Moth Story" podcasts. I was enthralled. These true, personal stories were the kinds of tales I had been longing to tell for 20 years since my first efforts at being a professional storyteller. Back in the 1990s, I had been a storyteller on KAOS-FM in Olympia, doing a weekly hour-long show. Then I did some storytelling for community access TV, which led to being selected as the 1998 National Storyteller of the Year—2nd Runner-up. This world of storytelling was more of a traditional form, filled with legends, myths, and yarns, and I had found it too "vanilla" for me.

So, hearing Moth stories reawakened my passions. When I recovered, I traveled to Moth open mics in Seattle. Getting there was epic, though. First, I had to ask a friend to drive me the 20 minutes to the bus stop in Spanaway, WA. There I got the #1 bus to Tacoma. After an hour's ride, I got off in downtown and walked a half mile to Sound Transit at the Tacoma Dome where I hopped on the express bus to Seattle. In the big city I had to take a #5 Metro bus to either the Fremont Abbey for one show, or the #49 bus to its sister stage at St. Mark's Cathedral.

Since the #1 bus shuts down at 10 p.m., I knew I wouldn't be able to get out of Seattle in time to make it home, so I had to arrange for an overnight in Seattle. The first night I was able to snag a bed with a friend in south Seattle, and on the second night I was able to rustle 30 bucks from my royalty check and pay for a bunk in the Green Tortoise youth hostel. The following day I reversed my trek, and had a second friend waiting for me at the #1 terminus. When I got home, I collapsed and slept for a day.

But I had gotten the ball rolling. At the open mics I made friends with other storytellers and learned of other venues, such as Fresh Ground Stories at the Olive Street Starbucks Coffee Shop. That has become my favorite place to tell, and is like a second home to me.

Then, in March 2018, my family sent me $2,500 out of the blue, saying," Go buy a car so you can take care of your life." I did. I bought a 1994 Toyota Camry, affectionately dubbed "The Red Rocket," from a local fellow in Eatonville, and then borrowed another $2,500 to pay for the insurance and repairs. Keeping my mind focused has been the key to getting through all the rough patches, and for me the mantra has been: "I tell my stories."

I've been zooming ever since.

50

Riding with the Orange Man
Corralling my judgments

As you've just learned, before I got the Red Rocket I took local buses to my storytelling gigs. Usually, I would take the aforementioned #1 bus to downtown Tacoma, where I would catch the express shuttle to Seattle.

One day, a portly man of about 50 boarded the #1 in Parkland, WA. He wore an orange cowboy hat, orange mittens, orange sneakers, and an orange sweatshirt that proclaimed: "Jesus is the Way!"

Oh, no, I thought, I'm about to ride with a whack-a-doodle.

As he walked down the aisle, I sunk down into my seat, breathed quietly, and hoped fervently that he would pass me by. However, the Orange Man plunked himself in the seat directly behind me, and I steeled myself for his Religious Assault.

But it never came. Rather, the Orange Man was silent. Peace reigned on the #1 bus as we rumbled through East Tacoma, chugging down Pacific Avenue toward downtown. Near the old Tacoma General Hospital, an older woman boarded who needed assistance. She had a wheeled-walker called a rollator, which had to be parked somewhere on the bus. So, the driver called back to us, "Can someone lift the handicap bench so she can put her walker there?"

I was the closest passenger, so I leaned over and slid my hands underneath the bench seat as I had seen others do on previous trips. But this was my first attempt, and I couldn't find the lever. An older gentleman nearby offered, "It's on the right side, by the driver."

I found it. It pulled easily and the seat lifted without a hitch. The Walker Lady secured her rig and sat adjacent to me. As we resumed our trip to Tacoma, the Orange Man leaned out of his seat toward me and said in a loud voice: "Jesus would be *so* proud of you."

"Thank you," I replied. "I love being a good Boy Scout."

The Orange Man continued. "Jesus wants us to help each other. That's what he teaches over and over." He proceeded with more Jesus-stuff, then took a breath. I figured I had to take command of the conversation or I was going to hear about Jesus for the remainder of my journey.

"So, I gotta ask you," I said to the Orange Man. "Why are you wearing so much orange?"

"Jesus wants the world to be colorful!" he replied with a big smile, "and I'm doing my part."

"You sure are, buddy!" I laughed.

"I have nine outfits," the Orange Man continued. "My favorite is my purple one because I was able to get a pair of really nice purple pants. I have a lot of trouble getting pants to match my outfits, so I have to buy a lot of women's clothes—the pants especially, because men's clothing doesn't include too many color choices."

I had never heard such a succinct fashion perspective from a guy who didn't have one iota of gayness about him. "Yeah, I can imagine that is a problem."

"Yeah, so I buy a lot of women's clothes, especially the pants, but they can be a hassle because the pockets are too small, and I can't get my hands into them—or they don't have any at all! It's a bummer."

At that point I realized that the Orange Man was wearing tan slacks, not orange. He must have been unable to find orange-colored trousers.

"I'm lucky," he continued. "I work at Goodwill and they're okay with my clothes. I've worked there for five years, too." The Orange Man proceeded to further describe his current fashion predicaments—in a loud voice—and with a side commentary on how Jesus was involved.

"I gotta get off soon," I interrupted. "I'm getting off at 25th Street."

"Oh, that's two more stops," the Orange Man joyfully announced.

As we approached my stop I headed toward the front door. Exiting, I turned and told my new friend, "I'll be keeping an eye out for that purple outfit. It sounds like a winner."

"Yeah, I even have a purple fur coat!"

Hearing that, I'm sure Jesus was laughing.

I know I was.

51

On Betrayal
Learning from old wounds

Betrayal spans a wide arc of human behavior, from the most basic "she's done me wrong" to complex manipulations that can destroy a person's life, like false accusations. Or harm even a country, as President Trump did through his role in the January 6, 2021 insurrection.

Betrayal can carry great weight, and I've encountered a few, especially through two marriages and divorces. But the keenest depths of betrayal, for me, involved my first girlfriend, Rachel.

We met during our first year in college, in September 1967. I was a freshman at Lehigh, and Rachel attended a small woman's college 60 miles away in Philadelphia. We were two oddballs who didn't fit in anywhere, and divine grace drew us together.

We reveled in exploring the world together — the streets and neighborhoods of Philadelphia, the rickety SEPTA trains, and historical sites, such as the Liberty Bell. She introduced me to the wonders of sweet-and-sour pork in a little eatery in Chinatown, and I taught her how to eat a hamburger with her hands, ditching the fork and knife from her European upbringing.

Rachel was quirky and had an odd history. She had been born in New Jersey, but was raised in Africa. She spent much of her childhood in the Belgian Congo; during its revolution in 1960 Rachel and her family had to flee in the middle of the night to nearby Rhodesia, which was still controlled by British colonialists.

After their escape, Rachel and her family resettled in Brussels, Belgium. That's where she went to high school, and where she was living when I met her. As a result, socially, she was more European than American. Besides hamburgers, she ate fried chicken with that damn fork and knife. Although she had lived on three continents, she thought going to Burger King was a super-duper treat!

The reason for such an unusual childhood, Rachel described, was due to the fact that her father worked as an executive for Arrow Shirts. Apparently, he was an important part of their African operation. At 18 I didn't question Rachel's explanation, but now it seems suspect.

Back then, we had the world to discover for ourselves. We were ecstatic in a deep, joyful way. We called it being "high on life," and the curious details of our parents' lives were never a topic of conversation.

Rachel spoke perfect French, and I loved her effervescent *Parisienne* charm. She would say, *"Oh, M'sieur Bruce,"* drawing out the "u" in a long, slow breath, "Bruuuuuuu…ce." I melted, and wrapped myself in her charm.

When Christmas vacation approached that first year of college, I prepared to head back home to New York, and Rachel to Brussels. Before leaving, Rachel gave me her address: 25 Avenue Air Marshal Cunningham. "Please write me," she implored. I did, but before she left I asked her about her unusual address.

"Why is your street named after an English guy? Why isn't it some French name, or Flemish? That's what they speak in Belgium, right?"

"It's a sign of respect. Air Marshal Cunningham was a British commander in the Royal Air Force during World War II, and the Belgians are very grateful to the Brits and the Americans for liberating them from the Nazis."

"Oh, okay."

I wrote a few times to Rachel in Brussels and was a little surprised that I didn't receive a letter in return. So, I was certainly eager to see her after our holiday vacation. However, our first phone call shocked me.

"Bruce, I can't see you anymore," she announced. "My father forbids it."

"Wha… Why not?"

"Because you're not Jewish."

"Yougottabekiddingme!"

"No, my family is adamant. My father's father is a rabbi, and my whole family is torn apart over my seeing you. I've told them how I feel about you, but it doesn't change anything."

I argued with her for over an hour, causing great consternation in my dorm because I was tying up the only phone for 20 guys. I told Rachel that I would marry her if that was what she needed to feel free from the grip of her family, but my proposal fell flat to the floor.

By the end of the conversation, I saw a glimmer of my old Rachel—the soulmate who connected so easily with me, the young woman who felt absolutely free and lived that freedom.

Hopeful, I called her the next evening, but we were back to square one.

"I just can't see you, Bruce. Please don't call me anymore," she said. "You're not Jewish, and that's just how it is. My father will not budge an inch."

That was it. I didn't see her and didn't call.

I suppose my broken heart was a testament to my first betrayal—a loss of a sweet love, the absence of a dear friend. Worse, though, is the deeper betrayal at the soul level. Rachel rejected our embrace of living a life free of social constraint.

She was choosing *not* to be "high on life." She was choosing *not* to fight for me, or to even find some means of compromise with her family. I was cut loose, pure and simple.

I was devastated. In a daze I walked for six hours in the rain, circumnavigating the vast base of Lehigh's South Mountain. I can still hear my feet sloshing in my shoes on every step.

However, a year later Rachel called.

"I'd like to see you," she said. "I'm getting married, and I'd like to see you to...oh, I'm not sure why. I guess, because I can somehow."

Rachel told me that she was marrying a friend of her family, some guy named Steve—Jewish of course—a rich lawyer who drove a red Corvette. I suppose his conventionality provided enough emotional cover for her to call me.

Regardless, any reason to see Rachel was good enough for me, so I hitched down to Philly.

We reconnected right away. We laughed, told stories, and enjoyed each other's company immensely. However, there were times when I went cold. Once, while walking down a street, I veered off to the opposite side of the roadway and walked alone for a block or two. I guess I was in shock over what was happening.

Something was rekindled, though. Rachel told me she was going to the Bahamas the next week for spring break with her roommate and her roommate's family. My spring vacation from Lehigh fell on the same week, so I told her I could meet her. *A week together in the Caribbean. WOW.*

Rachel gave me her address in Nassau—a fancy oceanfront condominium—but didn't discuss this plan with her roommate, apparently.

I hitched down to Florida and got a cheap flight to Nassau—29 bucks round-trip from Fort Lauderdale on a special student fare.

I arrived at the condo at 10 o'clock, and spoke with Rachel briefly, but was directed by the family matriarch to spend the night with her teenaged son, who had a whole wing of the house to himself. I was too tired to question the arrangements.

The next day, I cooked breakfast for everyone in the mother's wing, and endured an interrogation from the matriarch, who introduced herself as Rachel's "American Mother." Afterward, I rendezvoused with Rachel at the beach. Despite the enchanting turquoise greens and the deep azure blues of the Caribbean, my beach time with Rachel was short.

"You need to go, Bruce. You can't stay here," she said.

"Why not?"

"Oh, Bruce… you just don't understand."

I didn't.

I left the Bahamas and Rachel. Back at college a few weeks later, Rachel surprised me with a call, announcing that she had canceled her engagement. She was dropping out of school and returning to Europe, with a possible transfer to the University of Strasbourg in France. All of this, she said, was an attempt to find some psychological relief from her emotional confusion and torn loyalties. I hitched again, this time to JFK airport to see her off to Brussels.

When Rachel boarded her Sabena flight to Belgium, it was the last time I ever saw her — Gate 2 in the Pan Am building — and I remember it well. But through the decades I also began to understand what she had been trying to tell me.

First, I've come to appreciate how the pull of family can be so mighty. Plus, I've learned how deeply religious acculturation can penetrate, weaving into one's identity and forming a tapestry that supports a family's life. It's tough to shake. It's taken me 20-plus years in RSE to break free of my own Catholic indoctrinations and familial influences.

Nevertheless, I've never forgotten Rachel. Since I last saw her, I've learned a few things that have given me a broader perspective on her, too, especially her accounts of Africa. After 15 years as an investigative journalist, I believe I have a keener insight into what might have actually happened between Rachel and me, and why.

I doubt that her father worked as a business executive in the Belgian Congo. Rather, it is more plausible that he was a CIA operative, or more likely some kind of political agent looking to thwart the communist advances of the Congolese Revolution. I suspect his goal was to keep the minerals of Katanga Province flowing to the United States. Of course, he and his family had to flee when the bullets of the Congolese revolutionaries started flying. Finding eventual refuge in Brussels seemed a logical place to build a stable home, since Brussels is the headquarters of NATO and the center point of the European Union. It's an ideal place for an American undercover operative to park his wife and kids.

I doubt very much that Rachel's father was upset with his daughter dating a non-Jewish man. I believe it was a ruse to keep her—and himself—safe from unconventional and liberated fellows like me. If I was allowed into the family, I would never stop asking troubling questions, or be able to resist probing—hoping to discern—"What's really going on here?" I believe I was considered dangerous, along the lines of "loose lips sink ships." Blabbing my mouth in the wrong place at the wrong time could get Rachel's father killed. Hence, I had to be kept at arm's length, and my lack of Jewishness was just a convenient means of keeping me away.

But I haven't stayed put.

I've googled 25 Avenue Air Marshal Cunningham. The street does not exist with that exact spelling. However, I doubt it is a bogus address, as my letters were never returned to me by Belgian postal authorities. Rather, I think the real address is a CIA drop box for correspondence to field operatives and their families. I think Rachel got the letters—or at least her father did, and learned how serious our relationship was. The drop box worked perfectly from his point of view, and I doubt he ever gave his daughter the letters until he was sure she had formed emotional connections elsewhere.

As a result, I plan to visit Brussels and learn more of Rachel's truth. Besides investigating Avenue Cunningham, I'll peruse Belgium's famous outdoor *pommes frites* stands. There, I'll be looking for men and women eating hamburgers with their hands.

I might even find Rachel.

52

On Age
Savoring the journey

I remember President Eisenhower! I even remember his nickname, "Ike." I was born in 1949 and I love my age despite its vagaries of health. It has given me a delightful perspective on life, and especially on history. I remember a lot, in particular our wars. Not only Vietnam, but also the Korean War and its "flying boxcars" that used to soar over my childhood home in Garden City from their base at Mitchell Field.

Cultural changes, too. I remember seeing bathrooms in North Carolina that still had signs for "Colored" and "White" when I pulled off the highway in 1969 for a pee stop during a trip to Florida.

Simple things, too, like the introduction of ballpoint pens in 1959 when I was in 5th grade. Before then, everyone used fountain pens. We even had little inkwells cut into our wooden desktops to receive a small bottle of "Scripts" ink.

Of course, I remember the trivial. My first tank of gas as a newly licensed driver cost me $.29 a gallon. I also remember getting paid $2.50 per hour as a hospital aide and thinking it was a good deal.

All these remembrances give me a welcomed steadiness. Plus, age puts the sweetness of emotional maturity on my tongue, and any anxieties generated by today's headlines are softened by realizing that I've survived Nixon, JFK's assassination, and the dozens of American cities that burned when Martin Luther King, Jr. was killed.

But the biggest gift of age is seeing the evolution in my relationships. It's a splendid trajectory of change, acceptance, and love. BJ didn't talk to me for years after I left her in 1990 to join RSE. But now we're good friends and we treasure our 50-plus-year relationship.

Equally important, and perhaps more illustrative of age's benefits, has been my friendship with my buddies from Boy Scout camp. As described earlier, I had been part of a crew of provisional Scoutmasters for our Camp Wauwepex. These troops specialized in absorbing Scouts from home units that didn't have sufficient adult leadership for two weeks of camping. Wauwepex accommodated these Scouts by placing them in ad-hoc provisional troops, and I and my buddies — Bill, Geoff, Mick and Frank — were their leaders.

We loved that work, and we excelled at it. We were passionate about hiking and camping, swimming, and canoeing, and we knew plenty about nature and Indian lore. We embraced the sacredness of the woods, and reveled in its beauty. Our campsites were litter-free, and I can still smell the pitch-pine resin emanating from the crackly, dry needles on the floor of our forest.

Perhaps the most important time in these provisional troops occurred after dinner when we hosted "bullshit sessions," in our individual campsites. The young Scouts could ask us any question. They queried us about drugs and learned important drinking wisdoms, such as: "Beer after whiskey — very risky. Whiskey after beer, never fear."

Of course, we discussed girls, dating, and condoms. We problem-solved issues involving angry fathers and bossy mothers. We talked about Vietnam and why we participated in the March on Washington. We defended long hair and hippies, rock and roll, and why we cherished Crosby, Stills, Nash, and Young. We touched on all of the aspects of life that a suburban New York kid could encounter. Our Scouts loved us, and we loved mentoring them.

Beginning in 1967 and running through 1972, the guys and I forged our friendship. The bonds of good work at Wauwepex gave us a base, and after camp we continued by surfing at Gilgo Beach, followed by nights of clubbing and dancing. Over time, we explored the further reaches of the world: camping in Shenandoah National Park, rockin' at concerts like The Incredible String Band, and grabbing our own guitars and making music. I took LSD a couple of times with Geoff, and smoked pot with the others. We all confronted the norms of our families, who wanted us to be successful pillars of the corporate world. We were coming alive and felt on fire. Free. Excited. Connected. These were some of the sweetest times of my life.

As we grew older, we began to explore personal desires. I dropped out of college and went ski-bumming in Colorado. Bill went to New Mexico and studied photography. Geoff dabbled with a spiritual commune in Massachusetts, while Mick moved to Portland, Oregon to come out with his gayness. Frank began a life-long study of chess and met a woman named Kris.

The pull of our individualized quests eventually took us far afield from each other. By 1972, we didn't have the time or capacity to be summer camp Scoutmasters. We had college and careers. Then marriage and kids. With homes and bills to pay, our focus became very singular.

We didn't drift apart, exactly, for we saw each other intermittently for a few years and still felt a strong, magical connection. But our destinies lay in separate directions. By 1980, our friendships had entered a kind of vacuum that was real but inert. I went the next 38 years without any contact with my crew.

In the early months of 2018, though, I became haunted by memories of some of the irresponsible stuff we did as a group. We were good Scoutmasters, but we weren't perfect. The height of our irresponsibility occurred on a combined five-mile overnight hike to campsites along Long Island Sound. One spot was a Catholic orphanage, another was a state park, and my troop camped on lands managed by a local youth group.

As darkness fell and my campfire burned low, I was surprised to see Geoff and Bill enter the shadows.

"What are you guys doing here?" I asked.

"When my kids started going to bed, I decided to go for a walk down the beach," Geoff said. "I ran into Bill and his group a mile away, and we decided to come down to you. We're walking the beach. Want to join us?"

"Sure," I replied. I told my assistant Scoutmaster I was leaving for a little while and, since most of my kids were asleep or on their way, my ASM agreed.

Walking down the beach with Geoff and Bill was a delight—I thrilled in joining them on adventures. I had no realization that I was putting my Scouts at risk.

We three walked down the beach to the town park and entered a nearby pub, only to meet our boss, who fired us on the spot for our obvious dereliction of duty. Fortunately, the next day we were able to talk our way back into our jobs. But the fact that I could be so careless and irresponsible has lingered in my psyche for decades.

Then, one night in late 2018, my shame tanks burst open. I couldn't shake the nightmares. *Yes, I acknowledge that I messed up when I was a Scoutmaster...* I tried to console myself. *Yes, I made a mistake, but I learn from all things....* Nevertheless, the rationalizations failed to calm my soul.

That night, unable to sleep, I made some tea and sought emotional relief. As morning approached, I still ached terribly with guilt.

I decided to meditate and revisit the event, and see why it was staying with me so powerfully. I focused on the beach, Geoff and Bill, and the abandonment.

Mentally, I was transported back to summer camp, and instantly learned how much Wauwepex meant to me. I realized Wauwepex was a uniquely safe place, as it allowed me to feel so psychologically secure that I could truly express myself. My camp was *the* place for me to think, feel, and act in my own ways and not according to the expectations of others. Wauwepex was my place to make Really Big Mistakes, if that was what it took to become self-actualized.

As dawn brightened, I wrote this story and decided to send it to my guys. I scoured old address books, but I only came upon one working telephone number: Bill's, from 1980. Although he had moved a number of times during the ensuing years, he still taught at the same college in Amherst, Massachusetts, and had kept the same landline phone number. I dialed.

"Hello?" answered an unfamiliar woman's voice. I introduced myself and learned I was speaking to Jennifer, Bill's wife of 30-some years, whom I had never met. She put Bill on the phone.

"Hello," said a weak, hoarse voice. "Bruce… is that you?"

"Yeah, it's me, Bill."

"Wow…. Long time…. Everything… okay?"

"Yeah. I just wrote a story about us. About camp. I'd like to send it to you. What's your address?"

"Bruce, I'm dealing with cancer…I'm very tired…. We'll have to pick…this up tomorrow…or the next…when I have more strength."

When I called the next day Bill was stronger, and over the next few days we figured out how to reach the rest of the guys. Geoff's website for his counseling practice was valid, but he was doing so much in so many places that it took time to reach him. Eventually, though, we were successful.

Frank, Bill's assistant Scoutmaster and a frequent member of our escapades, was tough. Frank was a successful attorney in New Jersey, and we were able to locate his office. While the photos that accompanied Frank's contact information didn't look familiar, it proved to be legit.

Frank, in turn, had kept in touch with Mick, who ironically was living only a couple of hours away from me in Portland. He had been in the Pacific Northwest off and on for over 30 years and yet, somehow, we had never met. Once upon a time, though, we had been close. He'd lived a few blocks away from me in New York, and was a member of my patrol when we were young Scouts in Troop 166. In fact, we had worked together on the McGovern campaign in 1972. So, Frank gave me Mick's contact info, and eventually we connected—first by phone, then by email, and soon we found ourselves together at a Bangladeshi restaurant near Portland's famous Powell's bookstore.

When all of us agreed that we wanted to get together again, I suggested June since my mother was sending me a plane ticket to visit for her birthday. Mick agreed to fly to New York once a date was set.

On June 15, 2018, we rendezvoused. First, Frank, Mick, and I met at Geoff's place in New York City. Then we four drove to Bill's home in Massachusetts. He looked okay when we arrived, and announced that his cancer was "stable." But he warned us that his strength might not last more than an hour.

He was still going strong four hours later, though, and our reunion became more like communion. Quietly and steadily, we forged new bonds of heartfelt connection. Hours of catching-up, identifying kids and wives, homes and jobs, and trying to remember who did what and when, merged with discussions of addiction, divorce, and medical emergencies. Some of us had wine. Others celebrated their sobriety. For the record, I still don't remember seeing the Grateful Dead with Geoff and Bill at the Fillmore East in 1970, although they both swear I was with them.

Our hearts brimmed full, and we savored the gorgeous feast, especially the different kinds of vegetarian lasagna. Plus, we delighted in meeting Bill's wife, Jennifer, and their son Joshua, and learning about their daughter, Simone, who was living in Europe.

The good times were so lively and therapeutic that Bill and Jennifer invited us back the next day for brunch—and that lasted another four hours. When we left, Bill looked fine. In fact, I was the one pushing us to leave since we had a long drive back to NYC, and I knew construction delays at the LIRR's Penn Station awaited me before I could crawl into my bed on Long Island.

For the entirety of the return to New York, we four—Geoff, Mick, Frank and I—continued the "catching up," and the exploration of what it all meant to us.

Mick proclaimed the reunion one of the "finest days of my life," and described how he felt a new chapter was opening, with stronger connections and more openness. He even confessed that he preferred to be called, "Michael," instead of "Mick," which he had told us was his "coming-out name" and we had been using all weekend in place of his old camp nickname, "Mike." We practiced his *new-new* moniker of Michael for the last 10 minutes of our trip.

Frank also requested a name change. At camp I had always called him "Frank," as did most of the camp staff. In fact, when Bill called him "Francis," I thought it was some kind of inside joke poking fun at Frank's penchant for seriousness.

"But everyone calls me Francis, now," he declared.

"Francis it is, then," I proclaimed as I joined the Name Parade.

Geoff was able to resolve another haunt of mine—my God-awful acid trip with him when I went mute for hours, feeling like I was falling into an abyss.

"Could have been from not having experienced unconditional love in your life," Geoff suggested, based upon his

30-year clinical practice. He touched a nerve, and with a few brief words Geoff was able to soothe another old memory, and help identify an on-going dynamic within my family.

Later, when I told Bill about these name changes, he, too, spoke up: "I've been called 'William' all my adult life, so please make another adjustment!" So, a trifecta of name-changing emerged that visit.

We had come together easily and completely. Yes, there were moments of awkwardness when no one seemed to know what to say, but those were few and faded as the weekend progressed.

For me, perhaps the most telling example of this brotherhood is how everyone contributed, each in his own way. I got the ball rolling by writing the story and getting in touch with everyone. Francis drove us in his huge Nissan Armada. Geoff paid for the gas and lunch. Michael and Francis bought individual rooms in a luxury motel for each of us so we could all unwind and relax in our own way. Joshua, Jennifer and William prepared two huge, wonderful meals, with Joshua doing the dishes.

But a lingering thought may be the sweetest—all of this took 50 years to unfold. We met when we were teens, and now we were in our 60s and 70s. We romped into life together as youth—laughing and exploring, working and experimenting. Sometimes we created beauty and helped people, like our Scouts. Sometimes we screwed up royally, such as when we left those kids compromised.

Then, we all went off to live our lives as men.

But we were all back together, integrating the experiences of youthful exuberance with the wizened joys of adulthood. It takes time—a lot of time—to complete that kind of arc.

Age. Sometimes there just isn't any substitute.

53

Twists and Turns
Pre-med prepared me for quantum physics

I'm an adventurer. I'm like a dog that sticks his head out the window riding along in the car—always sniffing the breeze, wanting to see what's ahead and around the corner.

Others may want a more conventional life, one that includes raising a family. But not me. Although I've been married twice, along with two other long-term relationships, I haven't fathered any children. Nor have I felt a pull to have any of my own.

In my younger years, I never had a career path either, nor a clear idea of what I wanted to do in life. I rambled around—dropping in and out of college, finding strange pick-up jobs like driving a truck for the Salvation Army or flipping burgers at a ski resort. So, it was a surprise to my family when I announced in 1971 that I was going back to college to become a doctor.

In truth, I was already back in college, as my latest project—to attend a physician's assistant program at the University of Colorado in Boulder—had demanded that I first obtain some college-level biology and chemistry. As a result, I had enrolled at my local college, Hofstra University, as a non-matriculated student picking up the necessary credits.

But as soon as I saw all the baby-faced premed students in the seats around me, I decided I didn't want to be *their* assistant, and if they could be a doctor then I would become one, too.

I therefore switched my matriculation status and became a full-fledged student in premed. My parents were shocked by this turn of events and, in turn, I was shocked by their response—they began to like me! Actually, they began to be proud of me and *kvell* about me in front of their friends and neighbors. "My son, the doctor-to-be," became a refrain that was both amusing and frightening, since I knew their love was so conditional.

However, premed was tough, and I struggled in my science classes. Biology, chemistry, and physics were just not in my wheelhouse, and I had to study harder than I ever had before just to get a "B." I slogged through it, but I never got the "A's" I knew I would need to get into medical school.

However, my persona did make an impact on at least one of my teachers. When I needed a faculty adviser, Dr. Kerry Wells surprised me by volunteering for the job. I didn't have any particular affinity for the man, but he was a decent professor so I accepted his offer.

A significant part of applying to medical schools is a letter of recommendation, assessing scholastic work and offering a description of how any personal strengths would make one a great physician. On this task, Dr. Wells stepped up to the plate. Oddly, I had only met with Dr. Wells once to discuss my doctoring, and it was just a brief chat. Afterward, though, I was surprised to receive a phone call from his secretary.

"Mr. Smith, I felt compelled to call you because I just finished typing your letter of recommendation from Dr. Wells, and it is the finest letter of recommendation that I have ever seen—glowing and supportive. So, congratulations, and good luck getting into medical school."

Despite Dr. Wells' letter, however, I didn't get into medical school. My plethora of "B's" just didn't cut it. Upon graduation,

I didn't know what to do. As a result, I applied to graduate school and figured that I would reapply, knowing that any acceptance was a long shot. I also considered applying to medical schools overseas, such as Bologna, Italy.

But, more importantly, being a grad student allowed me to keep my federal work-study job at my local hospital, the Nassau County Medical Center. There, I worked two days a week as a recreational therapy aide in psychiatry where, as a graduate student, I got a raise to $2.50 per hour!

I plunged enthusiastically into my Plan B, but halfway through my first semester of grad school, my hospital director asked me if I would like to work full time as a regular employee since one of his therapists was going on a maternity leave and would be out for six months.

"You betcha!" I sang out.

Because I was starting a full-time job I had to bail on my graduate studies, which canceled medical school. My father freaked and warned me that the family would never give me another dime toward my education, but I didn't care. I knew I was on a better path.

After dropping out of grad school, I stayed at NCMC for another seven years. It was fantastic. My basic skill set of sports, yoga, art, and music that I had honed working in Boy Scouts camps and YMCA youth programs had given me a resumé that was ideal for working in psych.

Twenty years later, I heard about Ramtha and leapt at the chance to do something truly remarkable. Surprisingly, much of what he taught me about consciousness was based in the natural sciences, such as the biochemistry of emotions, genetic interplays within the body, and the neurophysiology of thought. These were all studies that I had struggled with many years before at Hofstra, and my background allowed me to grasp easily what Ramtha was teaching.

So, yes, I didn't get into medical school and had to witness the disappointment of my parents, but my life's twists and turns have delivered me to a wonderful place. I feel truly satisfied.

In fact, I have felt an inner contentment at RSE unlike any other time in my life. It was sublime and deep. There were days at the end of an event when I didn't want to leave the campus, and once or twice I was the last person out the gate. It reminded me of the total joy I felt at Wauwepex, but now I can recreate that bliss every day in my meditations, even if only for a few minutes. I taste it in my storytelling performances, too, and I am beginning to see the miraculous bloom in my daily life.

For instance, when I faced an escalating mound of bills for car repairs and health matters, I got a TV gig on DB Cooper that paid $250. Even better, I met other performers who told me about their careers—and salaries—and realized I was underpaid. With their encouragement I found the *cajones* to ask management for more money, within days receiving an extra $250.

Similarly, I also confronted WordPress, the folks who run Google ads at my online news magazine, *The Mountain News-WA*, over the fact they had never paid me. I demanded payment. Again, a check appeared, $471!

Further, I knew I could not depend solely on governments and corporations to reverse global warming. My severe asthmatic issues were greatly amplified by the smoke from the many forest fires in the summer. These conflagrations will continue, and I knew I could not continue to live for months at a time wearing a respirator, nor spend my summers indoors with air purifiers purring every minute. Therefore, I would have to create a bubble of pure, clean air around me—establishing a miraculous replacement to my breathing aids. Specifically, I envision a zone around me that ionizes the particles of contamination into nothingness, allowing me to walk around as if nothing is wrong.

In addition, my transportation needs once again required an intervention. My car, the Red Rocket my family helped fund, had been overheating and could need a head gasket along with other coolant-related items. As a result, I focused intensely on the Rocket being "solid and tight," and plugging that leaky engine. Fortunately, a few weeks after I began this focus, I learned that the car only needed a new radiator and fresh coolant. Yup, the Red Rocket's engine gasket was fine, so I was again back in the saddle.

While I may not have always known what I wanted to do in life, I have found my way to glorious places. It has taken a while, but I am where I want to be, learning the power of my mind and applying it to make my life better. In fact, engaging my consciousness and making it more robust is now a life-saver. Life is becoming too troubled, too desperate, and too problematic not to engage the power of a fully awakened mind.

The way I see it, I *must* develop my mind if I want to survive.

54

On Gratitude
Seeing my mother in a new light

Sometimes when you want to become the person you desire, you have to leave the confines of your past. You might have to leave your family, your home, and the way you've always done things. I certainly experienced that when I joined Ramtha's School of Enlightenment.

My family freaked when I left. My father thought I was running away to join a cult, and he worried I'd be drinking some crazy Kool-Aid and jumping off a cliff. Worse, the drama caused by my leaving added to the tensions already brewing beneath our relationship, as my father had often told me, "C'mon, Bruce, get your head out of the clouds and get your feet back down on the ground."

I would bristle hearing those slogans. Nevertheless, we maintained family connections. I think I just wanted family, even if it was half-assed. I'd travel back east for Christmas every year, and I was present for family gatherings, such as my sister's marriage in 2014 and my mother's birthdays in June. Plus, whenever I got jammed with the rent or car repairs, my family came through for me.

So, back a few years when Mom at 90-plus suffered a series of compression fractures brought on by osteoporosis, I returned to New York to help take care of her. Mom was in rough shape. Besides the bone loss in her spine, she had serious arthritis and could barely walk. She was overwhelmed with pain, and the hospital decided to transfer her to a rehab facility so that she could regain some strength and mobility.

Caregiving the frail and infirm is never easy, but with my mom it was even tougher for me because of the family *mishigas*. Mom and I had always been at loggerheads. As a kid I rebelled against her many rules, and some of them were crazy—like not being allowed to wear my sneakers for more than three hours a day. "They'll ruin your feet!" she'd say. Worse, when we went to the beach, she wouldn't allow me to go swimming for at least 15 minutes because I'd gotten sweaty lugging the food baskets and putting up the beach umbrella. My mom thought my muscles would cramp in the cold waters of the Atlantic and I'd drown. *Ah, Jeez, Mom.*

In adulthood, the conflicts escalated. My mom exploded with rage when I grew my hair long and stewed when I dropped out of college. She opposed my choices of girlfriends, especially BJ. Besides being 15 years older and having five kids was bad enough, but BJ was also Jewish—or more importantly, not Catholic. In general, mom was constantly harping on me and my values. It was as if she never stopped trying to pound the square peg of me into the round hole of her world.

Adding salt to these wounds, Mom never apologized for anything painful she ever said, nor recognized how tough it was to live with her. Most distressing, she never hugged me or told me that she loved me—well, not until late in life.

As a result, I developed a plan for emotional self-protection before I headed to New York to take care of her. First, I bought a round-trip ticket so my stay would have an end date. Then I brought lots of medications, including anti-anxiety meds like Xanax, in addition to my blood pressure pills.

More importantly, I brought a new attitude. I resolved not to fight, and to simply offer whatever assistance might be of help. Plus, I knew I would have to set boundaries on caregiving so I wouldn't get used up. I told my family I would not be available for any caregiving until noon, being a night guy who needs his sleep.

It worked, mostly. My BP did spike to 178/110 during my fifth week, but I quadrupled my meds and survived.

The most vital part of my plan, though, was meditating daily. In these sessions I focused on being open to love in whatever form it manifested. I also wanted to discover why it was so tough in my family to love and be loved.

In addition, I focused on sending healing energies to mom's knees and spine. I envisioned new bone molecules slowly bonding to her fissured vertebrae, building up bone density so they no longer impinged upon any nerves. Further, I pictured spiritual gels entering her joints to replace her depleted knee caps and cartilage, allowing her to walk pain-free on cushioned legs.

I think it worked—at least it may have added to the robust therapy she was getting in rehab. Regardless, after a month of her treatment and my focus, Mom was much better and able to take a few steps with a walker, and even get on and off the toilet independently. By the end of the sixth week, Mom was home, and my sister was arranging the caregiving team that would carry the work forward.

With things stable in New York, I returned to Seattle. Then I focused on me: What had I learned? Had I experienced a higher degree of love? If so, why did I get so stressed?

I was surprised to realize that underneath all the anger I had a lot of gratitude toward my mother. The first was the most obvious—she birthed me. That's not news to anyone, but in my meditation I began to savor it more lusciously, as if for the first time I was tasting the true sweetness of being her son. Not only did she give me life, she kept me safe. I was fed and kept warm. I saw a doctor when I was ill, and a dentist every six months. All of the predations prone to life were kept at bay. I was not molested, assaulted, or harmed in any way. Not every kid gets that luxury.

These insights expanded. I recalled how curious my mom has been about life and people. She had traveled the world, and even locally we drove through the slums of New York so I could see that not everyone lived as I did—in a white, upper-middle-class suburb—and that many people struggled mightily with discrimination, poverty, and lack.

Along those lines, mom took my sister and me to many museums and historic spots, like Washington, D.C. I've seen the White House and the Capitol, and we took a tour of Congress. Later, we went to the Treasury Building where I witnessed sheets of $10 bills rolling off the presses. One spring day we walked among the cherry blossoms at the Lincoln Memorial.

But more spectacularly, she took us to odd places of interest. Many Easter vacations she loaded Barbsie and me into the car and we'd go someplace *different*. It was like a *National Geographic* magazine come to life. One year we spent a week on a Mennonite dairy farm in Pennsylvania and visited their Amish neighbors, spending time in the village's one-room schoolhouse. Another year, we toured the Gettysburg battlefield. The following spring we hiked the Freedom Trail in Boston. Then we crawled through a whaling ship in Mystic Seaport and a submarine at the nearby naval base in Groton, Connecticut.

Yes, she occasionally overdid the "culture" thing, and needlessly took us to see the opera at Lincoln Center in New York City. But, more importantly, she took us to the beach two or three times a week during the summer. There we swam—*yes, after those long waits*—and took long walks along the strand and sang songs. Those experiences are not lost upon me when I consider that years later I became a commercial beachcleaner.

Mom's support for purposeful kids' play was manifested across the board. In Boy Scouts, she was first a Den Mother and then helped pay for my trip to Philmont Scout Ranch. During those times I heard her oft-repeated refrain, "Work hard, play hard."

She also instilled a deep sense of fairness and justice. She once threw a shoe at the TV set to show her indignation at Senator Estes Kefauver during some Congressional hearing. She was not a social activist, though. Rather, she simply never uttered a racist word or laughed at a cruel joke. Instead, she insisted that we all help each other. One day when I was about 10, she sent me out to shovel snow from a neighbor's walkway even though they hadn't asked and I wasn't getting paid. "Sometimes, we just have to do things to help each other, Bruce," she said. "Besides, they're old." Later, the neighbors sent me a box of chocolates, and I considered it a fair trade.

Mom also demanded that my sister and I do chores on an equal basis. I washed dishes on Mondays, Wednesdays, and Fridays while Barbsie cleared the table. We switched on Tuesdays, Thursdays and Saturdays. Yet, years later mom opposed the Equal Rights Amendment because she didn't want men *theoretically* using women's bathrooms — presaging the current anxieties about transgender folks using public restrooms — but she did vote for Hillary.

She also taught me simple yet important behaviors, like how to make friends in new places and how to advocate for myself. She taught me how to ride a subway, get uptown by bus, or catch the train to New York City — although my dad had to help me with the "changing at Jamaica" quandary that befuddled me for years on rides to Manhattan via the Long Island Rail Road.

As kids, Mom and Dad took my sister and me to fancy restaurants, and now I appreciate that I am not intimidated by the wealthy and powerful. I know how to treat waitstaff and how to tip. I even know how to dress, although I rarely sport anything more than basic apparel. The important thing is: Classy living is not foreign to me at all.

Mom has also shared her wealth. She has been paying for my dental care, and recently gave me a few bucks when I was short on car insurance. Yes, the negotiations were tortuous, but she did come through.

Most importantly though, she has tutored mindfulness. Her most powerful mantra was, "You can be anything you want as long as you put your mind to it." Ironically, that is exactly what Ramtha has been touting for the past many decades, so "Yes, mom, I agree I can be anything if I put my mind to it."

In fact, I'm doing it right now. I am putting my focus and energies on becoming a storyteller. I've taken all that I've been given and am carrying it to the storytelling stage. I am most grateful to be doing that, and I am doubly grateful y'all are here in my audience, even if only in book form.

Thanks to all of you.

55

Trista
Coming into life through loss

I got lost when I left the safety of the RSE bubble and floundered for several years. Fortunately, I found a psychotherapist named Trista, and the long, dark night of my soul began to see some light. I worked with Trista for 18 months, until one day when I walked into her office and she motioned me to sit quickly.

"Bruce, I have something very important to tell you. I'm starting a private practice and will be leaving the clinic. In fact, I've already put in my notice. So, I'm saying goodbye. I need to terminate with you. Today will be our last session."

I sucked in a breath of air and pondered what she had told me. It didn't quite compute.

"You're leaving me?"

"Yes."

A tsunami of emotion poured over me. I gasped. Then I grabbed my belly and started weeping and rocking back-and-forth. As I sobbed, I had to grab tissues, blowing my nose profusely. I only had the strength to drop the tissues to the floor. I writhed so violently I slid half out of my chair and almost had one knee on the floor. I had to grab an armrest to steady myself. I struggled for air. I could barely breathe between sobs. I wept for at least five minutes straight. Eventually, though, I was able to return to some degree of composure.

"I know this is tough," Trista said when I was able to sit upright and look at her.

"It sure is," I replied. "It's really tough."

Trista nodded, and we spent a few moments in silence.

I took another breath, and this time there weren't any waterworks. Trista and I spent the remainder of our time talking about the things I had accomplished in therapy—the book on DB Cooper, dissolving my depression and being able to get out of bed every day, finding joy working in the garden.

By the end of this last session, I had an additional insight. I realized that the intense weeping I had expressed at Trista's goodbye proved to me that I was able to develop real feelings toward another person—making deep and powerful connections—even while feeling alone in the world. That felt exquisite and powerful.

As I left Trista's office for the last time, I felt light and happy. I knew that to feel so deeply meant that I was not only able to love, I was also ready to live.

56

On My Way
How the Red Rocket got me there

I manifested a great miracle recently, and I did it unconsciously. In late July 2021, I was scheduled to work at the Washington State Fairgrounds in Puyallup to help set up the Good Guys car show. I wasn't certain I could do any intense labor, such as unloading a semi or building a stage, because I was 70 pounds overweight and short on stamina where just walking to the mailbox caused me to gasp for air. So, even though they promised it would be a light-duty assignment—attaching signage to cyclone fencing—I was concerned. Would it be too challenging for my body? But I felt I had to do it since they offered, and unemployment was asking me weekly if I had turned down any work. Plus, my body needed *some* exercise.

However, on the morning of my first day of work, my car, affectionately known as the Red Rocket, wouldn't start. The battery was good, but not the starter. It sounded dead, like it wasn't getting any juice. I lifted the hood and tightened all the electrical connections. Afterward, I slammed the hood closed, turned the key, and the engine started right up. *Hmmmm.* I was uncertain if I should drive off with a balky vehicle.

Nevertheless, I headed to work. When I got to the employee parking lot, I turned the engine off and restarted it a few times to see what would happen. *Maybe it's a starter relay and the heat of the engine has re-set the connections? Or is it something more?* My knowingness began to envision a deeper reality unfolding. *Could this intermittent starter be a manifestation? Maybe I'll get out of work and save my body from excessive stress?*

Even though the car started multiple times when I had arrived at the fairgrounds, I checked it again at lunch and it was as dead as a door nail. But my earlier inklings blossomed into a full knowingness. I smiled. I knew my car was helping me. I presaged that I would tell my boss I wouldn't be at work the following day because I'd need to get my car fixed. Thus, I would rescue my body from the heat, the sun, and all the kneeling I had to do to post-car show banners.

At the end of the workday, I was utterly exhausted and informed my boss I needed the next day off. I staggered to my car, but I *knew* it would start right up. I knew that my car had partnered with me to create the perfect alibi/reason to not work a second day. In a righteous affirmation, my car started on the first twist of the key. When I got home, I was so spent physically I could barely stand or walk. I felt feverish and flopped into bed. Even though it was the middle of July, I pulled the blankets and quilt over me and turned the heat up to max.

When I awoke the next day, however, I felt refreshed and alive. I went out to the Rocket, and she started without any hesitation. I debated whether I actually needed to show it to my mechanic. I knew intuitively there was nothing to fix, but I still had some lingering doubts. I was divided about 60/40. I had to go back to the car show the following day—this time to sell tickets—but what if the car didn't start again? What would I tell my boss? Or worse, what if all this "knowingness" was a woo-woo mind trip and I got stranded at the car show with a dead starter?

As a result, I headed to my local mechanic, Mike. I wanted him to check the whole system to satisfy any lingering questions. The doubting side of me was willing to get a new starter if Mike recommended it, but he agreed the starter sounded "strong" and replaced the relay. Ten bucks.

Over the previous weeks, I had been wondering what to do about this car show gig. I had worried about overdoing it and having another heart attack, and I think I created a perfect solution—and all done without any conscious awareness of it. Until now.

I believe my car is *quantumly entangled* with me and knew of my worries. Therefore, it took matters into its "own hands" to save my ass. When I told Mike my theories, he laughed good-naturedly and trash-talked my woo-woo. But he invited me to come over in the evening to sit around his campfire and repeat my starter story to his wife, because, "She likes this kind of stuff. She even reads books about it."

Regardless, I am beginning to see the remarkable manifest in my life. It's as satisfying as a lemon-lime popsicle on a hot summer's day.

Note: For those unfamiliar with The New Physics and quantum theory, the notion of "quantum entanglement" is a hypothesis developed from the scientific findings that a sub-atomic particle, such as an electron, seems to develop an uncanny relationship with its neighboring electrons in orbit around their atom's nucleus. Researchers have discovered that when one electron is separated from its twin and subjected to an electromagnetic pulse, the electron back in the pack acts exactly like its separated partner, and does so instantaneously. Thus, the electrons are said to be "entangled." This phenomenon has been adopted by those of us who study consciousness as a possible explanation of how our thoughts, feelings, and intentions impact our physical reality.

57

Realizations
Coming into my power

The thought arrived one night as I strode up and down my driveway—*I am the God I'm talking about*. It just popped into my head: I already *was* the God I was trying to become. I stopped.
WOW!

I had been engaging a walking-type of meditation where I fixated on a tree at the end of the drive and used it to focus my thoughts. This night I focused on healing my body, and in this semi-trance the realization dawned. After a few moments, I resumed walking and glimpsed at the shrubs and light poles, and then glanced skyward. Nothing out there had changed. But inside, emotionally, the world felt like it had turned inside-out.

More insights came in quick succession as I moved. I am divine *and* human. I am unlimited *and* fearful. I am immortal *and* aging, *and* scared to shit to send my manuscripts to publishers, but I do. It's all me. It's all God. It's all me and I'm all God. There is no separation. It's all one—messy and sublime. Blessed and mundane.

Life felt more stable after that, and I felt calmer. As before, though, distracting thoughts crept into my mind, saying,

"Okay, now what?" I smiled because that thought was an old friend. I continued to embrace my new realization, even though my external life hadn't changed in any dramatic fashion. I still struggled to get past my procrastination and write, focused endlessly on improved health, especially with my new symptoms of acid-reflex and annoying abdominal pains that got diagnosed as the mysterious IBS, Irritated Bowel Syndrome.

However, my newfound realization stayed easily in my mind, and I looked to strengthen my new perspective. Every focus session included long thoughts, savoring, "I am my God." When I went to bed, I repeated that phrase a few times as I lay down. It felt soothing and reassuring. Overall, I felt I was "getting somewhere" with my 30 years of exploring the science of consciousness.

A few months later on the same driveway, the Next Big Realization popped into my head: *I am my Christ.* Again, I stopped. I smiled. I breathed deeply, and savored the satisfaction of this new insight. *Yes, I am a brother to Jesus. Cool.*

Over time I focused primarily on "Christhood." At times, it felt scary. *Walk on water? Me? Whew....*

Nonetheless, I persevered and made cards that said: "CHRIST," and "IMMORTAL," and posted them over my desk. I didn't take them down, either, when films crews came to interview me for their documentaries on DB Cooper. If you see the HBO production of *The Mysteries of DB Cooper*, you can see them clearly in those scenes in which I appear. Surprisingly, no one has ever questioned me about them, which makes me smile. *I guess they're just not ready.*

But I had more growing to do myself. I realized I needed to claim these cards more decisively, so I pulled them down and added: "I AM MY CHRIST," and "I AM IMMORTAL."

Nevertheless, I debated removing them when FOX-TV News scheduled a DB Cooper interview and expressly wanted to film me in my 16-foot RV trailer. After a few moments of pondering, I said, *Nope, my cards stay up. If FOX freaks out, too bad.* Ironically, FOX's producer was so enamored with my garden and its scenic qualities that they filmed me in the midst of my 65 potato plants, and never bothered to poke their heads inside the trailer.

During the pandemic I decided I wanted to reach out to my schoolmates and see how they were doing with their journey to Christhood. Plus, we had lots of politics to talk about as the 2020 presidential campaign was roaring along. Within a few weeks, word of mouth and exchanges of emails gathered five guys together—all current or former RSE students—for weekly coffee at a bistro in Yelm. I challenged them on how they viewed their God-ness, especially how they dealt with frustrations in matters of health, since we all had slews of the aches and pains germane to 70-year-olds. But they did not seem to have the same passion for the subject as I, nor the same degree of angst.

I did learn lots from them, especially in the areas of marriage and the joys of being a father. Those subjects are quite foreign to me, so I observed and did my best to check my judgments.

Over the last six months of the pandemic, my RSE community experienced a large number of deaths—not from Covid, but cancer, mostly, and complications from diabetes. I loved the memorial services, but one ritual stuck in my craw.

My schoolmates toasted their dearly departed with the opening words: "Oh, my Beloved God...." *Who are they talking to? They sound like this "Beloved God" is someone outside of themselves.* I realized that they saw a separation between themselves and their divinity. It saddened me, but the appreciation of my realizations deepened. *I may be the only one who sees himself as a God-Realized human, and it's okay to be alone.*

I'd love to have some company on this quest, but hey, even it's a lonely journey, it's good to be a God.

58

Revisiting the Aliens
Seeking direct contact with Extra-Terrestrials

When the aliens left me in 1992, I left them as well. For nearly 30 years I didn't seek contact with the Extra-Terrestrials, nor did I hope they would come and visit. However, in 2019, I chose to revisit whatever truth inhabits this story.

The trigger was a call from the producers of RISK!, a Seattle-based podcast outfit seeking unusual sex stories. Since I was eager for a performance platform, I considered their offer. Giving the Risk! website a cursory look, it seemed that they specialized in stories celebrating the angst of young gay men coming out in the world. Not my cup of tea, exactly, but when I sent them a transcript of my "Sex with Aliens," they accepted the story and hired me to tell it on their stage before a live audience in Seattle.

Subtly, that impetus fueled a pull within me to investigate my abductions further, and I immersed myself deeply in the UFO mystery. First, though, I needed to take stock of what had happened to me 30 years before. Here were my musings:

1. *My story is real as told:* One race of Extra-Terrestrials, the Grays, even though advanced enough to transport themselves to Earth, are apparently not sophisticated

enough to genetically modify their own DNA to produce a more vital species. Hence, they're having sex with guys like me.

2. *My story is mythological.* Perhaps I've tapped into Humanity's Collective Unconscious and have created a modern tale of mythic proportions—like Noah and the Great Flood, or King Arthur and his magical sword. My story is a saga of how the aliens are endeavoring to reveal to us a grander truth about us, via our deepest dreams and memories. What that truth is, I don't know, but perhaps it is a way of preparing us to be space voyagers and citizens of the stars. Regardless, storyteller Michael Meade has famously stated: "Myths can tell us a truth that cannot be told any other way."

3. *My subconscious is talking.* My therapist may be correct and this story reflects my deep, unsatisfied longings. Perhaps I really do feel that romantic love is so unattainable that I have to go to Outer Space to find a girlfriend.

4. *Government conspiracy.* Perhaps the sex-with-aliens hybridization programs are just psi-ops conducted by rogue elements in government, and may be a scheme to stoke the current political turmoil regarding immigration and racial strife. Therefore, by going public it is possible that I'm kicking the hornet's nest of these powerful forces.

The last scenario is a real dynamic for me. As I developed this story for the RISK! production, I felt terrified. Would the bastards really come for me now? One day, I wept on the phone with Jeff, telling him about my anxieties from my RISK! exposure.

Seeking clarity or at least some kind of relief, I searched the internet for the latest postings on alien abductions. First, I was saddened to learn that Budd Hopkins had died several years before. Fortunately, his videos are plentiful, and they offered me much solace. I received similar assurance from Dr. John Mack, whose PEER research program on abductions I had joined 25 years earlier. Sadly, Dr. Mack, too, was deceased, killed in a traffic accident a dozen years ago.

But the videos that Mack and Hopkins have left behind reassured me of several key ingredients, namely some kind of benefit for the abductees — their fear and pain notwithstanding. Mack felt there was a kind of "connectiveness" between the abductees and aliens that was sublime and meaningful.

Hopkins didn't dispute that perspective, and added that although the abductees felt they were violated by being taken without their consent, they were generally open to helping the Extra-Terrestrials. They simply wanted them to explain their plans and be treated kindly.

Further, Hopkins declared the only real knowledge we have of the hybridization program comes from the abductees and what we remember, either consciously or under hypnosis. There is very little concrete proof of the aliens and their abductions — only a few indentations in the dirt from a small number of related UFO landings, or a couple of scars or "scoop" marks on the skin from a handful of abductees.

It begs the question: How completely can we trust our memories? Many experiencers have been given "cover" memories to lessen the shock. Remember, I thought I was having sex with a female being when I was actually engaging a metallic device. So, could all of our memories be false? Could the whole abduction scenario be One Big Memory Implant?

With the passing of Dr. Mack and Budd Hopkins, other researchers have taken center stage. One is Dr. David Jacobs, who appears grandfatherly in videos but whose perspectives are troubling. Jacobs says he has investigated over 1,000 abduction cases and feels the sex-with-alien breeding program has exploded in scale and scope. According to Jacobs, the sex is not just to replenish the gene pool of our Space Brothers, but also an attempt to create a new breed of humans here as well — humans adapted to *alien* life. Jacobs says that these hybrids look completely human, calling them "hubrids," adding that they are currently inhabiting Earth and living among us. Even getting apartments and jobs!

Jacobs has no concrete proof of this as, again, it all comes from hypnotic regression sessions with abductees. So, even though the scenario of hubrids is disturbing, it may be just another implanted false memory.

So, what is the point of all of this?

I contemplated these questions over the latter part of August 2019, and developed a new perspective. There may not be any abductions or hybrid people. Rather, the whole exercise may be a mental process designed to crack us open psychologically, freeing us from our social conditioning. Perhaps the abduction-hybrid scenario is a grand scheme to evolve our consciousness into something extraordinary. Consider:

The Sumerian legends that Zecharia Sitchin touted in his book, *The Twelfth Planet*, where ETs, in the form of the Nephilim, first engineered the development of *Homo erectus* hundreds of thousands of years ago from more primitive hominids. Then upgraded *H. erectus* again with frontal lobes—about 50,000 years ago—so they could achieve executive-decision-making capabilities, thus establishing the era of *Homo sapiens*.

Further, are the Grays and other ETs continuing to tinker with human development? How many of our recent technological advances are really our own, and how many come via alien assistance? Colonel Philip Corso in his book, *The Day After Roswell*, says that the US government has reversed-engineered plenty of stuff from aliens, such as fiber optics, transistors, and computer chips.

How about societal changes? Music? Art? Literature? How profound is the influence of the ETs? Are they in partnership with our own ascended masters and religious figures, such as Jesus and Ramtha?

Perhaps it's important to drop the labels we use to characterize all the beings we know who have impacted human development, and instead of calling them saviors or ascended masters, call them Beings From Elsewhere, or BFEs. Add to the mix other transformative fellows from history, such as Buddha, Muhammad, and Confucious. Maybe the Grays and the abducting aliens are BFEs, too, helping us become greater than what we have been. Thus, we may have a new understanding of how humans evolve. Perhaps ETs and enlightened beings—the whole BFE entourage—are critical to our growth. Perhaps the "Prime Directive of Non-Involvement" of Star Trek movies is utterly false. Perhaps the BFEs have been intervening in human history since the beginning of time, and it's been essential.

What does all of this mean? There is much talk currently in the woo-woo world of channelers and spirit mediums that this is a time of ascension—of a radical expansion of human consciousness. Could these days be comparable to when Neanderthals lived on the planet alongside the new *Homo sapiens*? Both groups survived for a while on parallel tracks, but ultimately the more advanced beings dominated. Ironically, many European-based humans have DNA that is 2% Neanderthal.

Perhaps those who are evolving in consciousness will become inter-dimensional beings, akin to the aliens who are "abducting" us. Perhaps we'll fly off to other universes in the near future and leave Earth for those who choose to remain with their old-fashioned, conventional consciousness. That may be the real mission of those beings we call aliens.

This is where my mind rested until early 2021. Then, I watched a film titled, *First Contact*, a documentary examining the teachings of a channeled fellow named Bashar. *First Contact* holds that the initial interaction between ETs and humans will come in the form of telepathy—and by extension, channeling—and Bashar has been communicating to human beings since the mid-1980s via a Los Angelino named Darryl Anka.

I find Bashar to be a kind and funny guy with savvy insights on how to live mindfully. "Follow your passion," seems to be his primary advice to humans, but his ultimate goal appears to be preparing us for an inter-dimensional life fueled by a super-powerful consciousness. In fact, Bashar is intimately involved in the Grays' cross-breeding program, and my understanding of his work is that humans will blend into the Grays and form a new species he calls *Homo galacticus*.

Bashar's documentary has not only expanded my views of reality, it has inspired me to seek direct contact with the aliens. As a result, I have taken steps to achieve that remarkable occurrence, such as listening closely to what Bashar has to say on the subject, and actively meditating on manifesting these relationships. I even sit at night in my garden and envision Grays popping into my field of vision for a late-night cup of tea and telepathic conversation.

When I contemplated Bashar's visions for the future, though, I often got tripped up by my anger at the Grays for violating me in the past.

Fortunately, Bashar has monthly sessions online that he calls "transmissions," and I signed up for one. When Bashar entertained questions from the audience, I asked: "How can the wonderful goals of expanded consciousness and hyper-dimensional living be reconciled by the rape and involuntary confinement that comes with the hybridization program? Thankfully, Bashar answered me.

The fear you experienced, Bashar stated, as I remember the conversation, *is rooted in the fact that your government, your society, and all the conditioning you received as a person growing up, has suppressed the knowledge that UFOs are real and that the hybridization program has been on-going for a long time. Add to that — remember — the beings that were abducting you did not have the capacity to understand what you were feeling, and they did not have the emotional basis to understand what you were experiencing. They just didn't know, which is exactly why the hybridization program was created in the first place.*

When I heard those words, my anger melted away.

Confusion still lingers, however, and now I ask: Why were the Grays so ham-fisted in their approach to me? Couldn't they have gotten supervision from other ETs who are emotionally mature?

Nevertheless, I want to develop a relationship with the Grays, and I'm looking for ways to achieve direct, physical contact with them. To that end, I've developed protocols that I insist the Grays follow:

1. I remain conscious during all contacts. No false memories, no paralysis, no forgetfulness.
2. Contact must be arranged prior to meeting. No surprises, no shocking encounters. Send a letter or leave a message on my phone.
3. All genetic and biological sampling must be consensual and done consciously, ie: sperm, sex, etc.
4. I am willing to work with the hybrid kids, teaching them how to be "more human."
5. I can terminate this contact at any time for any reason.

In the days since viewing Bashar's *First Contact*, I have not had any obvious sign of the Grays. But I have experienced anomalies: My bedroom clock stopped multiple times inexplicably, but now runs perfectly; the electric heater by my desk stopped working for days, but then resumed normal functioning and hasn't quit since. My sugar jar went missing for a day and a half until I found it in my refrigerator. Telekinesis, cosmic playfulness, or absentmindedness? I ponder all possibilities.

In addition, Bashar teaches an exercise designed to help us develop an expanded mind. He touts: *Can you envision an infinite number of infinite universes?* I find that exercise truly illuminating.

In addition, Bashar says, as I understand him, that he comes from a parallel Earthen universe in a future time, so it appears the future of *Homo galacticus* will involve multiple universes, parallel realms, and hyper-dimensional realities. No wonder learning how to communicate telepathically is our first step toward that degree of evolution.

All this has put me in a mental state where I am increasingly drawn to the world of spirit. This includes watching dozens of videos—from George Noory's "Beyond Belief" radio show to Alex Ferrari's "Next Level Soul" podcast and Theresa Caputo's *Long Island Medium* TV series. In particular, I've found Rueben Langdon's video series, *Interviews with EDs (Extra-Dimensionals)* very informative and satisfying. Langdon conducts interviews with dozens of channels who relay information from a plethora of BFEs, such as 12th Dimensional Beings from the Pleiadean star system, and a few that are even some of the hybrid children all grown up! Hearing them, my trust in the reality of the hybridization program has been restored. In fact, I am now in awe of it, as these kids—commonly called the Yahyel by Bashar and a delightful being named Bella—have been raised on other planets and have an advanced understanding of the nature of reality. As a result, I eagerly await contact with my kids and their peers, and hope they can teach me as much about the universe as I can them about being a human being.

Yet as I write these words, I am surrounded by anti-vaxxers, QAnon crazies, and folks running around my hometown with pistols on their hips. Therefore, I am actively focusing on creating a new world for myself. I don't know if it'll be a new Earth, or one of the many multiverses derived from the Many Worlds Theory of Quantum Physics, but I see our current world becoming more polarized, dangerous, and toxic. Hence, I want out.

Or rather, *in*.

I want to live *in* a new world—one that is safe and secure, filled with mindful people who take responsibility for their emotions. A world that is in balance with Mother Nature and has resolved climate change—where everyone drives an electric vehicle, or better, teleports. A place where I am respected, appreciated, and living in a culture of unconditional love.

Even though I have not heard back from the ETs after months of seeking direct contact, my life is bigger than having an encounter with beings from another planet. I am happier and more peaceful than at any other time.

As for a final word on sex-with-aliens, I wonder if we already are hybrids. The many of us who meditate and practice mindful living are certainly changing our DNA, and to some degree our bodies, as our efforts to heal ourselves are bearing fruit, even if modest in scale.

If that is the case, the new world I seek may already be here.

59

Resistance and Resolution
My fears nearly rip my guts out

By 2021 I had finished writing this book. Since it involved Ramtha, I submitted the manuscript to RSE for review. It was a practice I had performed for decades—certainly as a courtesy to the school, informing them on what I was saying to the world about my experiences, but also because they wanted a say in how the teachings of Ramtha were presented publicly.

For over 20 years, through numerous magazine articles describing my experiences and insights, my guidelines from RSE were: As long I confined my narrative to my personal interpretation of what I heard Ramtha say, my writings were acceptable. The key admonishment was: "Don't teach the teachings."

That meant I never quoted Ramtha or tried to tell the world what he was saying. Rather, I shared my understanding of what I'd heard Ramtha say and my integration of what it meant. So, my stories have been about me and my learning from Ramtha.

As a result, I was shocked when the RSE administrator responsible for publications, a fellow named Jaime, insisted I remove all mention of Ramtha, including Ramtha's School of

Enlightenment. However, he did concede that I could identify Ramtha by name once, along with RSE, in the introduction for the sake of clarity. Further, we agreed that I could replace Ramtha's name with the phrase, "my teacher," and RSE with, "my school."

When I submitted a revised manuscript sans Ramtha for his approval in 2021, Jaime accepted the new version. However, I felt unsettled, and let the manuscript sit on a shelf, awaiting clarity on how to proceed.

These events occurred during the aftermath of the pandemic, and part of my Covid journey was getting vaccinated. However, RSE went down the rabbit hole of QAnon conspiracies and the dangers of mRNA vaccines. Their fears reached the point where everyone who was vaccinated was barred from physically entering the RSE campus. Along those lines, I had one RSE student tell me to my face that he considered me "lethally dangerous" because I was emitting mRNA particles into the air he was breathing.

Facing that wall of resistance, I didn't address any issues concerning this book, and clarity on publication receded even further from view.

While the manuscript lay dormant, family matters took center stage. My mom was 97 and becoming frail, so when it was safe to fly in the latter part of 2021, I traveled to New York to check on her. She was stable, but required full-time nursing in her home. My sister managed that care, along with coordinating doctors' appointments, physical therapy sessions, and grocery shopping. I flew in to give my sister a break from her familial duties. In essence, my sister and I operated a miniature nursing home.

Mom was able to maintain her health through the holidays, so I returned home to Washington in January 2022. By April, however, she began to deteriorate and I returned to New York. She stopped eating in May, and then ceased drinking any fluids. By July she was gone. Her passing, coupled with the family's grief and the six months needed to clean out her house, never allowed me any time to focus on this book.

Finally, in January 2023, I left New York, exhausted. After a brief vacation in Puerto Rico, I returned to Washington. However, when I arrived, I had no place to reside. My little rental—a 16-foot RV trailer—had become uninhabitable due to water damage and vermin infestation. In response, I began an odyssey of couch surfing with friends, and finally rented a room from one of the few RSE schoolmates who wasn't scared of me.

By October 2023 I found a lovely home to rent in Eatonville. Then, it was time to dig into my life. I began by seeing a hypnotherapist, hoping to revisit my alien abduction experiences. However, my intake session on October 5, 2023 veered sharply away from Extra-Terrestrials, and instead focused on my "Home Run" story and my chronic fear of power. My therapist, Karen, directed me back to my Little League game and positioned me at home plate. "See the pitch coming in," she intoned. "Now swing away and see yourself hitting another home run."

I struggled to envision swinging and hitting a home run, but I finally saw one, as if through a haze. "Yeah, I got it," I said weakly.

"Now, see another pitch coming in, and swing," she chimed.

Yee-Gawds, Karen, why don't you come into this vision and hit these god-dammed home runs yourself?

Karen must have sensed my tension, so she switched my focus to my teammates and the general environment of the Little League game. "Look around, Bruce, remember how much you loved to play baseball. Now…remember that you did hit a home run. That's a fact. You do have the ability to do that. Even at 10 you demonstrated your prowess. It's real. It's real power. Let it sink in."

I did.

"Now go back up to the plate and hit another one."

Oh, Gawd, she's not letting this home run thing go, I screamed inside. But I took a deep breath and swung away. *This is what I came here to do. Make known the unknown. Accept my power. Not be afraid.*

I continued swinging away, and hit a few over the left field fence of the Stewart Manor Elementary School where this saga had all begun in 1960. That felt satisfying. It even put a smile on my face.

After that hypnosis session I decided to celebrate by eating dinner at a nearby Italian restaurant. However, moments after I had ordered a chicken parmigiana, I felt a sharp pain running laterally across my lower abdomen, as if I had been sliced by a knife. *Whoa, that session must have touched a nerve somewhere.* Then the pain vanished.

Feeling relieved, I sipped from my Italian lemonade. Moments later, though, another spasm ripped across my belly. *Ow, these hurt.* My guts felt like they were being eviscerated. I sent a wave of healing energy to my stomach. The pain subsided a bit, but came back fully in a few moments. This last spasm also triggered an urgency to move my bowels, so I headed to the toilet. There, a wave of diarrhea hit. After five minutes of sitting on the pot, I figured I was able to walk back to my table. I should tell the waitress to make that a To-Go order. I did and paid the bill, grimacing as I did so. The cramping was becoming near-constant.

I staggered back to Karen's office building, and feeling another bout of cramping I deposited myself on a toilet. After that stint, I felt strong enough to head to my car where I thought I'd wait it out. However, the stabbing pain continued and I gasped for relief. None came, and I realized I wasn't going to make it home. I needed help.

Fortunately, Karen's parking garage was directly across the street from Seattle's Swedish Hospital. As I walked into Emergency, I felt a super-charged cramp and had to beeline to the bathroom. For the next 14 hours I alternated between bathroom runs and medical testing—blood work, CT scans, X-Rays, and even an EKG. By morning I was spent, and my bowels were utterly devoid of contents. As the sun streamed through my hospital room's window, a physician by the name of Dr. Na entered, saying, "There is nothing wrong with you that we can find, Mr. Smith, at least nothing that we can fix. So, if you feel strong enough to drive home, you might as well head there and get some sleep. If your symptoms return, go to your local doctor."

I concurred and drove home. The next day I felt fine. In my morning meditation I realized I wanted to return to my book of stories. More importantly, I wanted to put Ramtha back in.

The next few days vacillated between absolute bliss as I re-entered Ramtha into my book and abdominal cramping and diarrhea as I confronted my fear of violating a directive from Jaime. I felt I was going up against Ramtha, JZ Knight, and RSE. What would JZ do? She had sued another classmate, Dr. Joe Dispenza, for supposedly transgressing the promise we students had made to "not teach the teachings." Would my book of stories be deemed a public teaching of Ramtha's material? What would Ramtha do? Would he block me in some fashion? Harm me?

I focused on what I wanted to do. Why was I writing this book? Why was I putting it out into the world? How would readers respond when I made RSE and Ramtha's teaching more public, even if indirectly? Was I trying to be a guru? Be famous?

I delved into these issues in my meditations. My passion to write was undeniable. I felt I could *not* not write my book. Yet, the fear was omnipresent. Even as I write these words my stomach tightens. But I knew I had to publish my book with Ramtha in it. It felt imperative. It is my truth. It is my reality. I wanted to honestly describe my journey.

Digging deeper, I realized I also wanted to share my little miracles—the spermy lights, the custodian at the open mic, the

Blue Angel—even fixing the Red Rocket's starter—because I knew these stories could offer solace to others like me, seekers who often lose hope.

My body's reaction, however, continued and was intense. Besides abdominal difficulties, my neck stiffened to the point where I couldn't turn my head. Further, my back tightened and I was unable to stand straight. Migraines ensued as well. Eventually, I realized my fear of RSE's response to this book was just one element oozing out of a deep pool of anxieties. Fear of power? Yes, but the fear of being alone and not having a place to live once my rental term was up was also part of my stress. So, too, watching my body age. I wondered: Will I really live for another 200 years without illness or pain, as I had toasted with Ramtha hundreds of times during events?

In response, I went to my local physician who prescribed pain meds. I also sought chiropractic care. In addition, I started with a massage therapist, along with continuing with Karen. All of this helped me peel back the layers of fear. By Christmas of 2022, I had found enough physical relief to write this chapter. I was strong enough to swing away.

All through 2023, I polished and edited the version of this book with Ramtha in it. By autumn, I had contacted a superb editor and book shepherd, Heidi Connolly, to prepare the manuscript for publication. However, in ensuing discussions with publishers, I realized I needed to secure agreements from the dozens of people mentioned in the book. That task brought my relationship with RSE back into focus. Hence, I contacted the chief administrator of RSE, Mike Wright, and asked him to reconsider Jaime's ruling from 2021. Mike reviewed both versions of this book, and in early 2025 decided that my description of my experiences with Ramtha was acceptable, whereupon he authorized my use of Ramtha and RSE. With that, I proceeded with publication.

I'm not sure what I will do in when someone asks me to show them how to see spermy lights or how to heal themselves. Similarly, some folks on podcasts have already asked me to talk about RSE. Some want to know who or what Ramtha is, or exactly what does he teach. I always approach the subject from my personal perspective. I tell them I don't know who Ramtha is exactly, but I can tell you what I've learned—quantum physics, neurophysiology, and the power of consciousness. Certainly, Ramtha has been a wonderful teacher to me, and I have been exposed to an amazing array of topics. However, my greatest gift has been receiving a comprehensive perspective on why we are here. Some aspects of my education have been philosophical, some hard science. Others have been experiential, such as learning how to meditate. To me, it's all good.

If people want to know more about how to become greater than what they have been, or even strive to become God-Realized, I advise them to find a secure place to learn. Big Ideas require a safe environment.

Regardless, I salute your journey.

A Song for the Journey

G – D
I've traveled light in my life

C – G
No kids, no house, no wife

Em – C – D
It's given me the chance to taste the nectar of a different kind of life

G – D
I'm like the wind, getting my stories

Em – C
By blowing from place-to-place

G – D
But, y'know the trees get their stories

C – G
By staying, all in one place

Refrain:

G – D
Stories, stories,

C – G
Stories from the journey of life.

Em – C, G – D
We've all been on a journey, and we all have some stories to cite

G – D, Em – C
But laugh or cry, the stories inside feed our hearts and minds

G – D
So, if you tell me yours, I'll tell you mine,

C – G
Yeah, stories from the journey of life.

Verse 2:

Sometimes we get busy, running 'round – and – 'round
Sometimes life gets peaceful, like we're restin' on the ground
Sometimes life gets rocky, with everything just going to hell
But either way the stories keep a-coming
There's always plenty more to tell.

Refrain

All Bruce's music can be viewed on his youtube channel at https://www.youtube.com/@BruceASmith-hn4zq

Acknowledgments

Please know that Ramtha® is a registered trademark of JZ Knight. Further, Ramtha's School of Enlightenment is a division of JZK, Inc.; PO Box 1210 Yelm, Washington 98597. For more information call (360) 458—5201, or visit Ramtha.com.

I have deep appreciation for Jaime Leal-Anaya reviewing this work. In addition, I owe heaps of gratitude to Mike Wright, my former editor at JZ Knight's *Golden Thread* magazine, for his precise editing of many of these stories and his wonderful encouragement. Also, I offer my profound gratitude to Ramtha for all that he has taught me, and for supporting me when I've faltered on the journey and teetered on the edge of despair.

A little closer to everyday life, I am grateful to the storytelling community of the Pacific Northwest, especially my friend Paul Currington, the host of "Fresh Ground Stories." The fabulous nights of storytelling he has hosted, first at the Olive Way Starbucks Coffee Shop in Capital Hill, and now at the Chabad in Seattle, have been my heart's true home.

Along those lines, I need to give a shout-out to Jen Kulik, the Director of Silver Kite Arts of Seattle. Jen hired me to tell stories in 2019 as part of her touring troupe and guided my early sharing of my inter-dimensional experiences with the public. I am truly grateful for that opportunity.

Another artistic director, Nancy Tribush Hillman, who sadly passed in 2019, was a long-time friend, mentor, and acting coach. I've cherished every minute I ever spent with her.

Also, Luby Missov helped with the formatting of this manuscript and gave me a solid read-through. In doing so, he has helped me deliver this manuscript to a most supportive literary agent and editor, Liz Kracht. Liz has given me solid advice and much appreciated encouragement. I salute her mightily.

Some folks have truly keen eyes, and they have cleaned the manuscript of troubling little glitches and typos. I am blessed to have had diligent and hardworking Beta readers, such as Jane Hachfeld of Minnesota, Clare Gladstein of NY, and Pat Sparks in Puyallup, WA.

A newcomer to this crew, Bob Akervick, has been a true friend and a vital contributor to this effort. Besides his editing and emotional support, he helped schlepp my 300-pound desk into the home where I now write these words.

Another newbie, Tammy Oughton Forman, has been an extraordinary editor. She caught so many errors in tense and offered countless ways of making my stories less confusing to the reader, especially the alien abduction tale. Her enthusiasm for the stories is warmly appreciated, and I am profoundly grateful for her skilled and diligent work.

My final read-throughs and edits occurred in the idyllic Sunshine Coast town of Sechelt, British Columbia. Many thanks to the folks at the Davis Brook Retreat Center, especially Lili DeCapite, who provided the peace and nurturance to bring these words into their full glory.

Lastly, thanks to Heidi Connolly of Harvard Girl Word Services for bringing this book to the finish line.

Lastly lastly, a thank you to my sister, Barbara, who applied her professional editing skills to the early versions of this manuscript, and whose contributions have guided my rewrites ever since. Plus, I am doubly blessed to have had her participate in the actual living of these stories. Thanks, Barbsie. I can still hear you sing out on a cold, wintry night, "Thank you, Mister-Man-Who-Wears-the-Star."

ABOUT THE AUTHOR

BRUCE A. SMITH has been on a spiritual journey his entire life, and spent twenty years studying at Ramtha's School of Enlightenment in Yelm, Washington. In his work life, he has been a commercial beachcleaner, an activity therapist in psychiatry, an investigative journalist, a stagehand, and a professional storyteller. He is the acclaimed author of *DB Cooper and the FBI – A Case Study of America's Only Unsolved Skyjacking*, and has been featured in several documentaries. All the stories told in the book happened to Bruce, and are shared in an authentic and light-hearted manner.

THE TARP COLLECTIVE

The TARP Collective is a group of beings channeled by Gayle Thomas, a young woman who lives in the UK. I first met the TARP Collective in October 2024, during a podcast hosted by Reuben Langdon at his "Membership Portal" site. During Gayle's channeling session of the TARP Collective, they announced that their prime mission on Earth at this time of ascension was to support and protect those humans involved in creative endeavors.

Excitedly, I raised my hand when Reuben opened a Q&A period and told the TARP Collective that I was an author writing a book on my spiritual journey and would welcome any support they could give me. Immediately, they said they were aware of me and my book, and would be happy to communicate with me whenever I could enter a "coherent state," which I took to mean a deep meditation.

Reuben then asked me for the name of my book, and when I said *Becoming God-Realized: Stories From My Journey*, the TARP Collective clapped.

We've been partners ever since.

Ms. Thomas says the TARP Collective is a group of Andromedin beings, and its name, "TARP," is not an acronym, nor does she know if it has any special meaning or relationship with tarpaulins or coverings.

www.ingramcontent.com/pod-product-compliance
Lightning Source LLC
Chambersburg PA
CBHW060107170426
43198CB00010B/795